Management for Professionals

More information about this series at http://www.springer.com/series/10101

M. Mercedes Galan-Ladero •
Helena M. Alves
Editors

Case Studies on Social Marketing

A Global Perspective

Springer

Editors
M. Mercedes Galan-Ladero
University of Extremadura
Badajoz, Spain

Helena M. Alves
Department of Business and Economic
University of Beira Interior
Covilhã, Portugal

ISSN 2192-8096 ISSN 2192-810X (electronic)
Management for Professionals
ISBN 978-3-030-04842-6 ISBN 978-3-030-04843-3 (eBook)
https://doi.org/10.1007/978-3-030-04843-3

Library of Congress Control Number: 2019930615

© Springer Nature Switzerland AG 2019

This work is subject to copyright. All rights are reserved by the Publisher, whether the whole or part of the material is concerned, specifically the rights of translation, reprinting, reuse of illustrations, recitation, broadcasting, reproduction on microfilms or in any other physical way, and transmission or information storage and retrieval, electronic adaptation, computer software, or by similar or dissimilar methodology now known or hereafter developed.

The use of general descriptive names, registered names, trademarks, service marks, etc. in this publication does not imply, even in the absence of a specific statement, that such names are exempt from the relevant protective laws and regulations and therefore free for general use.

The publisher, the authors and the editors are safe to assume that the advice and information in this book are believed to be true and accurate at the date of publication. Neither the publisher nor the authors or the editors give a warranty, express or implied, with respect to the material contained herein or for any errors or omissions that may have been made. The publisher remains neutral with regard to jurisdictional claims in published maps and institutional affiliations.

This Springer imprint is published by the registered company Springer Nature Switzerland AG
The registered company address is: Gewerbestrasse 11, 6330 Cham, Switzerland

Preface

In a globalized and interconnected world, societies face an increasing number of problems such as public health; social, cultural, and educational issues; or environmental challenges, among many others. Such problems need social marketing approaches to be resolved.

Thus, social marketing becomes a key tool to design and implement programs to promote socially desired attitudes and behaviors (or change undesired attitudes and behaviors). Importance, popularity and usage of social marketing have grown in the last few decades.

The aim of this book is to describe several cases to illustrate the application of social marketing in different areas, in different countries, and by different organizations. Thus, this book includes social marketing campaigns developed:

- By public and nonprofit organizations.
- In countries such as Argentina, Brazil, Colombia, El Salvador, Hungary, India, Norway, Portugal, Romania, Serbia, Spain, or the United Kingdom; or in several countries simultaneously (Latin America, or internationally).
- On topics such as environment (greenwashing, fire prevention, water pollution reduction), public health (childhood obesity, blood donation, Zika virus infection, HIV infection, antibiotics use, mental health, tap water consumption), social, cultural, and educational issues (child marriage, access to cultural events for socially disadvantaged children, work integration for vulnerable citizens, social innovation in solidarity economy, consumer protection), and safety and security (youth and gender-based violence, transportation accessibility for disabled people, road safety, abandonment, and mistreatment of animals).

This book focuses on contributing to social marketing literature from an international practical perspective. The objective is to offer a useful book for social marketing courses, and for social marketers or professionals that need examples of social marketing campaigns developed around the world to improve their ability to design and implement social marketing programs to reinforce or influence attitudes or behaviors, or promote behavior change.

Badajoz, Spain M. Mercedes Galan-Ladero
Covilhã, Portugal Helena M. Alves

Contents

Theoretical Background: Introduction to Social Marketing 1
Helena M. Alves and M. Mercedes Galan-Ladero

Part I   Social Marketing Cases: Environment

Greenpeace: The Threat of the Dark Side of Volkswagen 13
Antonio Chamorro-Mera

Plan of Action Against the Fire: Educational Programme "Bombi, the Firefighter" 25
Enrique Bianchi and Carolina Sánchez

Greenpeace's Detox Campaign: Towards a More Sustainable Textile Industry 37
José Manuel Ortega-Egea and Nieves García-de-Frutos

Part II   Social Marketing Cases: Public Health

Going Beyond Downstream Social Marketing: The Case of "Jamie's Food Revolution" 51
María José Montero-Simó and Rafael A. Araque-Padilla

How to Promote Blood Donation? The Case of the Blood Donor Association of Cantabria (Spain) 61
M. Mar. García-De los Salmones and Andrea Pérez

The Importance of Social Marketing in Global Health Emergencies: The Case of Zika Virus Infection 73
M. Mercedes Galan-Ladero and M. Angeles Galan-Ladero

Social Marketing Applied to HIV/AIDS Prevention: The Case of a Five-Year Governmental Response in Portugal 85
Beatriz Casais, João F. Proença, and Henrique Barros

Social Knowledge in Public Health: Case Study on Substantiating and Instrumenting the Social Marketing Campaigns in Romania 101
Ani Matei and Corina-Georgiana Antonovici

Vidyasagar Institute of Mental Health: Bringing People Together for a Cause 113
Deep Shree, Shiksha Kushwah, and Mahim Sagar

How to Encourage the Consumption of Tap Water: A Case Study on Águas do Porto 123
Ana J. Almeida, Ana P. Ribeiro, Rute D. Martins, Marisa R. Ferreira, and João F. Proença

Part III Social Marketing Cases: Society, Culture and Education

The Role of Social Marketing in a Controversial Cause: The Eradication of Child Marriage 135
Francisco I. Vega-Gomez and M. Mercedes Galan-Ladero

A Successful Festival for Kids in Győr 149
Ida Ercsey

Social Marketing for Social Innovation: The Employment Plan of the Spanish Red Cross as a Case Study 161
Marta Rey-García and Vanessa Mato-Santiso

The Role of Civil Society Organizations in Social Innovation as an Example of the New Social Marketing 171
Begoña Álvarez-García, Luis Ignacio Álvarez-González, Marta Rey-García, Noelia Salido-Andrés, and María José Sanzo-Pérez

The Social Role of Awareness Campaigns on Consumer Protection: An Extension of the Social Marketing Area 183
Ani Matei and Carmen Săvulescu

Part IV Social Marketing Cases: Safety and Security

Preventing Youth Violence in El Salvador: A Relational Social Marketing Model 195
Reynaldo Rivera

Equality and Gender-Based Violence in the University: A Practical Case of Social Marketing to Implement in the Framework of Non-Profit Marketing Studies 205
Juan José Mier-Terán Franco and Pedro Pablo Marín-Dueñas

Social Marketing and Their Related Challenges for the Limited Access for People Living with a Disability: A Serbian Case Study 223
Ana Vulevic, Dragan Djordjevic, Rui Alexandre Castanho, and José Cabezas-Fernández

Social Marketing in the General Directorate of Traffic's Campaign Called "Caminantedigital" 237
Estela Núñez-Barriopedro

Combat to Abandonment and Mistreatment of Animals: A Case Study Applied to the Public Security Police (Portugal) 245
Bruno Sousa and Daniela Soares

List of Contributors

Begoña Álvarez-García University of A Coruña, A Coruña, Spain

Luis Ignacio Álvarez-González University of Oviedo, Oviedo, Spain

Ana J. Almeida Porto Business School, Porto, Portugal

Helena M. Alves University of Beira Interior, Covilhã, Portugal

Corina-Georgiana Antonovici National University of Political Studies and Public Administration, Bucharest, Romania

Rafael A. Araque-Padilla Universidad Loyola Andalucía, Seville, Spain

Henrique Barros Institute of Public Health, University of Porto, Porto, Portugal

Enrique Bianchi Catholic University of Córdoba—Unit Associated to CONICET (National Scientific and Technical Research Council), Córdoba, Argentina

José Cabezas-Fernández Environmental Resources Analysis Research Group (ARAM), University of Extremadura, Badajoz, Spain

VALORIZA – Research Centre for Endogenous Resource Valorization, Portalegre, Portugal

Beatriz Casais University of Minho, School of Economics and Management, Braga, Portugal

Polytechnic Institute of Cávado and Ave, Barcelos, Portugal

IPAM Porto – Universidade Europeia, Porto, Portugal

Rui Alexandre Castanho ICAAM—Institute for Agrarian and Environmental Sciences, Évora, Portugal

Environmental Resources Analysis Research Group (ARAM), University of Extremadura, Badajoz, Spain

VALORIZA – Research Centre for Endogenous Resource Valorization, Portalegre, Portugal

Faculty of Applied Sciences, WSB University, Dąbrowa Górnicza, Poland

Institute of Research on Territorial Governance and Inter-Organizational Cooperation, Dąbrowa Górnicza, Poland

Antonio Chamorro-Mera University of Extremadura, Badajoz, Spain

Dragan Djordjevic Institute of Transportation – CIP, Belgrade, Serbia

Ida Ercsey Széchenyi István University Győr, Győr, Hungary

Marisa R. Ferreira School of Management and Technology, CIICESI, Porto Polytechnic Institute, Porto, Portugal

M. Angeles Galan-Ladero Andalusian Health Service, Almeria, Spain

M. Mercedes Galan-Ladero University of Extremadura, Badajoz, Spain

Nieves García-de-Frutos Department of Economics and Business, University of Almería (ceiA3), Almería, Spain

Shiksha Kushwah Department of Management Studies, Indian Institute of Technology Delhi, Hauz Khas, Delhi, India

M. Mar. García-De los Salmones Business Administration Department, University of Cantabria, Santander, Spain

Pedro Pablo Marín-Dueñas University of Cadiz, Cádiz, Spain

Rute D. Martins Porto Business School, Porto, Portugal

Ani Matei National University of Political Studies and Public Administration, Bucharest, Romania

Vanessa Mato-Santiso School of Economics and Business, University of A Coruña, A Coruña, Spain

Juan José Mier Terán Franco University of Cadiz, Cádiz, Spain

María José Montero-Simó Universidad Loyola Andalucía, Seville, Spain

Estela Núñez-Barriopedro University of Alcalá, Alcalá de Henares, Spain

José Manuel Ortega-Egea Department of Economics and Business, University of Almería (ceiA3), Almería, Spain

Andrea Pérez Business Administration Department, University of Cantabria, Santander, Spain

João F. Proença Faculty of Economics, University of Porto, Porto, Portugal

ADVANCE/CSG, ISEG, University of Lisbon, Lisbon, Portugal

Marta Rey-García School of Economics and Business, University of A Coruña, A Coruña, Spain

Ana P. Ribeiro Porto Business School, Porto, Portugal

Reynaldo Rivera School of Communication, Austral University, Buenos Aires, Argentina

InterMedia Social Innovation, Rome, Italy

University of Navarra, Pamplona, Spain

Carolina Sánchez Catholic University of Córdoba—Unit Associated to CONICET (National Scientific and Technical Research Council), Córdoba, Argentina

Carmen Săvulescu National University of Political Studies and Public Administration, București, Romania

Mahim Sagar Department of Management Studies, Indian Institute of Technology Delhi, Hauz Khas, Delhi, India

Noelia Salido-Andrés University of A Coruña, A Coruña, Spain

María José Sanzo-Pérez University of Oviedo, Oviedo, Spain

Deep Shree Department of Management Studies, Indian Institute of Technology Delhi, Hauz Khas, Delhi, India

Daniela Soares School of Economics and Management, University of Minho, Braga, Portugal

Bruno Sousa CiTUR and UNIAG, IPCA – Polytechnic Institute of Cávado and Ave, Barcelos, Portugal

Francisco I. Vega-Gomez University of Extremadura, Badajoz, Spain

Ana Vulevic Institute of Transportation – CIP, Belgrade, Serbia

Theoretical Background: Introduction to Social Marketing

Helena M. Alves and M. Mercedes Galan-Ladero

Abstract

Currently the importance of social marketing is unquestionable. Social marketing, also called marketing of social causes, has become a key tool for all types of organizations (public and nonprofit organizations and even companies). Since 1971, when the first definition was published, social marketing has grown in popularity and has been used in different areas.

In this theoretical chapter, some definitions and core concepts are considered, and social marketing approaches are analyzed. The main steps of a social marketing program are also explained. Finally, ethics and cultural differences are referred as key aspects in social marketing.

H. M. Alves
University of Beira Interior, Covilhã, Portugal
e-mail: halves@ubi.pt

M. M. Galan-Ladero (✉)
University of Extremadura, Badajoz, Spain
e-mail: mgalan@unex.es

> **Learning Objectives**
> - To discover the importance of social marketing for all types of organizations.
> - To define social marketing.
> - To analyze social marketing approaches.
> - To study the main steps of a successful social marketing program.
> - To understand ethical dilemmas that can appear in social marketing.
> - To consider the importance of cultural differences in social marketing campaigns, especially in an international context.

Introduction

Currently the importance of social marketing is unquestionable. Social marketing, also called marketing of social causes, has become a key tool for all types of organizations (public and nonprofit organizations, and even for companies).

Social marketing has grown in popularity and usage (Grier and Bryant 2005) in different areas since 1971, when the first definition was published:

- In Public health
  - Promotion of healthy food consumption—fruit and vegetables—, reduction of fat and sugar consumption, promotion of physical activity, ... to avoid health problems: obesity, high blood pressure, diabetes, cholesterol, heart attack, etc.
  - Prenatal care, breastfeeding promotion, implementation of hygienic measures, vaccination promotion, improvement of potable water access, etc., to reduce child mortality
  - Periodic reviews, tests, mammograms, ... to prevent cancer—or detect it on an early stage
  - Promotion of blood and organ donation, to save lives
  - Awareness to prevent several diseases (such as HIV infection and other sexually transmitted diseases)
  - Awareness about antibiotics use, to avoid they become ineffective
  - Reduction of smoking, drinking, or drug use
- In Education
  - Promotion of road safety, to avoid traffic accidents (e.g., do not drink when driving, rest from time to time, respect speed limits, etc.)
  - Awareness of the need of accessibility for disabled people, work and social integration for vulnerable people, etc.
  - Training in socially desired values (e.g., to avoid gender violence)
  - Education to avoid harmful traditions and cultural practices, such as female genital mutilation, child marriage, etc.
  - Awareness of pet care, to avoid abandonment and mistreatment of animals

Theoretical Background: Introduction to Social Marketing 3

- Information about consumer rights and awareness of consumer protection
– In Environment
  - Recycling promotion, to reuse materials
  - Promotion of responsible water consumption, to avoid wasting potable water
  - Reduction of environmental pollution, to protect and preserve nature
  - Forest protection, to stop desertification and improve air quality

A common problem is that social marketing is perceived by some professionals as a predominantly promotional or, even more narrowly, a communication activity—social advertising (Grier and Bryant 2005). However, social marketing is more than simple advertising, and it includes marketing concepts and approaches adapted to the social context.

Definition and Core Concepts

The first definition of social marketing was proposed by Kotler and Zaltman in 1971. They defined this new concept as "the design, implementation and control of programs calculated to influence the acceptance of social ideas and implies considerations of product planning, price, communication, distribution and marketing research" (Kotler and Zaltman 1971: 5). This definition was very innovative at that time, because it meant transferring the marketing mix scheme (the 4 Ps) to the realm of ideas as a new type of product (until then, marketing had only been applied to goods and services). However, this definition also made social marketing frequently be confused with social propaganda and social communication (Andreasen 1993). This distinction has since been fully resolved (O'Shaughnessy 1996). Social propaganda deals only with the strengthening of beliefs and is entirely didactic in nature, while social marketing is based upon studies of the needs of the respective target audiences (O'Shaughnessy 1996). Indeed, social marketing involves all the 4 Ps, not just one (Fox and Kotler 1980).

A later definition describes it as "the use of marketing techniques and principles to influence an objective public that voluntarily accepts, rejects, modifies or abandons behavior for the benefit of individuals, groups or society as a whole" (Kotler and Lee 2005: 115).

Moliner (1998: 27) considers that "social marketing is an extension of marketing that studies the relation of exchange that is originated when the product is an idea or social cause."

To sum up, social marketing focuses on accepting, modifying, changing, discouraging, or abandoning ideas, beliefs, attitudes, values, practices, and behaviors (Andreasen 1994). Donovan and Henley (2010) go further and include "involuntary" behavior in these definitions. These authors propose that the goal of social marketing is not just encourage individual voluntary behavior and change the environments that facilitate such changes, but also trying to influence and change the social structures that will facilitate individual changes. This will mean targeting the individuals that have the power to change policies and legislation. To achieve that, a combination of three approaches is advisable, namely, downstream approaches (addressing the problem by facilitating access to solutions), upstream approaches (acting upon the main causes of the problem), and midstream approaches (acting upon those that can help behavior change, like families, friends, coworkers, among others) (Donovan and Henley 2010).

In order for social marketing to become effective, four dimensions must be present (Hastings and Domegan 2014):

- **Client orientation**: identification of people's needs, aspirations, values, and priorities
- **Creative orientation**: Finding imaginative ways to engage them
- **Collective dimension**: Recognizing that social context matters
- **Competitive orientation**: Critically addressing the competition while reducing the price for the target

Social marketing scientists and practitioners have been supporting these orientations, in their practice and research, with the useful insights of several theories and models of behavior change (Donovan and Henley 2010; Hastings and Domegan 2014), namely, the Health Belief Model, the Protection Motivation Theory, the Social Learning Theory, the Theory of Reasoned Action, the Theory of Planned Behavior, the Theory of Trying, the Theory of Interpersonal Behavior, the Exchange Theory, the Stages of Change Theory, the Social Cognitive Theory, and the Social Capital Theory, among many others. All these models and theories contribute to understand the influences on behavior and hence provide a framework to develop the strategy and campaigns to fight social problems.

Social Marketing Approaches

Social marketing is characterized by the coordination of different complementary approaches, to achieve the realization or modification of behaviors or ideas. Thus, Santesmases (1999) points out four main approaches:

- A legal approach (with laws, regulations, sanctions, etc.):
  - To regulate traffic, there are laws and rules that drivers must respect (failure to comply them may involve fines, withdrawal of driver's license, and even jail sentences).
  - To avoid the consumption of tobacco, several laws have been enacted in many countries, which prohibit smoking in public places, regulate the advertising of this product, etc.
  - To prevent teenagers from consuming alcohol, the sale of this product to minors (under 18 or 21 years old, depending on the country) is prohibited by law in many nations. Also, to avoid excessive consumption of alcohol by citizens, in general, the sale and advertising of alcoholic beverages have been regulated in many countries.
  - To prevent the use of drugs, they are forbidden in many countries.

- A technological approach (based on innovations that facilitate the desired behavior):
  - To increase driving safety, airbags, seat belts, speed limiters, breathalyzers, and drug tests have been invented.
  - To avoid the tobacco consumption, gum and nicotine patches have been manufactured.
  - To avoid excessive alcohol consumption, alcohol has been eliminated in different beverages (e.g., beer, liqueur).
- An economic approach (reducing the cost of carrying out the desired behavior, or increasing the price to discourage unwanted behavior):
  - Fines for speeding.
  - To avoid tobacco consumption, the sale price has been increased.
- An informational approach (focused, above all, on persuasive information):
  - To reduce and avoid traffic accidents, the administration has distributed brochures, magazines, advertisements on TV, radio and internet, talks, etc.
  - To reduce tobacco consumption, warning labels, fear-appeal messages, and images have been included in the cigarette packs.

The Social Marketing Program

According to Kotler and Lee (2008) in order to create a successful social marketing program to change behaviors, the planning process should comprise several steps:

Step 1: Define the Problem, Purpose, and Focus In this step, the social marketer needs to identify what the problem is and what causes it, as well as who is affected by it, and try to find the numbers that bring evidence of the problem. At the same time, it is important to identify who is most likely to change and who is able to change.

Step 2: Conduct a Situation Analysis In this step, PEST and SWOT analyses are carried out. It is important to understand how macroenvironmental forces such as political/legal, economic, social, and technological forces influence the problem or its possible solution.

Step 3: Select Target Audiences This step comprises the identification of the target audience by identifying the segments most affected by the problems and the ones the organization can have access to. In order to achieve it, several criteria can be taken into consideration (Santesmases 1999; Andreasen and Kotler 2008; Hastings and Domengan 2014):

- Demographic criteria: age (children, teenagers, youth, adults, seniors), sex (males vs. females), ethnicity, etc.
- Psychographic criteria: lifestyle, values, and personality characteristics

- Behavior criteria: current behavior (heavy vs. light users; users vs. non-users), future intentions (new users vs. non-users), readiness to change (people willing to change vs. people not willing to change), and product loyalty (loyal users vs. not loyal users)

Step 4: Set Marketing Objectives and Goals On this stage, the social marketer needs to establish the main objectives and goals of the program, that is, to specify desired behaviors and changes in knowledge, attitudes, and/or beliefs. According to Santesmases (1999), four main strategies that can be followed in social marketing are the following:

- **A reinforcement strategy**: When attitudes are positive and behaviors are consistent (they are realized). In this case, the objective of the strategy would be to reinforce this situation. The actions to develop this strategy can be very varied (e.g., awards, rewards, economic or noneconomic incentives, legal norms, etc.):
  - Blood donations: Social recognition and awards for people with the highest number of blood donations; or gifts, every time a donation is made (e.g., a sandwich with a soft drink, a key chain, a beach ball, a pen, etc.).
  - Discounts on garbage collection taxes, if it is properly separated to be recycled. Or not to pick up garbage, or even give fines, if it is not properly separated and classified.
- **An induction strategy**: When attitudes are positive but socially desired behavior is not carried out. The objective of this strategy is to try to induce toward the accomplishment of that behavior. Actions are also very diverse (e.g., establishing social controls, facilitating material and human resources to carry out desired behavior, providing incentives, etc.):
  - Blood donation: To approach blood collection points to potential donors (work centers, universities, central areas, etc.).
  - Recycling: It can be facilitated by putting collection points close to homes. Or even picking up the product from home (e.g., used oil).
  - Many people know that they should eat fruit and vegetables, but they do not do it for the time it takes their preparation and the cost that they have. Making fruits and vegetables cheaper to purchase, easier to prepare them, or more available (in grocery stores and supermarkets, but also in all types of restaurants) can increase the attractiveness for them.
- **A rationalization strategy**: When a desirable social behavior is put into practice, but the attitude toward such behavior is negative. The goal of the strategy is to generate a change in attitude that is consistent with behavior, through actions such as persuasion, controls, etc.:
  - Speeding: To inform drivers about the reasons why they should not exceed speed limits and make them aware of being prudent on the road (and not just to avoid fines).
  - There are parents who send their children to school only to avoid be imprisoned (in countries like Spain, basic education is compulsory and,

according to the law, parents must take their children to school): To make them aware of the advantages their children will have in the future, if they receive an educational training.
- **A confrontation strategy**: When attitude and behavior are consistent but contrary to socially desired behavior. The goal of the strategy is to generate a change of behavior and attitude (this is the most difficult situation to change). For this strategy, economic sanctions, coercive actions, threat of punishment, or persuasive information can be used:
  - Parking in double row or in prohibited areas: To educate drivers so that they do not carry out this behavior, due to the traffic problems caused (fines are a common way to avoid this behavior).
  - Drunk driving—there are people who drink and drive, because "they always control": It is neccesary to make them aware of the problem and show them that alcohol always affects driving.

Step 5: Identify Factors Influencing Behavior Adoption Before defining the marketing mix, it is important to identify the barriers that prevent the audience of adopting the new behavior; the benefits they may realize when adopting the new behavior; the competitors' behavior, that is, the other more pleasant or convenient behaviors that prevent the target audience from adopting the new behavior; and the influencers of the desired behavior (who can help the persistence of the current behavior or help to change it).

Step 6: Craft a Positioning Statement The positioning statement should translate what the target audience feels when performing the desired behavior. This definition will help to design the marketing mix needed to achieve these feelings and differentiate this behavior from other unwanted ones.

For example, citizens want to believe that, when a victim of domestic violence calls the help line, a trustable person will help her/him and provide solutions.

Step 7 Develop Marketing Mix Strategies: The 4 Ps
First P: Product

The core product is intangible in social marketing: a desired idea, attitude, or behavior. But it can have a support (a tangible support, such as a good or even another intangible support, such as a service).

- For example, blood donation: To achieve this behavior, it is necessary to have medical services (to extract blood) and a physical space (such as a hospital ward).

Consumer orientation (orientation toward target audience) is desirable. Social marketers should offer the product with a social marketing program focused on the benefits the target audience values most (Grier and Bryant 2005). Marketing research is essential to understand the wants, needs, values, and motivations of these groups and to provide them with the best appeals to the target audience.

Second P: Price

Price can be monetary or non-monetary in social marketing:

- Monetary price: the cost for the promised benefits
- Non-monetary price: waste of time, effort, sacrifice, embarrassment, diminished pleasure, psychological hassle or psychic discomfort, etc. (Grier and Bryant 2005) for achieving the wanted behavior or changing the behavior.

In any case, the required considerations must be reduced to the maximum, so that the desired attitude or behavior is carried out.

A common characteristic in social marketing is that there is rarely an immediate, explicit payback to target audiences in return for their adoption of the desired behavior (Grier and Bryant 2005).

Third P: Place

Place focuses on providing appropriate distribution and response channels to transform motivations into actions (e.g., physical location where achieving the desired behavior: to consider its accessibility, comfort, operating days and hours, among others).

Channels can be direct or indirect (if intermediaries are needed to facilitate the behavior change).

Fourth P: Promotion

It is the most visible part of the marketing mix. Social advertising (similar to commercial advertising) is emphasized, above all. But the other elements of the communication mix should be considered, too (such as public relations, promotional activities, personal [face-to-face] attendance, and direct marketing, among others). Internet and social networks can help to achieve larger audiences sharing the social marketing campaigns quickly.

Messages used to change behaviors can be persuasive, but they also can include fear, humor, irony, or emotional appeals.

Step 8 Outline a Plan for Monitoring and Evaluation This step defines how the program will be monitored and how the outputs will be evaluated. Therefore, it needs to identify which processes and outcomes will be measured, what methods will be used to measure them, when the measurements will take place, and the costs involved in carrying out the measurements.

Step 9 Establish Budgets and Find Funding Sources Here, the total costs of the program are identified, including the costs to implement the program as well as the costs to control and evaluate it. It is also important to identify the funding sources that will support the costs.

Step 10 Complete the Plan for Campaign Implementation and Management At this step, the outline of the division of tasks is conceptualized: who will perform them, how much it will cost, and when they should be carried out, including the partners' roles.

Ethical Considerations

Social marketing can sometimes offer ethical dilemmas, especially for two reasons:

1. **For the behavior sought**: It may be an idea or conduct that is controversial according to a certain culture or religion and even contrary to traditional practices strongly rooted in a certain society. Thus, the proposed changes of behavior may influence and affect community traditions and also its cultural, social, and moral values.

   For example, topics such as family planning and promotion of contraceptives, organ donation, vaccination, eradication of child marriage or female genital mutilation, etc. can be very controversial in some cultures or religions.
2. **Because of the way in which the social marketing program has been designed, developed, and implemented.**

   For example:

   The language used in the campaign (political [in] correctness): For example, some terms and linguistic uses to refer to a person with a disability are not politically correct, and they should not be used in a social marketing campaign (e.g., subnormal, deficient, invalid person).

   Messages used to create sense of guilt, fear emotions, and fear appeals (or even panic): They can create anxiety and alarm, especially in sensitive people (and the improvements in the desired behavior are not significant, compared to other styles). For example, "Yellow fever kills!" and "Yellow fever arrived!!!!" campaigns, in Brazil; "Flu is here!", in Spain.

   Images used to recreate real situations (e.g., traffic accidents, sequelae of cancer): They may be disturbing to some viewers.

In addition, possible interests and interference of business lobbies should be sometimes avoided. Thus, for example, when it was discovered that tobacco consumption could cause lung or throat cancer, anti-smoking campaigns were not initially carried out because of the importance and power of the tobacco companies.

Or, for example, it has taken a long time for campaigns to reduce the consumption of soft drinks to be launched (and only in some countries), even though the high levels of sugar that carbonated beverages contain and their effects on health have been known for a long time.

To conclude, two main aspects should be highlighted:

1. Cultural differences should be taken into careful consideration in social marketing campaigns, especially in an international context. The success of a social marketing program will depend on the correct analysis of each situation and its adaptation to each society.
2. The end does not justify the means in social marketing. Not everything is valid to achieve a certain desired behavior.

   Ethics is a key aspect in social marketing.

References

Andreasen, A. (1993). A social marketing research agenda for consumer behavior researchers. *Advances in Consumer Research, 2*, 1–5.
Andreasen, A. R. (1994). Social marketing: Its definition and domain. *Journal of Public Policy & Marketing, 13*(1), 108–114.
Andreasen, A. R., & Kotler, P. (2008). *Strategic marketing for nonprofit organizations* (Pearson International ed.). Upper Saddle River, NJ: Pearson/Prentice Hall.
Donovan, R., & Henley, N. (2010). *Principles and practice of social marketing: An international perspective*. Cambridge: Cambridge University Press.
Fox, K. F., & Kotler, P. (1980). The marketing of social causes: The first 10 years. *The Journal of Marketing*, 24–33.
Grier, S., & Bryant, C. A. (2005). Social marketing in public health. *Annual Review of Public Health, 26*, 319–339.
Hastings, G., & Domegan, C. (2014). *Social marketing. From tunes to symphonies*. London: Routledge.
Kotler, P., & Lee, N. (2005). *Corporate social responsibility*. New York: Wiley.
Kotler, P., & Lee, N. (2008). *Social marketing influencing behaviors for good* (3rd ed.). Thousand Oaks, CA: SAGE Publications.
Kotler, P., & Zaltman, G. (1971). Social marketing: An approach to planned social change. *Journal of Marketing, 35*(July), 3–12.
Moliner Tena, M. A. (1998). *Marketing Social: La Gestion de las Causas Sociales*. Madrid: ESIC.
O'Shaughnessy, N. (1996). Social propaganda and social marketing: A critical difference? *European Journal of Marketing, 30*(10/11), 54–67.
Santesmases Mestre, M. (1999). *Marketing. Conceptos y Estrategias*. Madrid: Piramide.

Part I
Social Marketing Cases: Environment

Greenpeace: The Threat of the Dark Side of Volkswagen

Antonio Chamorro-Mera

Abstract
In 2011, Volkswagen launched a new version of its Passat model with an attractive advertising campaign entitled "The Force". This campaign starred a cute boy dressed as Darth Vader, from Star Wars. The success of the campaign was used by Greenpeace to protest about Volkswagen's policy of not supporting the measures to reduce air pollution that were being discussed by the European Union. The environmental group remade the original advert as a way of protesting against the German carmaker. The video quickly spread through the social networks. This protest campaign was reactivated in 2015 to denounce the fraud involving the CO_2 emissions of Volkswagen cars.

This case allows us to understand the concept of green marketing from the social perspective and the characteristics of an anti-advertising strategy to put pressure on companies to modify their behaviour and fight against greenwashing.

A. Chamorro-Mera (✉)
University of Extremadura, Badajoz, Spain
e-mail: chamorro@unex.es

Learning Objectives
1. To understand the concept of green marketing from the viewpoint of environmental groups.
2. To critically analyse the environmental communication campaigns carried out by companies that do not have a genuine culture of concern for the environment. Therefore, one must be able to spot the difference between true green marketing and greenwashing by companies.
3. To learn about the possible strategies that environmental groups can adopt to change the environmental behaviour of companies, being able to set out the debate between collaboration and confrontation.
4. To learn how an anti-advertising campaign is designed and disseminated.
5. To reflect on the existing gap between people's concerns for the environment and their actual purchasing and consumption behaviour.

Introduction

Environmental groups carry out vital actions to protect nature through working in the natural environment itself (e.g. reforestation actions) and through research projects (e.g. studying the melting in the Arctic). However, they also commonly have the objective of raising public awareness and denouncing poor political and business behaviour. Long ago, environmental groups realised that the power of marketing could be an ally for these awareness and denouncing actions. Green marketing, from a non-business point of view, can be defined as the set of strategies and actions carried out by non-profit and public organisations in order to influence the environmental attitudes and behaviour of the public, consumers, companies and politicians.

When focussing on companies, environmental groups can adopt opposite, albeit complementary, strategies. On the one hand, they can promote collaboration with those companies that show an interest in improving their environmental behaviour. On the other hand, they can carry out denouncing, pressurising or even boycotting campaigns against those companies and brands with the worst environmental behaviour or conducting greenwashing actions. This concept refers to misleading or exaggerated communication conducted by a company in relation to its environmental actions to take advantage of consumers' concerns about the environment.

One of the most attractive and aggressive ways of carrying out a marketing campaign against a company is what we can call *anti-advertising campaigns*. These can be classified as a type of *knocking copy*, which consists of remaking a company or brand's original advertisement with the objective of denigrating it or protesting against its environmental or ethical behaviour. We will now give an example of this type of marketing campaign.

Episode I: The Power of the Force

In 2011, Volkswagen launched the latest version of its Volkswagen Passat model with an attractive advertising campaign entitled "The Force". This campaign starred a child dressed up as Darth Vader, the evil character in Star Wars. To the tune of "the Imperial March", the boy tries to use "the power of the force" to move various different items in his house: the washing machine, the dog, a doll, etc. In one of the scenes, his father arrives home with the new Passat and parks it in front of his house. The boy comes closer and stretches his arms to try to use his power. The father watches him from inside the house and activates the car's automatic ignition with a remote control. The motor and lights turn on. Finally, the power of young Darth Vader has worked.

The 30-second-long TV advert was first shown at the start of that year's Super Bowl. The match took place on 6 February and involved the Pittsburgh Steelers against the Green Bay Packers. The manufacturer is believed to have paid between 2.8 and 3 million dollars for that advertising placement. A lot of money? The match was televised by the FOX channel and its audience surpassed 111 million viewers (TVbythenumbers.com 2011), making it the most-watched television programme in the history of the United States until then.

However, the great novelty of the launch campaign for the new Passat was the merging of its off-line and online strategies. The "The Force" campaign changed the concept of advertising linked to the Super Bowl. Four days before the Big Game, on the Wednesday, the advert was uploaded onto YouTube. This completely went against the strategy that most advertisers had followed until then, keeping the adverts that were going to appear during the Super Bowl practically secret.

On the Sunday, before its broadcast, it had reached 8 million views; and between its broadcast and the kick-off, it surpassed 17 million views (Sanburn 2015). Towards the end of 2011, the magazine Advertising Age (2011) estimated that the video had received 62.7 million views and said "with 600 placements, the video is on pace to become one of the most-watched viral ads of all time". YouTube itself (2017) created the "List of the top 20 Super Bowl ads on YouTube from 2008 to 2016". The campaign "The Force" remained in third place for the number of visits during the months of January and February in the year it was launched.

Its success with the audience and penetration was matched by its success in advertising festivals. The campaign, created by Deutsch Advertising Inc from Los Angeles, won two gold lions and a bronze lion at the 58th *Cannes Lions International Festival of Creativity*, the most prestigious advertisement awards in the world.

Although many aspects unrelated to its advertising success could have influenced the Passat's sales figures in the United States, the fact is that sales for this model grew by 82.71%, increasing from 12,497 units in 2010 to 22,835 in 2011 (ranked 126 among all car models sold in the United States). In 2012, sales grew even more, reaching 117,023 units, an annual growth rate of 412%, climbing to position number 37 among all models. On a worldwide level, in all its various international versions, the Passat model ended up as the eighth best-selling automobile in 2012 (OICA 2018).

Without a doubt, this comprehensive advertising campaign was the work of a company, Volkswagen, which has mastered The Force although this power might have taken them to the dark side.

Episode II: The Force and the Conquest of the Planet Earth

At almost the same time as the "The Force" campaign, Volkswagen also launched the "Think Blue." programme on the American continent after releasing it in Europe a year earlier, in 2010. The objective of this programme was to group all the Volkswagen brand's sustainable movement efforts under one motto. This programme was the visible side of the company's desire to "become the world's leading automaker in terms of both economy and ecology".

It was based on three lines of action:

1. Reducing polluting emissions by focussing on technological innovation. For motorisation and vehicle design, the company developed the *BlueMotion* technology for fossil fuel combustion engines, which included measures such as the Start&Stop system, brake energy recovery, the warning device for the optimal moment to change gears and optimised aerodynamics.

    In relation to production processes, the company started designing the *"Think Blue Factory"*. An example is the Chattanooga factory (Tennessee, USA) which received the Edison Green Award and LEED certification (Leadership in Energy and Environmental Design).
2. Offsetting the CO_2 emissions which, even with the technological advances, continue being emitted by Volkswagen vehicles. To this end, the so called Think Blue Forests were created in numerous countries, where the company would reforest degraded natural areas with trees. For every new vehicle of some of their models, they planted several trees to absorb the CO_2 that would be generated by the car with normal driving in its first year of use.
3. Raising public awareness about more efficient driving methods and, generally, about more environmentally friendly lifestyles. The programme includes cooperation projects with environmental organisations from numerous countries and in different areas.

Observing the *Think Blue. programme*, everything seemed to indicate that Volkswagen would use "The Force" properly to contribute towards sustainable development and protecting the planet Earth.

Episode III: Uncovering the Dark Side

While the success of the "The Force" advertising campaign was being enjoyed in the United States and Volkswagen was positioning itself as a Jedi that wanted to protect the environment, in another part of planet Earth, there was a debate about the speed at which we had to progress in the fight against climate change and the decarbonising of the economy.

In 2009, the European Union committed to reducing its greenhouse gas emissions by 20%, to below 1990 levels, by the year 2020. In 2011, the debate was about increasing the reduction target to 30% by the year 2020. Over 90 major companies such as Google, Ikea, Sony, Unilever and Philips support a 30% target, many of whom have signed public statements in support of this more ambitious target (Greenpeace 2011).

The burning of oil in vehicle engines creates significant amounts of GHG emissions. The European Environment Agency estimates that cars are the single largest source of transport emissions, representing around half of the total. In 2009, it was established that by 2015, the average emissions from all cars sold in Europe must not exceed 130 g of CO_2 per km driven and, by 2020, 95 g of CO_2/km. With this new legislative proposal, the intention was to make the standard that new cars had to comply with stricter 80 g of CO_2/km by 2020 and no more than 60 g of CO_2/km by 2025.

In this context and taking advantage of Volkswagen's successful advertising campaign, Greenpeace published the technical report "The Dark Side of Volkswagen" in June 2011. In this, the environmental group accused the German manufacturer of being "one of the driving forces in the lobbying campaign against the introduction of these vehicle efficiency standards". As well as the pressure exercised through the European Automobile Manufacturers Association (ACEA), the report calculated that Volkswagen "spends at least 2.3 million € per year on EU lobbying alone". For this reason, it can be argued that the "Volkswagen Group is not just a big economic player in Europe, it is a political player too". The German company highlighted the negative effects that this environmental policy would have on Europe's economic growth and on the number of jobs.

As one of every five cars sold in Europe at that time was from this company (VW, Audi, Seat, Skoda, Bentley, Bugatti, Lamborghini), Greenpeace stated that "as the biggest car company in Europe, the Volkswagen Group has the biggest climate footprint of any car manufacturer in Europe" and its support for the new objectives was the key to its success. Greenpeace estimates that the new cars sold by the company in 2009 emitted over 5 million tonnes of CO_2 per year, representing an estimated 23% of the total oil use and related CO_2 emissions of new European cars.

Furthermore, the German company's advances were worse than those of other competitors. In the period between 2006 and 2009, Volkswagen reduced "its fleet's average per-kilometre emissions by 7.8%, whereas rivals BMW and Toyota achieved reductions of 18% and 14%, respectively" (Greenpeace 2011).

The strange thing is that the company had designed the BlueMotion technology to produce highly fuel-efficient vehicles. However, instead of applying this to all its fleet, it was incorporating it exclusively as an "accessory" in some models of its brands while adding a price surcharge. Just 6% of the Volkswagen Group's global sales in 2010 were of its most efficient models.

The report by Greenpeace stated that in 2011 there were "nearly 70 different variations of the Volkswagen Golf. Its most efficient 'BlueMotion' model has an efficiency rating of 99 g of CO_2/km. But the majority of the Golf models without BlueMotion emit more than 130 g of CO_2/km (petrol) and 120 g of CO_2/km (diesel) ... the cheapest and most basic model of the Golf emits 149 g of CO_2/km".

Moreover, "Volkswagen's 'efficiency' versions of their cars are also sold at a much higher price than the standard models. In Germany, the Golf BlueMotion 1.6 TDI 77 kW is sold at 21,850 €, whereas the comparable Golf 1.6 TDI 77 kW without BlueMotion costs 20,825 €, a discrepancy of nearly 1000 €. The actual cost of the technology package, according to leading technology consultants PA Consulting, would only be 260 €, suggesting that Volkswagen is adding a considerable mark-up for the BlueMotion brand" (Greenpeace 2011). Even the planting of trees in the *Think Blue forests* to offset the emissions during the first 20,000 km was sold as optional equipment for an average price of 150 €.

The desire to become "the most eco-friendly automaker in the world" and the *Think Blue project* were more of a greenwashing campaign than any real concern embedded in the company's philosophy and organisational culture. Volkswagen had not mastered "The Force" and had gone to the dark side: taking advantage of environmental concerns to sell more automobiles.

Episode IV: The Rebellion of the Green Jedis

A public rebellion against this greenwashing was necessary. The situation revealed in the technical report had to be conveyed to the public to turn them into Green Jedis that could force Volkswagen executives to move away from the "Dark Side".

The success of the "The Force" campaign was used by Greenpeace to design an anti-advertising campaign in protest at the German company's behaviour. It created the website www.vwdarkside.com and designed a video mimicking the original advert, which was uploaded to Greenpeace's YouTube account. The new Passat was replaced with an old one in poor condition. And in front of the little Darth Vader stand a little Skywalker, Princess Leia, Yoda, Chewbacca, C3PO and R2D2. They all face Darth Vader and watch as spaceships take off from the Death Star, designed with the logo of the German brand. The video ends with the message "VW is threatening our planet by opposing cuts to CO_2 emissions. Join the rebellion".

In a second video, the story continues and a banner is displayed from the Death Star which reads: "*Save your Planet! Greenpeace*". It ends with a fun dance by all the characters. Furthermore, the environmental group performed several street marketing actions and in several printed press channels changed the company's logo "*Das Auto*" to "*Das problem*".

The initial video, published on 27 June, spread quickly on the social media, and its viral success was of the level seen for Volkswagen's advertisement. The social impact of the protest could be considered a battle won by the environmental activists. However, victory in the environmental aspect would have to wait almost 2 years. In March 2013, Greenpeace published a statement welcoming the automobile manufacturer's change of attitude. This is an extract (Ayech 2013):

The force is with you and together you made Volkswagen (VW) do a handbrake turn on improving the efficiency of its cars. Something they said they could not do until you cried BS to make VW turn away from the Dark Side! ...

But 526,000 Greenpeace supporters across the planet have forced VW to change its policy and its cars.

For the past two years VW refused to back a key European law which would make cars more efficient and help reduce our dependence on oil. VW were a major obstacle against strong targets. As the biggest and most powerful car company in Europe they used their might to lobby politicians and block progress.

But after more than half a million people stood against them, a parody of their Star Wars advert went viral across the internet, thousands of activists dressed as storm troopers protested at their dealerships and on the streets, and direct actions at car shows across Europe, VW have caved in to pressure from across the globe and announced they will meet and support climate targets.

This victory couldn't have happened without you. Back in June 2011 when we started this campaign, VW preferred to remove our videos from YouTube rather than talk about the efficiency of its cars or how it was lobbying against strong EU climate laws. VW has now publicly agreed to live up to its promises to be the world's greenest car company, setting an example for the rest of the industry. This is what we can achieve when we act together! ....

A battle had been won by the Green Jedi, but had the dark side of Volkswagen been defeated forever? The company still had a very strong weapon in its favour: car sales. During the year of the conflict, 2011, the highest selling car models in Europe were from Volkswagen (Golf and Polo), with a third (Passat) among the top 10. Furthermore, in 2012 the company achieved record sales worldwide with 9.07 million automobiles, 11% more than in the previous year (OICA 2018).

Episode V: The Return of the Dark Side

We had to wait until September 2015 for the dark side of the Volkswagen automobile group to come to light. It had been operating in the shadows during the last few years despite its good intentions proclaimed in political forums and its commercial communication. The scandal known as "Dieselgate" unearthed the company's greenwashing once again.

Following scientific research, the United States Environmental Protection Agency (EPA) proved that the German manufacturer had been lying about the atmospheric emissions of its diesel vehicle engines, installing software which detected when the vehicle was undergoing a test and lowering polluting gas emissions only at that time. The software was installed in most diesel vehicles sold between 2008 and 2015. Almost 11 million vehicles of several of the corporate group's brands were affected: VW, Audi, SEAT and Skoda. According to EPA figures, those cars emitted up to 40 times more nitrogen oxide (NOx) than the amount established by North American and European regulations. Thanks to that, the company saved 600 € per vehicle (Rubio 2016).

In light of this situation, the Green Jedis at Greenpeace had to team up once again. The 2011 video went viral again on the social networks. By February 2018 the video had been viewed 1.79 million times on Greenpeace's YouTube page.

New street marketing actions against the company began. The first was a gathering in front of Volkswagen's Wolfsburg headquarters, under the motto "No more lies", written on placards and images of Pinocchio. In addition, there were placards where the advertising slogan "Das Auto" had been changed for "Das Problem" and others where in the carbon dioxide formula, CO_2, the O had been replaced with the round trademark of VW.

As well as other actions in the brand's car dealerships, there were activist protests in the United Kingdom to hinder the unloading of containers carrying the company's cars. And Volkswagen was included in the "Justice for people and planet" report (Greenpeace 2018), which includes 20 cases of corporations that have repeatedly abused and violated human and environmental rights.

The severity of the facts made the movement by the Green Jedi to discredit the brand the least of the company's problems. After the fraud was revealed, the value of its shares on the Frankfurt Stock Exchange fell by 36.6% in one month: from over 159 € per share on 2 September to just 101 € on 2 October.

Despite the Volkswagen group having achieved record figures in 2014 for profits (over 11 billion €), sales (10.14 million vehicles) and turnover (over 200 billion €) and in the first quarter of 2015 having surpassed Toyota as the leading worldwide seller of cars, the Dieselgate scandal meant that it ended the year with 4069 million € in operating losses and 1582 million in net losses. Behind this financial crisis were the huge compensation figures the company was starting to face. In September 2017, the company estimated that the cost of fines, trials, buybacks and repairs all over the world had reached 25.1 billion € (El País 2017).

Company CEO Martin Winterkorn had to resign, and several executives were given prison sentences in the United States. Once again the dark side seemed to have been defeated, but . . .

Episode VI: The Fume Threat

. . . in January 2018, several German media outlets unearthed another scandal that directly affected the German carmaker and its policy of irresponsibility towards human health and the environment, with the sole objective of continuing to increase sales of fossil fuel vehicles.

In 2014, ERGEHTS, an association created and financed by Volkswagen, BMW and Daimler, had commissioned an experiment by a North American laboratory to prove that the diesel engine of a VW Beetle was much less hazardous to human health than the engine of a Ford van from 1999 (Ewing 2018). To do so they had to establish the effects that the gases emitted have on the respiratory system and blood circulation.

The experiment was initially carried out on ten macaque monkeys locked in crystal cubicles for 4 hours while inhaling the gases that both car models emitted. Afterwards, experts examined the respiratory tracts of the monkeys with the help of a special endoscope. The controversial experiment had the opposite results to those expected, but the company never made it public. Even more surprisingly, days later

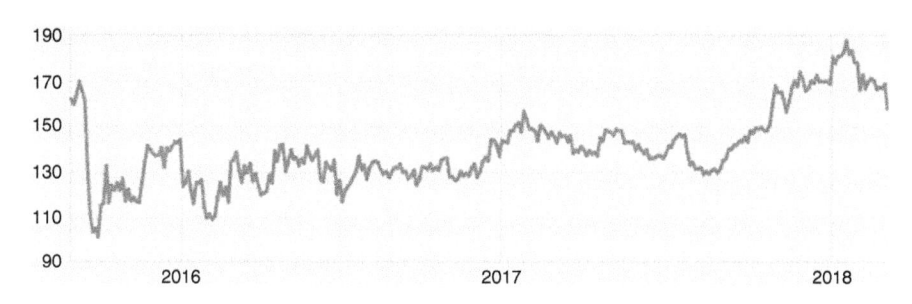

Fig. 1 Price of Volkswagen shares over time. Source: own creation based on trading prices

it was also leaked that the experiment had been carried out on 25 people, who they forced to inhale nitrogen dioxide (NO_2).

Episode VII: The Final Defeat?

Following so much disdain for its clients, human beings and the planet, the question that remains is: Can a company like Volkswagen survive in the market or can the force of thousands of citizens acting as Green Jedi defeat it and make it change its behaviour?

Unfortunately, financial and commercial figures seem to suggest that defeating Volkswagen's dark side still has some way to go. The evolution of the German group's share price can be seen in Fig. 1 and does not show any punishment in the medium and long term for the unearthed scandals.

Following the 2015 losses, the Volkswagen group returned to profit in 2016: 7103 million € of operating profit and 5144 million € of net profit. Turnover for the group was 217,267 million €, and its worldwide vehicle sales reached the record figure of 10.29 million units. And it became the largest automobile manufacturer worldwide ahead of Toyota! The year 2017 closed with new sales records. It continues to lead the worldwide market with 10,413,355 units (including all its brands), and three Volkswagen brand models are ranked in the top 10 best-selling (Golf, Tiguan and Polo).

Conclusions

The story outlined in this educational example allows us to draw some important conclusions, for both company executives and those running environmental groups.

(a) Companies must reflect and carefully design their positioning strategies as environmentally friendly brands. Behind a green marketing campaign, there must be a company that is truly concerned with reducing its impact on the

natural environment. Even though one can always receive criticism, this will be lessened if a credible and honest environmental commitment is conveyed.
(b) Environmental groups have the social networks at their disposal to convey their messages to the public and consumers in an efficient and relatively cheap way. If the campaign is original and creative, it will be disseminated virally on the Internet and the social networks.
(c) Concern for the environment is increasing among consumers, but that does not always mean that this concern is transferred to their purchasing decisions and behaviour. Environmental attributes are usually secondary for consumers, and there are various factors that make responsible purchasing difficult, such as pricing, brand image, a lack of knowledge, confusion, etc.

Discussion Questions

1. In your opinion, why have the automobile sales of the company not been negatively affected by the aforementioned scandals?
2. Why do many consumers still not reflect their concern for the deterioration of the planet in their purchasing and consumption behaviour?
3. Do you think Greenpeace's campaign was effective? Reflect on the indicators of success that should be used to evaluate this type of campaign.
4. Look for other confrontation or anti-advertising campaigns carried out by Greenpeace and note the similarities in implementing and designing them.
5. Look at the WWF group's website and compare their campaigns dealing with companies to those carried out by Greenpeace. How do they differ? Which of the different strategies do you favour most?
6. Reflect on how the greenwashing that many brands carry out can be fought.

References

Advertising Age. (2011, December 12). *What we shared: Top 10 viral advertising campaigns of 2011*. Retrieved from http://adage.com/article/special-report-book-of-tens-2011/top-10-viral-advertising-campaigns-2011/231497/
Ayech, S. (2013, March 6). *Greenpeace takes on Europe's biggest carmaker... and wins!* Retrieved from https://www.greenpeace.org/international/story/7515/greenpeace-takes-on-europes-biggest-carmaker-and-wins/
El País (2017, September 29). *Volkswagen eleva en 2.500 millones más el coste del 'dieselgate'*. Retrieved from https://elpais.com/economia/2017/09/29/actualidad/1506705470_497861.html
Ewing, J. (2018, January 25). 10 Monkeys and a beetle: Inside VW's campaign for 'clean diesel'. *The New York Times*. Retrieved from https://www.nytimes.com/2018/01/25/world/europe/volkswagen-diesel-emissions-monkeys.html
Greenpeace. (2011). *The dark side of Volkswagen*. Retrieved from https://www.greenpeace.org/eu-unit/Global/eu-unit/reports-briefings/2011%20pubs/6/The%20Dark%20Side%20of%20Volkswagen.pdf

Greenpeace. (2018). *Justice for people and planet*. Retrieved from https://storage.googleapis.com/p4-production-content/international/wp-content/uploads/2018/01/29bf8b6b-justice-for-people-and-planet.pdf

OICA. (2018). *2005-2017 Sales statistics*. International Organization of Motor Vehicle Manufacturers. Retrieved from http://www.oica.net/category/sales-statistics

Rubio, G. (2016). Greenwashing y su impacto en la responsabilidad social corporativa. El caso de Volkswagen a través de un análisis con opciones reales. *Economía Industrial, 401*, 129–139.

Sanburn, J. (2015, January 30). The Ad that changed Super Bowl commercials forever. *Times*. Retrieved from http://time.com/3685708/super-bowl-ads-vw-the-force/

TVbythenumbers.com. (2011, February 7). *Super Bowl XLV breaks viewing record, averages 111 million viewers*. Retrieved from http://tvbythenumbers.zap2it.com/featured/super-bowl-xlv-poised-to-break-viewing-records-ties-1987-with-highest-overnight-ratings-ever/81684/

YouTube. (2017). *The Big Game on YouTube. AdBlitz 10-year anniversary report*. Retrieved from http://services.google.com/fh/files/misc/the_big_game_on_youtube_10yr.pdf

Plan of Action Against the Fire: Educational Programme "Bombi, the Firefighter"

Enrique Bianchi and Carolina Sánchez

Abstract
Between 2005 and 2010, within the framework of the Policy of Wildfire Prevention implemented by the Government of Córdoba Province (Argentina), the "Primary School Sessions on Prevention of Fires of Hills and Grassland" took place.

This educational plan of action was jointly carried out by the Department of Preschool and Primary Education (Ministry of Education), the Bureau of Environment of Córdoba and the Foundation of Environment, Culture and Development. The complexity of the issue of fire required an approach that integrated institutions related to prevention, fighting and remediation of fire; therefore, a jointly work was coordinated.

This social marketing programme not only attained awareness increase within the population, but it also eventually allowed to diminish fire hotbeds in the province.

"Bombi" is the name chosen in a contest for a little fox, the pet of the Provincial Plan of Fire Management. It can be considered a short form of the word firefighter in Spanish (*bombero*).

E. Bianchi (✉) · C. Sánchez
Catholic University of Córdoba—Unit Associated to CONICET (National Scientific and Technical Research Council), Córdoba, Argentina
e-mail: enrique.bianchi@ucc.edu.ar; licsanchezc@ucc.edu.ar

> **Learning Objectives**
> The pedagogical aims of the case are:
>
> - To value the role of sensitization and social awareness about the issue of fire and the forest fires through children educational programmes that seek to reach families and the general community
> - To evaluate the fulfilment of the objectives and the quality and scope of the Programme "Bombi, the Firefighter", an animated cartoon that protects nature and the native forest
> - Discuss different social change strategies as from the behavioural profiles identified in relation to the caretaking of the forest and the risk of forest fires

Introduction

> Once upon a time, there was a little fox from Córdoba that lived very, very placidly in the mount with his lovely family. One day, the little fox noticed a lot of smoke near the stream and came closer to see what was going on. At that moment, he saw that smoke changed into a big campfire due to some glass left on the grass by some neglected people. What a scare! He immediately put his tail in the water to splash it onto the fire. As he realized that he could not put the fire out, he run to the village looking for help... When he reached the fire station, he signalled for help to the firefighters and asked them to follow him. The firefighters acted quickly and put the fire out; then, they talked about how courageous the little fox had been and decided to name him the official pet of the fire station... his name would be BOMBI, the firefighter fox faster than a fire engine! (Efraín Osvaldo Rost, 6 year old, from Alcira Gigena, Córdoba, Argentina, winner of the 2004 contest "A name for our little fox")

Between 2005 and 2010, within the framework of the Policy of Wildfire Prevention implemented by the Government of Córdoba Province (Argentina), the "Primary School Sessions on Prevention of Fires of Hills and Grassland" took place.

This case addressed the complexity of the issues of fire by integrating institutions related to prevention, fighting and remediation of fire, such as the firefighters, the police, schools and the overall community.

First of all, this work presents the situation of the fires in the province, the risks, causes and consequences of fires. Then, it describes in detail the educational programme "Bombi, the Firefighter", its characteristics, its pedagogical proposal and how families and the community can be involved. Last, this work shows the results of the educational programme and its impact on fire management.

Case Development

The Province of Córdoba

Córdoba is one of the 23 provinces that constitute the Argentine Republic. It is located in the Centre Region, 710 km from Buenos Aires; it has a surface of 165,321 km^2, and it is the fifth largest province of the country and the second most populated one.

As regards its geography, two morphologically well-defined areas can be observed: a hilly area to the west and a predominantly flat area to the east. Thus, plains, hills and valleys characterize the landscape of Córdoba.

For the above-mentioned reasons, Córdoba is a classical tourist destination of Argentina. The hilly systems with rivers and streams surrounded by unique natural landscapes invite tourists to enjoy nature, the typical gastronomy and cultural events, like the outstanding festivals during summer. The dams and the reservoirs of Córdoba are visited by fishing and water sports lovers; adventure sports like trekking, climbing or parapenting invite those who enjoy the adrenaline while the peaceful Jesuit *estancias* or farming estates and churches allow to discover the Spanish and Jesuit legacy.

Furthermore, Córdoba is an important economic, financial, educational and cultural centre. International events like the Rally Dakar and the Rally of Argentina attract argentine and foreign visitors (900,000 visitors). People from Córdoba participate in these events with a lot of passion and fanaticism while having the traditional *asado* or barbecue at the side of the road.

On the other hand, it is worth mentioning the diversity of plant formations of the native forest composed of the Chaco forests, the espinal forests and upland forests. Though this natural richness, Córdoba has a sad record: it has recorded one of the highest deforestation rates of the native forest of the world. During the last century, Córdoba lost 95% of its native forest (Fundación Vida Silvestre 2016) due to numerous factors: agriculture growth, unsustainable forest exploitation, unplanned urbanization and uncontrollable forest fires.

Care for the Forest: Fire Risk and Issue

The fires of forests, scrubs and bushes due to natural causes or human actions have always been present in the geography. Deforestation as a result of urban development and agricultural production, the logging for forest use and the overgrazing of fields have contributed to the dramatic reduction of the area covered by forests. At the beginning of the twentieth century, there were approximately 12 million hectares of native forests; in 2012 there were only 594 thousand hectares left (Groshaus 2015).

The fire season in Córdoba coincides with the dry season, from the beginning of winter until the end of spring. It is characterized by the presence of abundant plant material that becomes dry because of frosts and drought. Moreover, the frequent winds of August and September worsen the fires. The combination of these factors

(Days in the month)

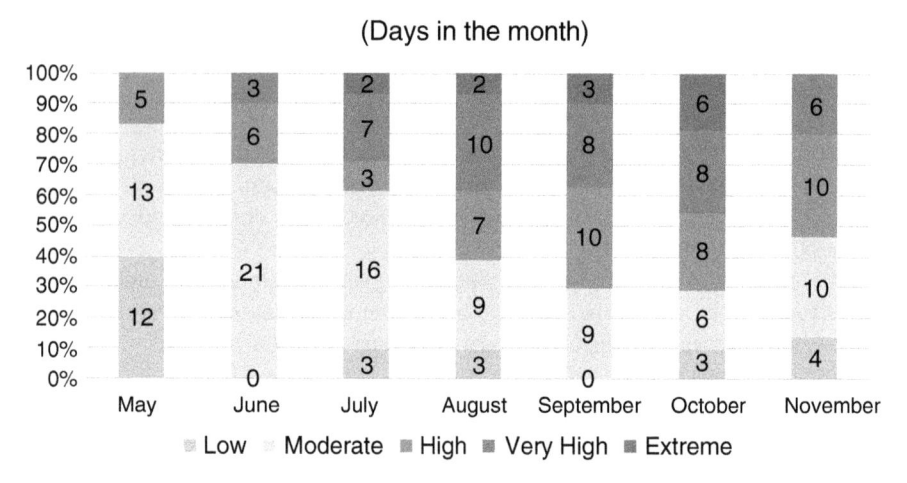

	May	June	July	August	September	October	November
Extreme	5	3	2	2	3	6	6
Very High		6	7	10	8	8	10
High	13		3	7	10	8	
Moderate		21	16	9		6	10
Low	12	0	3	3	9 / 0	3	4

Fig. 1 Fire weather index. Source: Guía de prevención de incendios [Guide for the prevention of fires] (2007)

allows to forecast, through the fire weather index, the seasons of highest fire risk, as indicated in Fig. 1.

Moreover, the following deep-rooted human habits are added to the above-mentioned natural conditions that may cause fires:

- To light a fire intentionally to weed, ward off rodents, collect firewood and get regrowth of grazing land to feed livestock
- Accidental fires because of not extinguishing embers after the preparation of a barbecue in the open air and the tossing of hot cigarette butts and the disposal of wastes from residues that act as combustible material in a rural or forest area

Forest fires cause severe damage to the ecosystem, thus having a negative impact on nature. The main effects are shown in Table 1.

The Plan of Fire Management of Córdoba

The mission of the Provincial Plan of Fire Management involves preventing forest fires, extinguishing them in a fast, coordinated, efficient and secure way and reducing their environmental and social impact by helping the affected places.

The authority in charge of implementing this plan is the Former Bureau of Environment of Córdoba (the current Secretary of Environment). The secretary works together with the Department of Firefighters of the Córdoba Police, the Federation of Volunteer Firefighters and the Provincial Department of Civil Defence in the elaboration of the Annual Plan of Prevention and Fight against fires. This plan is financed by the funds for prevention and fight against fires which consist of the resources from the General Budget of the province of Córdoba, collections that come from the payment of fines and sanctions, donations and other taxes collected by the enforcement of the law.

Table 1 Problems of the rural fires

Ecological problems	The flora and fauna habitat is destroyed; old trees are burned; naturally originated seeds and seedlings are lost; animals die; biodiversity is reduced; levels in the trophic chain are eliminated (plague can appear); forest fires contribute to soil erosion; the regulatory capacity of water diminishes (high risk of floods); waterways are contaminated, the atmospheric humidity diminishes; gases are released, which increases the greenhouse effect
Economic problems	Destruction of forests for forest production; loss of harvest or pasture and livestock; loss of farm facilities (perimeter fence, posts, stockyards, houses) and reduction of livestock production
Social problems	Impoverishment of the population due to the gradual loss of farm productivity; reduction of quality of life
Health problems	Respiratory diseases; burn injuries; traffic accidents caused by the loss of visibility; loss of human lives

Source: Elaborated by the authors

As mentioned above, prevention is one of the aims of the plan. The legal prevention comprises all those legal norms that regulate, prohibit or punish the use of fire. At federal level, the National Penal Code establishes this in its 186 Article. At the provincial level, the Provincial Law 8751 of Fire Management, in its Article 4, states that "it is forbidden to use fire in the rural and/or forest environment", the infringers will be punished with a fine, notwithstanding the penal responsibility for the commission of the crime. In addition to legal prevention, an effective power of control to enforce the law is crucial; this enforcement authority is represented by the Environmental Police (which reports to the Secretary of Environment).

Cultural prevention involves both influencing the population so that it has an active role at the issue of fire and managing to change inadequate behavioural patterns in relation to the use of fire. In order to raise awareness about the prevention of fires and the importance of having an active role in its early warning, different means are available: (a) approaching the problem from the educational system; (b) dealing with the topic in the mass media; (c) placing signposts at roads, information posters at stores and stickers at vehicles; (d) distributing flyers to neighbours and to toll stations; and (e) raising awareness in an individual manner among local producers and vehicle drivers during the critical season.

Within the framework of the cultural prevention and taking into account the need to increase society awareness as to the prevention of fires, the "Primary School Sessions on Prevention of Fires of Hills and Grassland" and the educational Programme "Bombi, the Firefighter" herein presented were developed and implemented.

The Educational Programme "Bombi, the Firefighter"

Aims and Basis of the Programme

In order to reach the substantial reduction that can be observed in Fig. 2 in relation to the number of burned hectares, the support of the educational system was crucial since it allowed to deal with the issue in a systematized manner and on a large scale.

[Bar chart showing number of burned hectares (in thousands) by year from 1993 to 2010, with values decreasing over time from around 230 in 1993 to near 0 in 2010.]

■ Number of burned hectares (expressed in thousands)

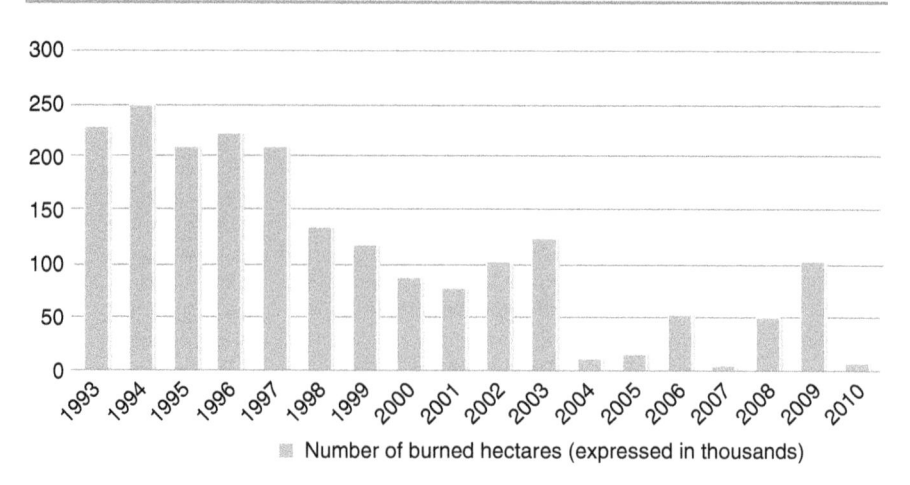

Fig. 2 Fire statistics: burned hectares. Source: Guía de prevención de incendios [Guide for the prevention of fires] (2007)

Furthermore, the unconditional support of 50 volunteer firefighter brigades located in the risk areas, the participation of 29 lookout posts of fires and the power of control of the Environmental Police by verifying compliance with the legal regulations were added.

Furthermore, working with children was key to the educational programme "Bombi, the firefighter", since the teachings received during the first years of education are kept until later years. In addition, these teachings have a multiplier effect because each child spreads their knowledge at home, thus becoming little "teachers" and guardians of nature and making it possible to spread the message to the local community.

Characteristics of the Programme

Materials were distributed to 2148 provincial and municipal primary schools (public and private) so as to reach 400,000 children and 20,000 teachers. The materials kit for each student, teacher and school consisted of:

- The booklet for children: *Do not burn our future!*
- The games: "Bombi Firefighter" and "Firebusters"
- A three-page leaflet for parents, teachers and the school library
- The book *2005 Educational Sessions on fire prevention of hills*
- Posters with information about fire prevention to hang in the classroom and in other places of people flow (town hall, supermarket, grocery store, filling station, etc.)
- The video "Bombi Firefighter" and the Chest of Prevention
- A circular and assessment sheet of the educational "sessions" for each school

The educational sessions lasted, at least, 3 days and covered two situations: one working with students and the other one with the community through extension activities. At the end of the session, the participants filled in a form to evaluate the activities.

The Educational Session Dynamics: Suggested Activities

It was proposed that, before carrying out the "session" at the school, teachers thoroughly studied the following materials so as to know them and to plan the classroom activities: the booklet for children *Stop the fires!*, the games "Bombi Firefighter" and "Firebusters 2", the video "Bombi Firefighter", the Chest of Prevention and the guide to "Sessions on Prevention of Hill and Grassland Fires from Primary Schools".

In the first place, at the beginning of the "sessions", it was suggested to work with the students on concepts related to fires with the help of the booklet for children. This began by the motivating and triggering reading of each concept with "The story of Bombi" and "The Fourth Element". Once the concepts of the booklet were taught, it was necessary to integrate and internalize such concepts. At this point, the games "Bombi Firefighter" and "Firebusters 2" were used, the first one intended for younger children, the second for older children. Before playing them, the students had to make a dice and cut the cards and game pieces that made up the game. The opposite side of the "Firebusters 2" game cards had a simple puzzle for younger children. In order to present or integrate the topic, a video titled "Bombi Firefighter" and a Chest of Prevention were also available. In summary, at this point the aim was to reinforce concepts related to fires: causes, consequences and prevention.

Once the previous aim was achieved, the next objective involved sharing these learnings with the family. To do this, a three-page leaflet was given to each student so as to take it home and share it with parents and other members of the family. The family also participated in filling the last pages of the booklet. This stage was very important because the school invited adults to actively participate in the process of fire prevention with the purpose of changing deep-rooted behaviours and local habits related to fire management. In order to accomplish this objective, the activities mentioned below were suggested to be carried out at the school:

- The community was invited to a theatre play performed by the students.
- The volunteer firefighters were invited to give demonstrations and deliver informative talks.
- Parents and neighbours were invited to constitute a "Committee for the prevention and early warning of fires".

Pedagogical Material: Stories and Tales Written

The kit of pedagogical materials used in the sessions included the stories, tales and theatre plays described below that were especially written for this programme by specialists.

The Story of Bombi

By the end of 2004, the contest "A name for our little fox" was organized by volunteer firefighters with the purpose of inviting children and teenagers from 6 to 15 years old to create a story and name for the pet of the plan. One thousand, four hundred and fifty children and teenagers participated in the contest, and the winner was Efraín Osvaldo Rost, of 6 years old, who named the little fox "Bombi" and wrote the story included at the beginning of this case.

The Story "The Fourth Element (Land, Water, Air and ... the Fire")
This story for children and adults was written by the teacher Fanny Pérez.

> Life exists in the world due to three elements that can be touched: earth, water and air. However, for life to be possible, another element outside earth is needed: the sun. The fourth element is fire.
>
> This element has something in particular: though fire was far from the reach of men, it is the only substance that can be manipulated. Fire seems to be alive, it gives light and heat but it can also consume everything. It can cause suffering and death.
>
> For this reason, it is said that, at the beginning of the creation, fire was owned by the gods and that it could only be manipulated by them. You may remember that the first men did not know how to make fire. There were neither matches nor lighters. They ate raw food or they used the heat of the sun to cook certain food.
>
> Fire was present in the sun, in the lightning of storms, in the heart of Earth that shows through volcanoes. It was always far from the reach of mankind.
>
> Words has it that when the Greek god Zeus got angry with human beings, he threw bolts of lightning over the Earth without rain, which caused fires. But, that only happened when Zeus got angry. In their early imagination, men attributed fire to the gods because they were aware of its danger.
>
> Today, we can make and use fire. It would be difficult to think about our civilization without the use of fire. However, this element can cause fires. We know that these are rarely caused by nature; lightning might strike and burn trees, but it rains immediately after this, or humid weather may prevent burning from happening.
>
> But, we also know that we need to be "careful with fire" because it can get out of hand and cause a catastrophe and, this time, the guilty ones will not be the gods.

Performance of the Theatre Plays
Table 2 summarizes the theatre plays written to be performed within the framework of the educational sessions.

Videos of Bombi, the Firefighter, and His Friends
A series of cartoon videos that included episodes of fire prevention was made. By using the cartoon characters "Bombi, the firefighter and his friends", these videos incorporate a playful and entertaining sense. In addition to Bombi, the characters that appear are his friends Verón, Sandro and Bola, an old firefighter called Anatoli and Flame (the fire). The structure of the cartoon follows the logic of programmes for children: the fight of good and evil, the triumph of good, the reestablishment of order and a moral teaching. Table 3 presents a synopsis of each of the seven episodes, which last 4 minutes in average.

Table 2 Theatre plays for the educational sessions

Play	Description
"Fear at the forest of the mistol"	Bringing the world of nature nearer 5–7-year-old children and being capable of distinguishing characteristics of the native flora and fauna were the main objectives The story takes place in the forest. The talking parrot brings rumours about a fire that is burning near, which causes concern. At the end of the play, the little fox, Bombi, the firefighter, appears; he looks tired after extinguishing the fire and tells the audience about the causes of the disaster
"Luciano and the Time Machine"	Luciano and his group of friends are fans of scientific experiments. They invented a machine to travel through time. The play is divided into three scenes Scene 1: Trip to the prehistory. They learn how fire was invented Scene 2: Trip to a forest on fire. They observe the dreadful consequences and sadness caused by a fire Scene 3: They travel to the moment before the fire starts to find out its causes and prevent it from happening
"The Explorers"	This plays tells the story of some explorer boys who learn to identify when there is danger of fire and to act accordingly. This proposal is intended for children between 8 and 10 years old

Source: Elaborated by the authors

The prevention campaign was also addressed to a more general and undifferentiated public through the mass media. The presence of Bombi was omitted from these actions. Some of the actions and messages transmitted are emphasized below:

(a) Campaign of alert signs: a thermometer that warns of the level of fire risk, depending on weather and atmosphere conditions, was made known.
(b) Road alert signs, warnings and recommendations in areas that are prone to fire risks due to their environmental characteristics. It can be noticed that these signs are placed all through the province of Córdoba, mainly in the hilly departments of the province.

Conclusions

The Results of the Programme and Its Impact on Fire Prevention

Santesmases Mestre et al. (2007) indicate that social communication has to be measured in relation to the change it can cause not only in behaviour but also in attitudes. The implementation of the Provincial Plan of Fire Management and the Sessions on Prevention of Fires provides very positive results which can be measured in terms of the reduction of the number of burned hectares, the number of fires recorded by year and the important levels of participation and achievement of the activities proposed in the plan.

Table 3 Synopsis of the episodes of the cartoon Bombi, the firefighter

Episode	Title	Synopsis
1	The Brigade	Bombi meets the Flame again and remembers the fire that affected his family when he was a child. He can confront him now together with his friends Verón, Sandro and Bola so as to protect our hills. Due to Bombi's efficient way of fighting the fire and, above all, due to his courage, the firefighters name him Chief of the Brigade of Animal Firefighters Youtube Link: https://www.youtube.com/watch?v=MXe83qIgkis
2	A new fire station	The members of the Brigade meet their new fire station and discover the equipment available: fire engine, firefighting plane, intercom equipment and all that is needed to fight forest fires. Their first mission takes them to talk to their neighbours so that these people become aware of the burning of grasses. The Brigade also faces their first challenge against fire which they successfully overcome Youtube Link: https://www.youtube.com/watch?v=jfxR_KT-90o&t=45s
3	Anatoli	This episode brings a surprise. A quiet night at the fire station is interrupted by a strange visit: the legendary Anatoli. He is a great firefighter from a different time who will join the team to share his experience and to collaborate in the following missions, thanks to his deep knowledge of the hills of Córdoba Youtube Link: https://www.youtube.com/watch?v=Gh1C1MRHVfQ&t=1s
4	Ninja cigarette butts	Bombi and his team have to deal with various incipient fires caused by hot cigarette butts in an area of complicated access. The confrontation is tough, but our friends successfully overcome another challenge. At the same time, they teach us that starting a fire in an unauthorized place is forbidden by law. Link Youtube: https://www.youtube.com/watch?v=p-ZYf15h1X0&t=2s
5	Children and the fire	A group of children are playing firefighters just when a fire caused by an unextinguished campfire starts close to the children. Fortunately, Bombi and his friends will arrive on time to extinguish the Flame. Together we learn that fire is not child's play and that, above all, we must call a specialist Link Youtube: https://www.youtube.com/watch?v=w7mxfmaw0CY&t=1s
6	Rally in Argentina	The firefighters prepare themselves to work for a new edition of the Rally in Córdoba. Our friends achieve the objective by avoiding risks that are not usually taken into account and by providing information about how to behave and prevent fires in the hills from happening Link Youtube: https://www.youtube.com/watch?v=AA-sj3TFgxE
7	The ambush laid by the Flame	After a fright, Bombi, Sandro, Bola, Verón and Anatoli analyse how to deal with difficult situations by reflecting on the importance of teamwork and organization to face each challenge. They arrive to the conclusion that we must all help in prevention by taking all the precautions we have learnt Link Youtube: https://www.youtube.com/watch?v=Uon-7UQH45k

Source: Cabás and Viale Linares (2010)

Córdoba has gone through years of devastating fires. In the last years, it can be noticed a decreasing trend: with 9800 burned hectares, 2016 is the year with the smallest surface burned by forest and rural fires. Nevertheless, the task of prevention should not be considered over at all. Statistics show that there were periods of increase in the number of fires, like the devastating fire that took place in 2013 at the area of Calamuchita, where 152 thousand hectares were blazing (a hilly area of high forest and environmental complexity).

Although the comparison of burned surfaces by year gives relevant information for making a diagnosis, it does not show a key data: the environmental and economic impact, since the affected areas take years, or decades, to recover from fires.

The economic costs derived from fires are usually estimated by taking into account the losses recorded in terms of burned forest resources (natural or planted), livestock or fodder resources and the costs incurred to extinguish the fire (in relation to human and technical resources), among others. However, these costs, as a whole, represent only 10% of the total losses since these estimations do not measure the recreational or the ecological value caused by the fire (Kopta et al. 2005).

Human beings are responsible for 95–98% of forest fires. In addition, the members of the community itself are the ones who can prevent these fires from happening. Educational and prevention actions (physical, cultural and legal) performed through the educational sessions on fire prevention has proved to be the adequate path to prevent Córdoba from even more fires.

During these sessions, a great participation of the community (parents, volunteer firefighters, neighbours, police officers) was recorded; almost 100% of the participants considered the results of the sessions as positive (excellent, very good, good). Moreover, the constitution of committees for prevention and early warning of fires was achieved from the schools, which involved an increased commitment of adults to organizing themselves so as to contribute to the solution of the problem. In addition, teacher's great commitment to deal with the topic was stressed. An example of this is the percentage (70%) of schools that performed the plays proposed. On the other hand, a positive evaluation of the distributed materials was obtained, with an average evaluation of 95% (excellent and very good). All these indicators show that there is a great interest, willingness and concern of the whole community in relation to the issue of forest fires. They also reveal that joint actions among the different social participants can be coordinated so as to have an active role and, as a whole, to manage the prevention of future hotbeds.

Discussion Questions

1. Which is the importance of cultural prevention in relation to forest fires within the Integral Plan of Fire Management?
2. In order to change undesirable behaviour in society, different actions from social marketing are proposed. One of them is education and information. Do you consider that educating children so as to reach adults is an effective and productive action to raise social awareness in the community?

3. Throughout the case, attitudes, behaviours and actions of citizens that can provoke forest fires are described. (a) According to those behaviours, can you create or define different citizen profiles? (b) For each of the above-defined profiles, identify their attitudes (positive or negative) and their behaviours (desirable/undesirable).
4. Based on question 3, what strategies of social marketing are relevant to implement: reinforcement, rationalization, induction or confrontation? Why?
5. In your opinion, which profile (question 3) matches the programme "Bombi, the firefighter"? To which strategy of social change (question 4) corresponds the programme? Explain.

References

Cabás, P. A., & Viale Linares, F. (2010). *Antes que todo se queme. La estrategia comunicacional del Plan del Manejo del Fuego para Córdoba*. V Congreso Latinoamericano de Ciencia Política. Asociación Latinoamericana de Ciencia Política, Buenos Aires. Retrieved from http://cdsa.aacademica.org/000-036/472

Fundación Vida Silvestre Argentina. (2016). *Córdoba: peligran los últimos bosques nativos de la provincia*. Retrieved from https://www.vidasilvestre.org.ar/sala_redaccion/?16260/Crdoba-peligran-los-ltimos-bosques-nativos-de-la-provincia

Groshaus, L. (2015). *Córdoba perdió 150 mil hectáreas de árboles en 12 años*. UnCiencia. Agencia universitaria de comunicación de la ciencia, el arte y la tecnología. Retrieved from http://www.unciencia.unc.edu.ar/2015/octubre/cordoba-perdio-150-mil-hectareas-de-arboles-en-12-anhos

Guía de prevención de incendios. (2007). *Plan Provincial de manejo del Fuego*. Gobierno de la Provincia de Córdoba, Abril de 2007. Retrieved from http://www.cba.gov.ar/wp-content/4p96humuzp/2012/06/Guia-para-la-Pevencion-de-Incendios-Forestales.pdf

Kopta, F., Colombati, M., & Pérez, F. (2005). *Jornadas 2005 de prevención de incendios de montes y pastizales desde las escuelas primarias de Córdoba*. Agencia Córdoba Ambiente. Gobierno de Córdoba. Retrieved from: http://www.cba.gov.ar/wp-content/4p96humuzp/2012/06/Jornadas-de-Prevencion-de-Incendios-de-Montes-y-Pastizales-2005.pdf

Santesmases Mestre, M., Sanchez De Dusso, F., & Kosiak de Gesualdo, G. (2007). *Marketing: conceptos y estrategias*. Madrid, Ediciones Pirámide.

Greenpeace's Detox Campaign: Towards a More Sustainable Textile Industry

José Manuel Ortega-Egea and Nieves García-de-Frutos

Abstract

The apparel industry has been criticized for its unsustainability, with dominant fashion firms promoting continuous changes in clothing trends, product obsolescence, and ever-increasing consumer purchases. Apparel firms have also been criticized for using highly pollutant, insecure, and unhealthy production methods, setting irregular work conditions, and paying exceptionally low wages, among other unsustainable practices.

Greenpeace's Detox campaign was a major response to the need for profound supply- and demand-side sustainability changes in the textile industry. The main goal of the Detox campaign was to reduce water pollution caused by toxic chemicals stemming from the global textile industry by targeting and securing commitment from major clothing brands. This case study draws attention to the agent/developer (i.e., Greenpeace as an NGO), main targets (brands), and the scope of the Detox campaign. It will also consider the barriers to and benefits of the pursued goals, approaches, strategies, marketing actions taken to address those barriers and benefits, and the societal outcomes and industry consequences.

J. M. Ortega-Egea (✉) · N. García-de-Frutos
Department of Economics and Business, University of Almería (ceiA3), Almería, Spain
e-mail: jmortega@ual.es; gdn779@ual.es

© Springer Nature Switzerland AG 2019
M. M. Galan-Ladero, H. M. Alves (eds.), *Case Studies on Social Marketing*, Management for Professionals, https://doi.org/10.1007/978-3-030-04843-3_4

Learning Objectives
1. To gain insight into the hidden unsustainability problems in the clothing and apparel sectors and current consumer shopping behaviors
2. To discover the process followed by an NGO to best develop an environmentally oriented social marketing campaign
3. To understand how Greenpeace turned the main goal of the Detox campaign into concrete actions
4. To learn about the actual societal and industrial consequences of a social marketing campaign

Introduction

Excessive and nonconscious consumption contributes to the depletion of natural resources and waste generation (Thøgersen and Grunert-Beckmann 1997). Unsustainable production patterns can also be linked to local and global environmental problems such as climate change. The apparel industry is illustrative of such unsustainability problems, with dominant fashion firms being criticized for shortening manufacturing and delivery times, promoting continuous changes in clothing trends, and fostering product obsolescence, thus encouraging ever-increasing and frequent consumer purchases. Apparel firms have also been criticized for using highly pollutant, insecure, and unhealthy production methods, setting irregular work conditions, and paying exceptionally low wages, among other unsustainable social and environmental practices.

The need for profound demand- and supply-side changes has led for-profit and nonprofit organizations to develop different social marketing campaigns for a more sustainable future. Greenpeace's Detox campaign is illustrative of a social marketing campaign developed by an NGO and targeted at the textile industry. The main goal of the Detox campaign was to reduce water pollution caused by toxic chemicals stemming from the global textile industry by targeting and securing commitment from major clothing brands.

Following the conceptualization of social marketing by Kotler and Lee (2005), and the approaches and strategies outlined by Santesmases Mestre (1999), this case study outlines the characteristics and development of Greenpeace's Detox campaign. Such a study is done in light of the agent/developer (i.e., Greenpeace as an NGO), main targets (brands), and scope of the campaign, barriers to and benefits of the pursued goals, approaches, strategies, and marketing actions taken to address these barriers and benefits, and the societal outcomes and consequences for the apparel/fashion industry (McKenzie-Mohr 2011).

Agent: Greenpeace

Founded in 1971 as a nonviolent, direct action environmental NGO, Greenpeace has become one of the most influential and largest sustainability NGOs, with offices in approximately 50 countries (Greenpeace 2018a). Starting with a direct protest against a nuclear weapons test, the scope of Greenpeace's campaigning has expanded to include environmental issues such as climate change, oceans, forests, toxic pollution, nuclear power, and sustainable agriculture (Greenpeace 2018b). As to their methods, in addition to direct action, Greenpeace also employs lobbying, research, and ecotage (i.e., an environmental sabotage) to achieve its environmental goals.

The Textile Industry: Unsustainable Trends

The textile and apparel industry includes companies involved in the design, production, and distribution of yarn, cloth, and clothing, based on the use of natural or synthetic raw materials or chemical products. It is a major industry that accounts for a significant share of the economy and exports in developing countries. In 2016, the largest exporting countries of textiles and apparel were China and Bangladesh, representing one of the most important trends in the industry since the 1950s (i.e., the shift of textile production for global markets from North America and Western Europe to Asia). China is currently the premier provider of clothing and footwear in most Western markets—an illustrative example of economic success in a global industry that hides environmental degradation in the producing country.

The textile and apparel sectors have been criticized as one of the top polluting industries, mainly due to the use of persistent hazardous chemicals in the manufacturing process. Such chemicals can evaporate into the air or be absorbed through the skin, thus causing serious health problems like cancer. Huge environmental damage is also caused when wastewater (e.g., from dyeing processes) is dumped directly into rivers (common practice in some Asian countries). In response to the public visibility of such health and environmental risks, consumers in Western markets are increasingly becoming concerned about the unsustainable conditions surrounding the origin and manufacture of textile and apparel products, as well as the undesirable consequences of excessive and nonconscious clothing purchases (Kim et al. 2013).

The Detox Campaign

Greenpeace launched the "Detox My Fashion" campaign in July 2011 to expose the hidden link between the textile manufacturing facilities in Asia and the release of hazardous chemicals into the environment and to urge the commitment of top clothing brands to create toxic-free fashion (Greenpeace 2011). According to Greenpeace (2016), the Detox campaign has secured commitments from

76 international clothing brands (e.g., Levi's, Zara, Benetton, Victoria's Secret, or Puma). Leading fashion brands were targeted because of their influence on suppliers, retailers, and trends in the fashion industry. Such a strategy has triggered political and policy changes in both Europe and Asia. More recently, Greenpeace has shifted the focus from detoxing the textile industry brands to slowing fast fashion (i.e., slowing the rate at which clothes are made, bought, used, and thrown away) and excessive consumption.

Targets and Implementation of the Campaign

First Stage

The considerable fragmentation of the textile and clothing industry led to targeting only *sportswear brands*. Such brands were viewed as influential players in the clothing industry, with a dissonance between promoting healthy lifestyles and lacking the policies and systems to ensure that hazardous chemicals were not released into the environment during production. It was thus thought that they were well positioned to lead the shift toward a toxic-free future (e.g., through on-the-ground action and collaborative policies) (Greenpeace 2011). Connections were identified between the sportswear brands Adidas, Nike, Puma, Bauer Hockey, Converse (a Nike brand), and Li (a Chinese brand) with two major polluting manufacturing plants in China. Nike and Adidas were challenged to champion the elimination of the release of all hazardous chemicals across their entire supply chains. In view of the pressures and public activism against Nike and Adidas—a confrontation strategy (Santesmases Mestre 1999), Puma leaped ahead of these two competitors and voluntarily committed to comply with the Detox requirements. Such an offensive strategy saved Puma from being targeted by the Detox campaign while also becoming a model for the whole industry. Further activism pressure (e.g., asking people to redesign the Nike and Adidas logos in a way that truly reflected their toxic practices and signing Greenpeace's Detox petition) led to Nike and Adidas joining Puma in the journey toward toxic-free fashion. Other sportswear brands and fashion brands followed: Li-Ning, Levi's, and Burberry, among others.

Second Stage

The next step taken in the Detox campaign was to target *fast-fashion retailers*. H&M was identified as the largest clothing company in Greenpeace's Dirty Laundry (Greenpeace 2011), with the potential to set the trend for the rest of the fashion industry. It was criticized for maintaining very low prices at the expense of manufacturing processes in polluting facilities in China. Greenpeace activists and supporters exerted pressure on H&M (e.g., by pasting massive "DETOX our water" and "DETOX the future" stickers onto H&M shop windows or rebranding H&M stickers and making these viral on social media) once more utilizing a confrontation strategy (Santesmases Mestre 1999), until the company complied with Greenpeace's Detox demands. Other fast-fashion retailers that became targets and ultimately joined the Detox challenge include, among others, C&A, Marks & Spencer, Zara, Mango, and Primark.

Of note, as of February 2012 (i.e., 7 months into the Detox campaign), Greenpeace prepared a step-by-step Detox plan (Greenpeace 2012) to aid fashion companies convert their Detox commitment plans into concrete actions. That is, an induction strategy was followed and seen appropriate at this point to facilitate bringing about the desired changes toward a toxic-free fashion production.

Third Stage

More recently, Detox pressures have focused on leading supermarkets such as Lidl and Aldi (both have committed), as well as outdoor fashion companies such as Paramo and Gore Fabrics (the maker of GORE-TEX® products)—a major supplier of membranes and coatings to outdoor brands such as The North Face and Mammut. These latter pressures are part of the spin-off Detox Outdoors campaign aimed at urging big outdoor brands to eliminate PFCs (and other hazardous chemicals) from their products. Even a company like Patagonia®, with a strong commitment to the adoption and expanding the use of more sustainable materials, has been criticized by Greenpeace's Detox campaign. Detox efforts are also being directed at fashion consumers with the goal of counteracting consumers' excessive and nonconscious consumption. The survey "Does shopping make you happy?", commissioned by Greenpeace in 2017, found that people buy far more than they need or use and questioned the "false" idea that shopping makes people happy. Results from this survey, coupled with segmentation analyses, could be used to devise new reinforcement, induction, rationalization, and confrontation Detox strategies (Santesmases Mestre 1999), to be targeted at different types of fashion consumers.

Marketing Mix

Product

The objective of the Detox campaign is to change pollutant practices of the textile industry by urging clothing companies to stop using hazardous chemicals that contaminate water, not only during the manufacturing process but also every time garments are washed. Facing individuals against such an ambitious objective may generate them feelings of powerless. That is, they may feel that they have little to do to force the giant textile industry to change its hazardous practices. Hence, the first step for Greenpeace consisted in breaking down this larger objective into smaller and more reachable goals.

Their first attempt to raise awareness of the environmental problems caused by the textile industry consisted in the launch of the "Dirty Laundry" report where it stated: "Brand owners are therefore the best placed to bring about change in the production of textiles and clothing" (Greenpeace 2011, p. 7). As previously mentioned, Greenpeace did not focus on the whole industry, but started targeting globally recognized brands such as Nike and Adidas.

Individuals may also be uncertain about the best way to induce companies to change. In response to this uncertainty, Greenpeace provided several action plans, which varied in terms of difficulty. Thus, individuals were encouraged to share information about the campaign and its events, address pollutant targets and complain about their unethical behavior, participate in different kinds of live protests, and stop consuming clothes from the targeted brands. This helped individuals to choose the action best suited to their personal interests. More importantly, the broad and abstract objective of changing the environmental practices of the textile industry could become as simple as sharing one petition.

Promotion

The Detox campaign has been active since 2011, but as previously mentioned, it gradually adapts its specific plans of action and broadens the number of targets. When a target company finally commits to the NGO's requirements, new targets are set. Hence, the main lines of the communication plan have been maintained, such as the media mix and the main content of the message. However, other parts of the campaign have undergone several adaptations, such as the language and style of the message. This is a way to better address the specific type of consumer of each brand targeted by the campaign. Some important elements in the communication plan of the Detox campaign are the following:

Message Framing

As mentioned, one of the key features of the Detox campaign is its evolving and adapting nature. Messages are adapted in order to engage with the specific type of consumer of each targeted brand. For example, when Greenpeace launched the Detox campaign to challenge Nike and Adidas, they launched a video that imitated the advertisements of both brands. The people, music, and actions were similar, but some elements were added: chemical symbols to represent the hazardous substances that are released in the water by clothing production. At the end of the video, both companies are explicitly addressed and urged to detox their production. Since Nike and Adidas are sport brands, Greenpeace framed it like a challenge and wondered which company would become the "Detox champion." Finally, the video combines the Detox message with a play on words with the slogans of both companies by asking them whether they are "all in" (Adidas' slogan: "Adidas is all in") and demanding that they "just do it" (Nike's slogan: "Just do it").

In contrast, when the NGO addressed children's clothing companies, such as Disney and American Apparel, they created the microsite "Little Monsters" (Greenpeace 2014). The little monsters were depicted as drawings of small ugly creatures, used to represent hazardous chemical substances such as phthalates or PFCs. The language used imitated a fairy tale, starting with the "once upon a time" formula. The images related to this part of the campaign showed children that were visibly angry or scared because of the little monsters. This report was linked to a microsite where further information about the problem was provided, using colorful typography for titles and evoking children's writing.

In addition, other elements of the campaign have been maintained over time. Perhaps, the most important element is the symbol chosen to represent the Detox campaign. This is a Chinese character called *shui* (水), which represents water. The Chinese ideogram was selected to emphasize the need to clean the water from polluting chemical substances, especially in China, where the problem is more serious because of the large number of companies comprising the textile industry. The *shui* character is often employed as part of the Detox word, substituting the final x character. Yet, it is also depicted alone, usually tattooed on activists' skin. For example, in the Adidas versus Nike video, the *shui* symbol can be found as part of the Detox word in graffiti or a party invitation but also tattooed on people's skin. In the little monsters microsite, the *shui* symbol also appears tattooed on children's bodies.

In most of the videos and reports of the Detox campaign, Greenpeace makes an effort to show citizens how the brands and clothes they purchase every day are linked to water pollution. In order to do so, they offer images of branded clothes with vivid colors and then trace the manufacturing process back, showing the factories and the polluted rivers, all dyed in the same color—i.e., pink. They also show images of people doing the laundry, in order to connect the whole cycle. Other imagery of the Detox campaign shows famous models posing in factories or rivers in order to make the fashion-pollution connection more evident.

There is a combination of rational and emotional appeals. On the rational side, Greenpeace provides results of laboratory tests on chemical substances and the harmful effects that each one of these substances may have on human health. This is to foster cognitive reasoning and information processing. On the other hand, they also use pictures of environmental degradation, i.e., polluted water, which evoke negative feelings toward factories and brands. Connecting these images with the ones of average people doing their laundry helps to enhance feelings of proximity to the problem, reinforcing negative emotions toward brands.

Media and Formats
The Detox campaign uses different channels and formats to attract the attention of the companies and the public, but the main media employed to spread their message is the Internet.

Online On the Internet, the NGO wisely combines the publication of content on their various websites—i.e., Greenpeace International, national Greenpeace websites, and microsites—with a very active campaign in different social media, i.e., Facebook, Twitter, Weibo, Instagram, and YouTube. Greenpeace employs a variety of formats to provide content in the abovementioned online channels. Periodic *reports* offer relevant information about the problem in a detailed and scientific way, pointing to the main challenges and contributors to the problem but also manifesting venues for citizen action. Reports also help individuals to keep track of the achievements of targeted brands and companies. Reports are offered in pdf format, but the information can also be displayed in a microsite, to allow greater interactivity—i.e., individuals can automatically share a certain part of the information provided or read more about a certain target. Information about the campaign is also provided in shorter formats such as blog entries or microblogging postings. The company also employs richer formats, such as different types of *videos*—i.e., animated, documentary, or advertising-like—which have been launched to briefly inform about the problem and the severity of its consequences and promote citizen action.

Offline The Detox campaign places a great deal of attention on *outdoor elements*. In a guerrilla-marketing tactic, they organize different interventions on targets. They use elements such as stickers or banners with the symbols of the campaign and place them in stores owned by those companies that have been previously selected as targets. The NGO also organizes press conferences, sometimes programming simultaneous conferences in different locations. This helps to transmit the idea of the global reach and level of organization that Greenpeace is able to exhibit. Numerous news media have echoed some of the most important findings in the Greenpeace reports and have published news covering their interventions in different stores around the world. The media also publish the reactions of the companies to the pressure of the campaign.

Place

Online One important venue for campaign development is the Internet and especially social media. Given the global nature of the campaign, Greenpeace has employed social media such as Facebook or Twitter, which are used in many countries around the world, but they have also turned to more locally known alternatives, such as Weibo, which is a Chinese social media site and little known outside of the Asian giant. In social media, Greenpeace and its followers directly addressed targeted brands and companies in their own fan pages, filling them with critical messages demanding action. Users also explicitly addressed the targeted companies by using the "@+name of the company" formula in their messages, to make sure companies received their notifications (Brunner and DeLuca 2016).

Offline The NGO has carefully selected the locations where to promote the campaign and address specific targets. Most offline actions have been placed in flagship stores of targeted brands. Such stores tend to be located in the center of large cities, where many people pass by every day. Hence, the election of these locations is made in accordance to the relevance of the store for the brand and the visibility of the protest location. This has occurred in cities around the world, particularly in Europe, America, and Asia. Protest actions have also been carried out on factories that are the direct pollutants and supply textiles and garments to the targeted brands, for example, in China or Mexico.

Price
Greenpeace aims to convince targeted companies that the costs of changing their environmental practices are small. To do so, they place emphasis on the high

environmental costs caused by their manufacturing practices and highlight the benefits of changing their policies regarding toxic chemicals. The NGO challenges companies to become sustainability leaders. Therefore, they are indirectly telling targeted companies that by complying with their requirements, the companies will improve their environmental reputation. In fact, Greenpeace publicly praises each company that committed to detox their products. In addition, the NGO designed a roadmap on how to improve the environmental conditions of garment manufacturing and offered it to companies that were committed to the Detox objective. This collaboration also lowers the costs for companies.

For individuals, the costs of taking action are minimized by offering them different ways to collaborate. Those more engaged in environmental activism could take part in the public acts and interventions in stores located around the world. However, the NGO also offers other options, so individuals do not need to leave the comfort of their homes to feel they are doing the right thing. Thus, it is possible to participate in the campaign by merely clicking on a button on the Greenpeace webpage. For example, in one of their latest microsites "the catwalk Detox," the NGO offers the possibility of sharing a prewritten tweet or Facebook message specifically targeting one of the different companies that have been analyzed. Hence, the costs of thinking of a message, writing, and posting it are simplified.

Consequences of the Campaign

Extant studies manifest that brands targeted by the Detox campaign suffered damages in terms of more negative attitudes toward them and lower intentions of purchase of their products (Grappi et al. 2017). However, this effect seems to be moderated by the reaction of the brand itself to the demands of Greenpeace. Thus, when targeted companies finally comply with the NGO's requirements, the effects on attitudes and purchase intention become weaker compared to those brands that choose to ignore the Detox campaign. Consequently, effects on companies and brands depend greatly on the response they demonstrate to the NGO's demands. At a broader level, several brands, including some of them owned by the biggest players in the industry, have committed to detox their manufacturing processes and are taking steps in that direction. An important policy achievement of the Detox campaign was the banning of the toxic chemical NPE from textile imports to all EU member states (Greenpeace 2018c).

Conclusion

This case study shows how an ambitious objective, such as changing the practices of an entire industry, can be effectively addressed by an NGO. In this case, Greenpeace's Detox campaign is used as an example of how, by breaking down comprehensive objectives into smaller goals and with an ever-changing campaign, positive results are possible.

Discussion Questions

1. Critique Greenpeace's decision to first target sportswear brands in the Detox campaign. Why not first address counteracting consumers' unsustainable shopping behavior?
2. Was the selection of the confrontation strategy appropriate? What other strategies (e.g., reinforcement, induction, or rationalization) could be used, and how?
3. The messages used in the Detox campaign are adapted to the characteristics of each specific brand target. What are the advantages and disadvantages of this approach?
4. Think of a different sector (e.g., electronics), and sketch a suitable social marketing plan, drawing on the example of the Detox campaign.

Acknowledgments The authors gratefully acknowledge the financial support of the Spanish Ministry of Economy and Science and the European Regional Development Fund -ERDF/FEDER (National R&D Project ECO2015-66504-P), from the University of Almería (UAL, ceiA3), and CySOC.

References

Drumici, E. A., & DeLuca, K. M. (2016). The argumentative force of image networks: Greenpeace's panmediated global detox campaign. *Argumentation and Advocacy, 52*(4), 281–299.
Grappi, S., Romani, S., & Barbarossa, C. (2017). Fashion without pollution: How consumers evaluate brands after an NGO campaign aimed at reducing toxic chemicals in the fashion industry. *Journal of Cleaner Production, 149,* 1164–1173.
Greenpeace. (2011). *Dirty laundry. Unravelling the corporate connections to toxic water pollution in China.* Retrieved February 25, 2018, from https://www.greenpeace.org/archive-international/Global/international/publications/toxics/Water%202011/dirty-laundry-report.pdf
Greenpeace. (2012). *The step-by-step detox plan.* Retrieved March 2, 2018, from https://www.greenpeace.org/archive-international/en/news/Blogs/makingwaves/the-step-by-step-detox-plan/blog/38962/
Greenpeace. (2014). *Little monsters: Greenpeace.org.* Retrieved March 15, 2018, from https://www.greenpeace.org/archive-international/Global/international/code/2014/littlemonsters/index.html
Greenpeace. (2016). *The detox catwalk: Greenpeace.org.* Retrieved February 20, 2018, from https://www.greenpeace.org/international/worldwide/
Greenpeace. (2018a). *Our offices: Greenpeace.org.* Retrieved February 10, 2018 from https://www.greenpeace.org/international/worldwide/
Greenpeace. (2018b). *What we do: Greenpeace.org.* Retrieved February 10, 2018, from https://www.greenpeace.org/archive-international/en/campaigns/
Greenpeace. (2018c). *Detox timeline: Greenpeace.org.* Retrieved March 5, 2018, from http://www.greenpeace.org/archive-international/en/campaigns/detox/timeline/

Kim, H., Jung Choo, H., & Yoon, N. (2013). The motivational drivers of fast fashion avoidance. *Journal of Fashion Marketing and Management: An International Journal, 17*(2), 243–260.
Kotler, P., & Lee, N. (2005). *Corporate social responsibility*. New York: Wiley.
McKenzie-Mohr, D. (2011). *Fostering sustainable behavior: An introduction to community-based social marketing*. Gabriola Island: New Society Publishers.
Santesmases Mestre, M. (1999). *Marketing. Conceptos y Estrategias*. Madrid: Piramide.
Thøgersen, J., & Grunert-Beckmann, S. C. (1997). Values and attitude formation towards emerging attitude objects: From recycling to general, waste minimizing behavior. In M. Brucks & D. J. MacInnis (Eds.), *Advances in consumer research* (Vol. 24, pp. 182–189). Provo, UT: Association for Consumer Research.

Part II

Social Marketing Cases: Public Health

Going Beyond Downstream Social Marketing: The Case of "Jamie's Food Revolution"

María José Montero-Simó and Rafael A. Araque-Padilla

Abstract

Until the mid-1990s, much of the focus in social marketing was on individual behaviour change, the so-called downstream social marketing. In recent years, scholars have proposed a broadening of social marketing's horizons beyond the individual to attempt to influence those that help shape the determinants of human behaviour, namely, the structural and immediate social environment. This broadening highlights the necessity to go upper stream in search of the causes of social problems (upstream social marketing).

This case study addresses how a more comprehensive social marketing approach can be applied. To do that, "Jamie's Food Revolution" campaign is analysed. This campaign looks for engaging different agents in an attempt to take into account their role in the change and push governments to improve their food and nutrition policies. This campaign offers us a good example for examining the potential of an upper stream social marketing approach to address a social problem.

M. J. Montero-Simó (✉) · R. A. Araque-Padilla
Universidad Loyola Andalucía, Seville, Spain
e-mail: jmontero@uloyola.es; raraque@uloyola.es

© Springer Nature Switzerland AG 2019
M. M. Galan-Ladero, H. M. Alves (eds.), *Case Studies on Social Marketing*, Management for Professionals, https://doi.org/10.1007/978-3-030-04843-3_5

> **Learning Objectives**
> - Differentiate between down and upstream social marketing. Understand what is meant by moving upstream in social marketing.
> - Recognize how important it is for social marketers to think beyond the individual and to ask themselves what kind of causal behaviours should be changed.
> - Understand that regardless of the person whose behaviour you are trying to change, the same basic social marketing principles are applied.

Introduction

Childhood obesity is one of the most serious public health challenges of the twenty-first century. The problem is global and steadily affects many low- and middle-income countries, particularly in urban settings. The prevalence of childhood obesity has increased at an alarming rate. According to the World Health Organization (WHO), the number of overweight or obese infants and young children (aged 0–5 years) has increased from 32 million globally in 1990 to 41 million in 2016. In the WHO African Region alone, the number of overweight or obese children increased from four to nine million over the same period. The vast majority of overweight or obese children live in developing countries, where the rate of increase has been more than 30% higher than that of developed countries. If current trends continue, the number of overweight or obese infants and young children will increase globally to 70 million by 2025. Without intervention, obese infants and young children will likely continue to be obese during childhood, adolescence and adulthood.

Overweight and obese children are likely to stay obese into adulthood and more likely to develop non-communicable diseases, such as diabetes and cardiovascular diseases, at a younger age. However, overweight and obesity, as well as their related diseases, are largely preventable. Prevention of childhood obesity therefore needs to be a high priority. The WHO Member States in the 66th World Health Assembly have agreed on a voluntary global non-communicable disease target to halt the rise in diabetes and obesity.

In the case of the UK, the situation is worrisome. Children and adults in the UK lead the numbers of overweight individuals in Europe: there are seven thousand amputations a year due to diabetes suffered by three million people. Two out of three adults are overweight, and one in four adults suffers from obesity. To the point, the problem is serious enough that different initiatives have recently been launched to try to remedy the problem of obesity. One of those campaigns constitutes the content of the case that is presented.

A necessary starting point to understand the case is analysing what typical British families eat and what is influencing their choice of food and drink. According to The Food Foundation report (The Food Foundation 2016), typical British families have four members: two adults, a primary school-age child and a secondary school-age child. These families have a total household income between £37,000 and £52,000, the middle-income band in the UK in 2013. Approximately 1.5 million families of four members in the UK have an income at or below this level. Parents in these typical families are administrators, teachers, health professionals and builders.

Starting with national data sets, primary data collection, secondary sources and key informant interviews, the cited report outlines three main findings:

1. The diets of typical British families now pose the greatest threat to their health and survival. None of the UK family members meet all seven dietary standards that directly protect their health. Two-thirds of their calories come from highly processed foods, many of which are low in fibre and high in fat, sugar or salt (HFSS). Adults are eating too much red and processed meat. The diets of children are particularly concerning: 47% of primary school children's dietary energy comes from HFSS foods, 85% of secondary school children are not eating enough fruit and vegetables, more than 90% are not eating enough fibre, and all are eating too much sugar. Families are spending nearly one-fifth (18%) of their money on food, throwing much of the food away (equivalent to six meals per week), and not receiving value for their money.
2. Many factors in the food environment prevent UK families from eating healthy:
   - Food and drink advertising reaches UK family members, including children, through multiple channels. Adverts for prepared convenience foods and confectioneries account for 60% of food advertising spend.
   - There is an abundance of food conveniently available to UK family members. The number of places to eat out has increased by more than 50% in the last 10 years, and the single largest category is quick-service restaurants (QSRs), which typically sell less-healthy meals.
   - Promotions cause people to buy one-fifth more than they otherwise would. Supermarket and eating out promotions are biased towards unhealthy foods.
   - Healthy choices within the UK family's popular product categories are limited. Only 5% of items in four product lines bought by typical families (ready meals, breakfast cereals, bread and yoghurts) have low levels of fat, saturated fats, sugar or salt.
   - Labelling is confusing due to inconsistent use of traffic lights, no consistency in the use of portion sizes, continued use of display until and sell by dates and inconsistency between nutrient claims and traffic lights.
   - School meals offer children protection from all these factors during the school day and during term time, but uptake is only high among infants for whom the meals are free.
3. The balance of prices of their food is wrong, tipping them even further towards unhealthy diets. Healthier foods are three times more expensive than HFSS foods as a source of dietary energy, and the price difference is growing. QSR meals, which tend to be less healthy, are £10 cheaper on average than meals in pubs, restaurants and hotels.

In summary, the children in the UK typical family have very poor diets; one in three children is overweight and obese, with all the concomitant psychological and health consequences, and a growing number are even experiencing type 2 diabetes in adolescence. These children are tomorrow's parents and the future workforce. If nothing else, changes in the food system must be done to help ensure that they can eat more healthily.

Case Development

As a response to the challenges above, Chef Jamie Oliver (of The Naked Chef) launched a cross-platform campaign called Jamie's Food Revolution.[1] Currently, the Food Revolution is an ongoing, global campaign of the Jamie Oliver Food Foundation and its partners at the Good Foundation to provoke debate and inspire positive, meaningful change in the way we access, consume and understand food. From food education programmes delivered at a local level to national and international campaigns that influence policy on key issues, the campaign aims to revolutionize the way people feed themselves and their families.

The project tries to involve different stakeholders—families, schools, hospitality industry and policy makers—in a joint effort to discuss the solutions that could provide children with access to good, fresh, nutritious food for generations to come. This project has established four main objectives:

1. *Food education*. Good food education enables people everywhere to develop a better, more understanding and balanced relationship with food.
2. *Nutrition*. Ensuring that children have access to good, nutritious food is vital to helping them grow up to be healthy and happy.
3. *Food waste*. Globally, we waste enough food to feed the world's hunger four times over. Food waste is not only immoral but also unnecessary.
4. *Our planet*. To sustain nutritious food for now and for the future, we need to care for the planet that produces it, linking individuals, food and the environment to create a sustainable, healthy food system on both commercial and domestic levels.

The Strategy: A Multi-stakeholder Approach

A. Working with Families
The project promotes initiatives at different levels, from education at home to support for campaigns:

---

[1]All the information about Food Revolution Campaign has been obtained from the following websites: www.jamiesfoodrevolution.com; www.jamieoliver.com; www.jamiesministryoffood.com.au and https://timecounts.org/foodfoundation.

1. *Campaigning for better school food policies and standards.* Change can start at home simply by learning to cook a few nutritious meals and passing those new skills onto friends and family. For example, the initiative invited families to obtain downloads such as the ones shown below and to join their "kids' Food Truth gang". Additionally, it is possible to check out Jamie's Food Revolution breakfast recipes.
2. *Raising awareness through social media, blogging and recipe sharing.* For example, one can sign up and receive all the latest news straight to his/her inbox and share on social media.
3. *Fundraising and supporting Jamie's projects or starting a new initiative.*
4. *Choosing something that excites and inspires.* Local groups and local ambassadors should be able to get started and be acquainted with the current events and campaigns in a local area.
5. *Proposing new initiatives.* One does not have to just stick to these exact actions. If people have other ideas or are already working on other initiatives, they are invited to let the project know.

B. Schools as a Change Agent

Through Jamie Oliver's Kitchen Garden Project, primary school teachers are empowered to integrate growing and cooking into the school day. By teaching children about food, where it comes from, how to cook it and how it affects their bodies, resources and recipes equip children with the knowledge and confidence to cook from scratch. The work also extends to secondary schools through Jamie's Home Cooking Skills, a BTEC (Business and Technology Education Council)-accredited programme.

These resources are also available online through the Food for Life schools and early-year programmes. This means that one can access both programmes' high-quality resources for a single subscription, giving even more support to bring food education to life as well as the support needed to take the first steps to a whole-school approach to food.

Food for Life is an award programme that provides resources, support and guidance to help schools and nurseries provide freshly prepared, nutritious lunches, make lunchtimes a positive part of the day, and give children and parents the opportunity to learn how to cook, grow food and understand where their food comes from.

Through the programmes, schools can achieve awards that demonstrate their commitment to children's health to the wider world. Schools can work to meet criteria at the bronze, silver and gold levels, while nurseries and children's centres apply for a single tier award.

C. Influencing Food Hospitality

Since 2002, Jamie Oliver's Fifteen restaurant in London has trained more than 164 young adults to become chefs. Today, 80% of graduates are still in the hospitality industry. Building on this success—and continuing Jamie's mission to add more new chefs to the industry—his apprentice programme will now be in action across all of Jamie's 46 UK restaurants, including Fifteen London.

The Jamie Oliver Restaurant Group is composed of all Jamie's restaurant brands: Jamie's Italian, Jamie's Italian International, Barbecoa, Fifteen, Union Jacks, Jamie Oliver's Diner, Jamie's Pizzeria, Jamie's Deli and The Jamie Oliver Cookery School. Each brand has its own culture and values based on Jamie's approach to life. These brands inspire everything from the way the staff interact with guests and teammates to how managers develop their staff.

D. In Search of Political Action

In lobbying the UK government to introduce a strong and robust multisectoral childhood obesity strategy, together with medical experts and professionals, Jamie Oliver launched a six-point plan to tackle childhood obesity in the UK. He works with partners all over the world to raise awareness and pressurize governments and businesses to become serious about making sure children have access to the right food. This plan details a range of proposed policies, initiatives, incentives and community-based interventions, which together try to create a powerful tool to change the way children access and consume food and drink:

1. *Sugary Drink Tax*: To pressurize the government into bringing a sugary drink levy. The revenue will be invested in health initiatives and food education.

    Recent results from the Carbohydrates and Health Report (Scientific Advisory Committee on Nutrition (SACN) 2015) show that soft drinks are the largest single source of sugar consumption for school-age children and teenagers. The suggestion of an introduction of a 20 p levy per litre on all sugary soft drinks could not only drive down consumption but also raise revenue of up to £1 billion per year. The UK government should also be encouraging food manufacturers to show sugar content in teaspoons on their products, with the aim of this labelling to eventually become mandatory throughout the EU.
2. *Sugar Reformulation*: Mandatory targets to reduce excessive sugar in all products and penalties for non-compliance.

    A soft drink levy will kick-start the task of reducing childhood obesity levels, but in the long term, food reformulation is needed. The government must ensure that all food available for purchase in the UK is as healthy as possible as soon as possible. A compulsory long-term programme to reformulate all food and drink products with excessively high levels of sugar must be put in place. A compulsory strategy must be pursued since the voluntary Responsibility Deal between government and industry, conceived 5 years ago in an attempt to improve public health, failed. Ultimately, penalties should be imposed on any food companies that fail to meet the targets.
3. *Fair Marketing*: A ban on food advertising targeted at children and cutting the promotion of sugary products.

    The affordability and marketing of food need urgent attention, and policies to reduce the cost of healthy foods are required. Regulations should be put in place to promote healthier choices and limit the quantity, frequency and amount of time that food and drinks that are high in fat, salt or sugar (HFSS) can be promoted.

The introduction of a buy-one-get-a-reduction-on-another scheme for healthier food products should be implemented, and supermarkets should be encouraged to provide on-premises cooking classes for customers, with government grants for in-store kitchens. Supermarkets should be incentivized to work more closely with organizations such as FareShare (which has estimated that food waste could provide 800 million meals for British people living in poverty) and FoodCycle, so that nutritious food can be made more available to people on lower incomes.

Restrictions on the types of food businesses allowed to set up near schools should be put in place to limit the unhealthy choices available to children. The saturation of HFSS food in corner shops and the checkout aisles of supermarkets must also be addressed.

4. *Clearer Labelling*: Mandatory and clear on-pack sugar information, such as traffic light labelling, in addition to restrictions on portion sizes for confectionary and sugary drinks.

    Both the SACN and WHO have published guidelines recommending that everyone should consume far less free sugar daily, but current EU-governed labelling legislation around sugar is not proving adequate. Product labels do not currently differentiate between the quantity of natural sugar in a product and any free sugars (sugar found in honey, syrups and fruit juices as well as refined sugar added to the product by the manufacturers). It is therefore extremely difficult for consumers to judge how well they are keeping to the SACN and WHO guidelines. In addition, front-of-pack traffic light labelling should be made mandatory, and restrictions on portion sizes should be legislated, where appropriate.

5. *School Food*: Access to healthy food at school for all children, prioritizing food education in schools.

    The project considers that it is every child's human right to learn about real food, where it comes from, how it affects their body and how to cook it. The ongoing delivery of the actions in the UK government's School Food Plan is vital and should be made compulsory for all schools. Free school meals should be made available to all families, and school food standards must apply to packed lunches, with guidance from the Department of Health and Change4Life. Other suggestions include the following. To further build on the success of the School Food Plan (Ofsted), school inspections must report on how schools ensure children are eating well and leading active lifestyles. Basic nutritional training must be embedded in all teachers training, and educational programmes must be offered to parents, parents-to-be and healthcare workers—particularly doctors, midwives and health visitors. Out-of-term clubs would be a great opportunity for children who might otherwise go hungry during the holidays to receive cooking lessons, using donated food that might otherwise be destined for the landfill.

6. *Education*: Clear national guides on what nutritious daily meals look like, practical resources for both parents and teachers and better consistency between the classroom and home.

    Parents should be armed with the tools to help their children be the healthiest they can be. One way of doing so is by extending the National Child

Measurement Programme (NCMP) in schools. The NCMP currently measures the weight and height of children in the reception class and again in year 6. Ideally, it should be implemented from preschool years and then annually throughout primary school so that early signs of obesity can be identified and preventative measures put in place, where required. It is extremely important that such a programme is sensitively run so that it does not lead to an increase in eating disorders among children and young people. Expertise on this matter should be sought so that the NCMP leads to only positive outcomes for young people.

Conclusions

This case shows us the power and creativity of social marketing to tackle complex social problems, such as childhood obesity. In these situations, social marketers must adopt a broader perspective of intervention. They have to be concerned with changing the social context in which individuals make decisions about their behaviour, going beyond individuals' behaviour, "moving upstream" and recognizing that there will be occasions when this strategy will provide more effective and efficient social marketing solutions. All levels of intervention are needed if social marketing is going to move from isolated behaviour change to ongoing social change (Hastings 2008).

Regardless, upstream social marketing involves the adaptation and application of marketing and other approaches to change the behaviour of decision makers and opinion formers, which alters the structural environment and has a resultant positive influence on social issues (Gordon 2013). One author used a metaphor to illustrate this broader perspective of intervention in social marketing:

> Some bystanders on a riverbank notice a person swept up by the river's current and clearly in trouble. One shouts: *Why don't you know how to swim?*; a second offers swimming lesson coupons; and fortunately, a third jumps in and pulls the drowning person out. Over time, more and more people float down the river in trouble. Researchers take demographic profiles of these people. The whole effort proves very expensive. Some who are saved end up falling back in. Eventually there are so many in the river, it is impossible to save them all. Too many were falling in. The growing group that hung around the river finally got the bright idea that perhaps they should look upstream to see why so many people were falling into the river in the first place. Once they got upstream, they found all kinds of signs saying things like: *Jump in. It's fun. Don't worry*. The endorsers on the ads were attractive role models. The few signs urging caution could hardly be seen. When these river marketers were criticized, their answer was that they felt it was the responsibility of each individual to know his/her own swimming abilities. It was up to the family to teach their kids. Some of the investigators present agreed and decided to work toward better swimming curricula in the schools and greater family involvement. But others thought that the real problem was the upstream environment. They argued that the signs should be taken down and that commercial free speech was not deserving of the same protection as political speech. Others worked for counter advertising that might alter the environment. Still others thought that, although the marketing and advertising environment was a problem, it might be wise to look even further upstream. They found that there were large parts of the population in specific areas that were sliding into the river. These were the areas where there was high unemployment, racism, lack of education and economic opportunity, and limited access to health care. The story

concludes with the argument that these latter upstream factors are the ultimate source of public health problems and that it is critical to link these problems with downstream conditions. (Goldberg 1995)

Undoubtedly, the more we keep going upstream, the more stakeholders are involved, the more difficult it is to bring changes and more necessary it is to appeal to different strategies of action. However, otherwise, a focus on only individuals' behaviour without paying attention to the causal conditions is not enough to influence rooted social habits.

Working at different levels implies identifying the key stakeholders and understanding how the different factors influencing a social problem are related. In this line, it is crucial to count on a good analysis of the situation. Jamie's Food Revolution project has been supported by scientific reports, such as The Food Foundation Project, which brings stronger rationales to the proposed strategies.

The wider focus of upstream social marketing requires applying the social marketing concepts and strategies to different stakeholders, which must be considered as not only target adopters but also intermediaries in many cases. For example, the hospitality industry could be a target adopter when a change in their products or promotion practices is needed to obtain social change; however, at the same time, it is an intermediary as long as it can play a key role in raising awareness of healthy food habits in families (e.g. involvement in public campaigns or the use of communication strategies to inform and educate).

Finally, the design of proposals for decision makers and opinion formers is usually more controversial than actions trying to change an individual's habits. Unfortunately, changing structural causes is not an easy task because there are diverse intermingled interests. The search for influence upstream requires a long-term approach, continuous public debates, refining of proposals, searches for the support of other social agents and a great dose of patience and persistence.

Discussion Questions

1. Explain how Jamie's Food Revolution project has sought to go upstream in search of greater effectiveness in social change.
2. How have the basic social marketing strategies been applied to influence the diverse behaviours to be modified?
3. In your opinion, which key stakeholders (families, schools, industry, government) have been the most weakly addressed in the project? Propose some possible actions for them.

References

Goldberg, M. E. (1995). Social marketing: Are we fiddling while Rome burns? *Journal of Consumer Psychology, 4*(4), 347–370.
Gordon, R. (2013). Unlocking the potential of upstream social marketing. *European Journal of Marketing, 47*(9), 1525–1547.

Hastings, G. (2008). *Social marketing. Why should the devil have all the best tunes?* Oxford: Butterworth-Heinemann (Elsevier).

Scientific Advisory Committee on Nutrition (SACN). (2015). *Carbohydrates and health report.* Norwich: The Stationery Office.

The Food Foundation. (2016). *FORCE-FED. Does the food system constrict healthy choices for typical British families?* London. https://foodfoundation.org.uk/wp-content/uploads/2016/07/The-Food-Foundation-64pp-A4-Landscape-Brochure-AW-V32.pdf

How to Promote Blood Donation? The Case of the Blood Donor Association of Cantabria (Spain)

M. Mar. García-De los Salmones and Andrea Pérez

Abstract
The present case study focuses on the application of social marketing principles to the promotion of blood donation. In this regard, many lives depend on the availability of safe blood supplies for transfusions and medical procedures, and the voluntary contribution of people is key to the success of the blood donation system. Specifically, we introduce the demographic profile of blood donors in Spain, paying special attention to the younger segment as a relevant target in promoting donations. We also detail the restraints and motivations that guide people's behaviour regarding blood donation. Later, we describe the actions carried out by the Blood Donor Association of Cantabria (i.e. the main non-profit association in charge of creating the permanent blood bank in this geographical region) to promote voluntary donations, paying special attention to young people and experienced donors. The case study ends with conclusions and discussion questions.

M. M. García-De los Salmones · A. Pérez (✉)
Business Administration Department, University of Cantabria, Santander, Spain
e-mail: gsalmonm@unican.es; perezran@unican.es

> **Learning Objectives**
> - Define the importance of blood donation as a prosocial behaviour.
> - Analyse factors influencing donor behaviour.
> - Analyse how social marketing can be applied to promote blood donation.
> - Describe the actions carried out by the Blood Donor Association of Cantabria in terms of convenience and communication, specifically targeted to young people.

Introduction

Blood is necessary for life. For surgery and/or transplants, hospitals require blood to be successful. Many lives depend on the availability of safe blood supplies for transfusions and medical procedures (Lemmens et al. 2009). The necessity is permanent, so the contribution of people is key for a reliable, constant supply and for satisfying a demand that otherwise could not be met.

There are three main sources for collecting blood (World Health Organization (WHO) 2017): (a) replacements that come from relatives of the patient, (b) paid blood donations and (c) voluntary unpaid blood donations. According to the WHO, the last source is the most important as it is the only system that ensures a reliable supply of safe blood for patients whose lives depend on it. In fact, the challenge of the WHO is to get all countries in the world to implement fully voluntary, non-remunerated blood donations in the short term. In the same vein, the Council of Europe has presented several reports with measurements to guarantee the self sufficiency of the European Community by means of unpaid blood donations. Although most European countries report collecting blood from 100% (or almost 100%) voluntary, non-remunerated donors (WHO 2017), there are still some exceptions. For instance, in Germany some organizations offer a reimbursement for whole-blood donors to cover their expenses. On the contrary, in Spain any type of payment has been forbidden since 1985, and blood donation constitutes a totally anonymous, voluntary and free act. The implementation of this non-remunerated system forces the development of awareness programmes to attract new donors and retain existing ones; this is where social marketing comes into play.

Furthermore, young people's attitude towards donating has been recently identified as a significant challenge to the stability of the voluntary donation system established in most developed countries. In this regard, the willingness of the younger age groups to donate is significantly lower than older age groups, while these older people are entering the age when they need to receive (rather than give) donations (Solomon 2012). Thus, young prospective donors, with their long-term donation potential, constitute an especially attractive target for blood collection agencies (Hupfer 2006). For this reason, the identification and development of good social marketing campaigns oriented to this group are especially useful.

Based on this information, the present case study considers the Spanish context and analyses the application of social marketing principles to blood donation. In this regard, Spain maintains record numbers of transplants and organ donations, and its donation system has been a world leader for the last 26 years (National Transplant Organization 2017). In the case of blood donation, the Spanish rate has always remained close to the value recommended by the WHO (i.e. at least 40 donations per 1000 inhabitants to be self-sufficient in national blood supplies). These good results are supported in a very effective donation system, frequent awareness campaigns and, above all, much solidarity.

More precisely, the case focuses on presenting the social marketing actions implemented by the "Asociación-Hermandad de Donantes de Sangre de Cantabria" [i.e. Blood Donor Association of Cantabria (Spain)]. This association is the main non-profit organization in charge of creating the permanent blood bank in this geographical region, and it provides an interesting example of an organization strongly committed to the promotion of voluntary donations among young donors.

Throughout the case study, the demographic profile of national and regional donors, as well as motivations and restraints of common people regarding blood donation, will be shown as a first approximation to the topic. Later in the chapter, the social marketing actions carried out by the Blood Donor Association of Cantabria will be described. Specifically, and taking into account the importance of attracting young people to ensure the replacement of generations, the current case study details some of the most relevant marketing strategies targeted to this group. Results that measure the success of the social marketing strategy of the organization will also be shown. Finally, the chapter ends with the proposition of a set of discussion questions that will allow the reader to delve more deeply into the work of the Blood Donor Association of Cantabria, as well as reflect on social marketing and its applicability to blood donation.

Market Segmentation and Factors Affecting Blood Donation

Market segmentation is defined as the division of a market into distinct subsets of customers having similar needs and wants, each of which can be reached with a different marketing mix (Kotler 1994). The advantage of segmentation is that it allows an organization to tailor a marketing mix to the needs and wants of homogeneous subsets of customers that are not shared by the general consumer (Mowen and Minor 1998).

In the context of blood donations, profiling and segmentation studies indicate that the majority of donors are male, owing to a higher dropout rate of females, in their mid-30s (or older), and have higher educational, occupational and income levels than non-donors (Grant 2010). As shown in Fig. 1, in the Spanish context, people between 31 and 45 are the most frequent donors (Spanish Federation of Blood Donors 2017). In Cantabria, there is also a high proportion of donors aged 46 and over, while younger donors aged 30 and below only represent 23% of the pool of donors.

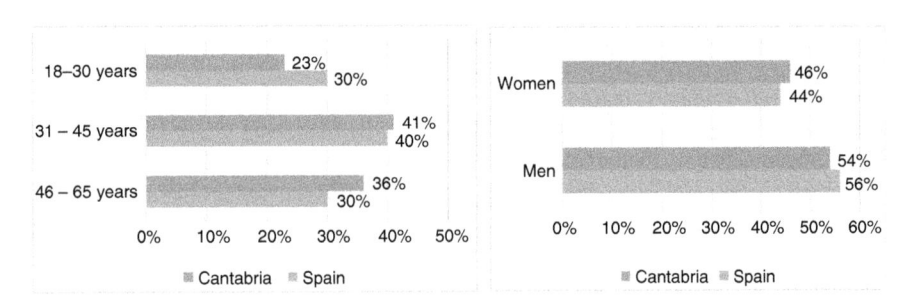

Fig. 1 Demographic profile of blood donors in Spain and Cantabria. Source: Compiled by the authors on the basis of the 2016 annual reports of the Spanish Federation of Blood Donors and the Blood Donor Association of Cantabria

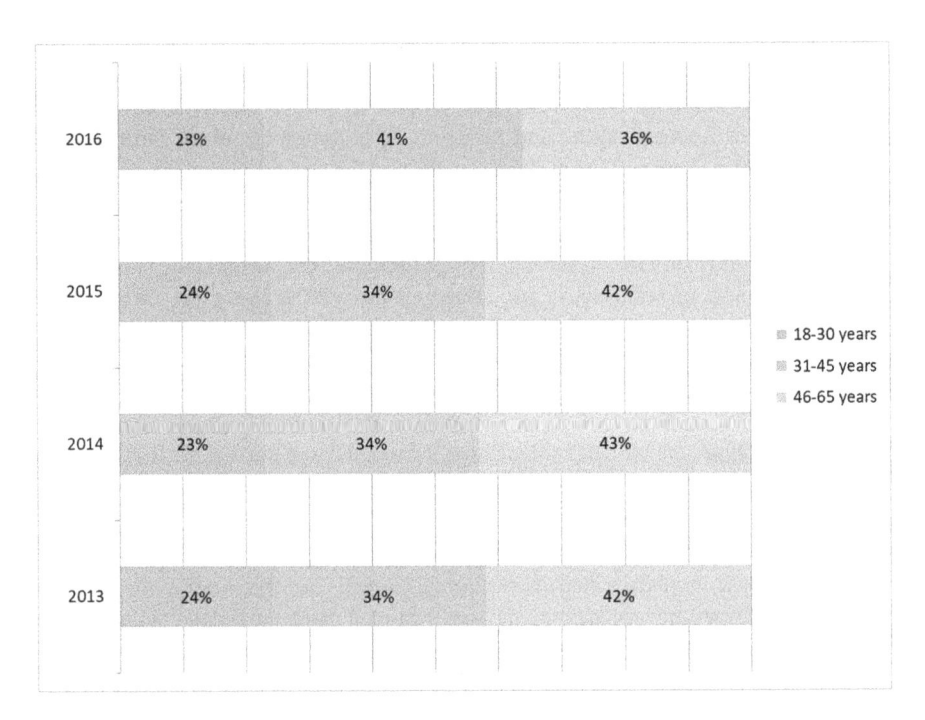

Fig. 2 Profile of blood donors in Cantabria according to age. Source: Compiled by the authors on the basis of the 2013–2016 annual reports of the Blood Donor Association of Cantabria

Focusing on the region of Cantabria, Fig. 2 shows that the donors' profile according to age has remained stable during recent years. The youngest segment represents the smallest percentage of donors, whereas the group aged 46 and over has usually been the largest. Furthermore, according to the Blood Donor Association of Cantabria, young people are not very loyal compared to older donors, in the sense that they do not have the habit of donating regularly. These data confirm the need for raising blood donation awareness among young people, attracting this segment and making them loyal to this social activity.

In order to design appropriate marketing strategies to attract blood donors in general, and younger people in particular, it is important to correctly identify the factors that affect these figures. In this regard, blood donation constitutes a process that tends to generate fear and aversion, which obviously hinders donation levels (Beerli-Palacio and Martín-Santana 2008). Specifically, some barriers identified in previous market research are, among others, fear of needles, fear of feeling dizzy or sick, pain or discomfort, feeling unpleasant seeing blood, previous negative experiences, lack of intimacy in the donation act, schedule conflicts and the extraction location being too far from home (Aldamiz-Echevarría and Aguirre-García 2014). Lack of information, ignorance and being unaware of the need for blood or other aspects of the donation process have also been consistently identified as negative factors in potential donor decision-making (Gillespie and Hillyer 2002).

Some of these impediments are psychological issues, which can be difficult to solve from a marketing point of view. Nonetheless, with a good strategy, acting on trust, convenience and communication, many of the worries that currently hold back blood donation can be overcome. For this purpose, the important thing is to reduce the perceived costs and increase the perceived benefits of donating, placing greater focus on the positive feelings derived from the act of donating blood (Pentecost et al. 2017). With regard to this, solidarity or altruism has been considered the primary motivation to donate blood (Beerli-Palacio and Martín-Santana 2008). However, Misje et al. (2005) point out that the habit of continued blood donation is not exclusively linked to altruistic reasons but also to a combination of other motives that include social reasons (such as the influence of friends and family), strengthening of one's self-esteem, positive experiences associated with the donation and moral obligation to donate.

All these issues will be considered in the next sections of the case study, where the authors analyse the social marketing actions related to the convenience and communication strategies carried out by the Blood Donor Association of Cantabria to reach young donors in particular.

Social Marketing in the Blood Donor Association of Cantabria

The Blood Donor Association of Cantabria (www.hdsc.org) is the main non-profit association in charge of creating the permanent blood bank in this geographical region. It was created in 1970 with the purpose of "promoting the habits of social solidarity and contributing to stimulate the altruistic donation", in order to "totally and completely cover (with altruistic donations) the needs of blood and plasma of any health facility in Cantabria". In December 2016, the association had more than 95,700 members, which represents almost the 20% of the total population of Cantabria. As reward for its important work, it has been recognized with the highest regional distinctions for its extraordinary merits, such as the Golden Medal of

Santander City (2002) and the Golden Medal of the Government of Cantabria (2005).

Convenience: How to Break the Barrier of the Distance

Convenience or distribution strategy refers to the process of organizing all the blood donation units. As noted above, possible obstacles to donation could be schedule conflicts or the extraction location being far from home. In order to overcome these potential dissuasive barriers and to avoid long displacements of volunteers, the Blood Donor Association of Cantabria has established a wide network of fixed and mobile units throughout the region. Specifically, the fixed blood donation centre is located in the Bank of Blood and Tissues of Cantabria (located at Marqués de Valdecilla University Hospital in Santander, the capital city of Cantabria). This unit collected 31.7% of the total blood donations in 2017. The other 69.3% of donations were collected by the mobile units (Spanish Federation of Blood Donors 2017). These provide service in various parts of the region, according to a schedule that can be consulted regularly on the Blood Donor Association website. Furthermore, the association has established numerous agreements with private companies and other public institutions to bring blood donation units to their workplaces periodically, making it easier for employees to donate. In the case of young people, the association has established an agreement with the University of Cantabria under which mobile units visit the different university centres regularly (at least three times a year). The university community is informed of these visits through various channels of internal communication (i.e. website, intranet, agenda). The association also displays mobile units in local primary and high schools, where students over 18, teachers and administrative staff can donate (Fig. 3).

Fig. 3 Mobile units of the Blood Donor Association of Cantabria. Source: www.hdsc.org (2018)

Communication: How to Inform and Persuade

When facing its communication strategy to promote donations, the Blood Donor Association of Cantabria faces two main challenges:

- How to effectively reach different targets (i.e. young donors vs experienced donors) with diverse motivations, lifestyles and attitudes towards social marketing (Hupfer 2006; Solomon 2012)
- How to solve seasonal issues of blood donation (Grant 2010), which can jeopardize the stability of the voluntary donation system in the region

Reaching Different Targets

As far as the first challenge is concerned, it is evident that developing an effective way to communicate with people as they reach the age to donate is a critical step to be taken (Solomon 2012) and persuading them to give blood may require specifically tailored marketing communication (Hupfer 2006). Based on this idea, in recent years, the Blood Donor Association of Cantabria has started to design specific communication measures to target the young market segment successfully. Actually, the association differentiates two targets within the youngest segment: (1) the target of "potential donors over 18" and (2) the target of "non-donors under 18". The Blood Donor Association of Cantabria designs communication activities to both targets, with a special focus on the "non-donor" segment, which is considered the future of blood donation worldwide. In this segment, the communication activities focus on raising awareness among young people who are close to the age of donation.

Communication for Young Donors

The coordinator of all the implemented activities is the Young Donation Network, a project promoted by the Blood Donor Association of Cantabria that aligns with the goals of national and international initiatives such as the National Committee of Young Donors (Spain), the Ibero-American Meetings of Young Donors (international) and the International Youth Committee (international), among others. The project, which was proposed based on the success of a similar initiative carried out in Catalonia (Spain) (www.donantsdesang.cat), is an educational programme for children and young people from ages 6 to 18 to acquire knowledge and values through the promotion of blood donation and the organization of a specific communication campaign for the Blood Donor Association. The idea is based on a learning-service model: "learn by doing service for the community". First, the students enrolled in the programme identify a problematic situation in their local community to whose improvement they want to commit themselves. To alleviate the social problem, they develop a social project that puts into play their knowledge, skills, attitudes and values. In the specific case of the Blood Donor Association, the social problem refers to the shortage of blood donations in Cantabria, for which the students create a campaign to promote the donation among society that, the hope is, ends with a massive blood collection. The programme consists of four stages:

- Stage 1. *Training*, in which participants learn concepts related to blood, donations, equality and altruism and acquire knowledge to create their own communication campaign and raise social awareness.
- Stage 2. *Creation of materials*, in which the educational centre prepares all the materials needed for the communication campaign for blood donation. Specifically, the students work in groups to create logos and slogans to personalize each campaign, design letters to the families of the centre and the neighbourhood, create banners, devise gifts for donors, etc.
- Stage 3. *Service*, in which children and youngsters put into practice all the knowledge they have learned during the programme. In this stage, they are responsible for raising awareness in their environment with their communication activities. Within the service stage are two key moments: before the donation campaign and the day of the campaign.
- Stage 4. *Valuation and acknowledgements*. The Blood Donor Association makes a critical reading of the campaign to generate learning and derive improvements from the experience. In addition, participants are identified and recognized. In this sense, recognition is essential to generate commitment and a positive attitude of these young people towards future donation. Finally, the generated resources are given visibility. Specifically, and if the materials are sufficient, award competitions are held with public and media coverage.

Along this line, the role of new communication technologies and social media among young people also represents a great challenge for the communication of the Blood Donor Association. Accordingly, the association has a website that was updated in 2017, on which ample information is displayed such as stories, facts, figures and the importance of donations. On the website, the entire donation process is explained in order to overcome the barrier that a lack of information or awareness about the need for blood represents.

Furthermore, the association is also especially focused on social media as one of the most effective communication channels for reaching young donors. Specifically, the Blood Donor Association is present on four social media platforms: Google Plus, Facebook, Twitter and Instagram. It is vital that the association understand social media as a useful and necessary way of promoting donation. In this regard, sharing an image with friends and family of one in the process of donating blood is the simplest and most practical form of promotion. A phrase, a testimony of someone who has given or received blood, inspires others. As for the content of the posts, most of them are primarily informative, describing how, where and when users can donate at the permanent facilities of the association or the mobile units that travel the region. Emotional messages are also posted through the use of pictures of actual donors along with encouraging messages to promote blood donation.

Finally, the young segment is also reached through volunteerism. In this regard, an interesting initiative has been promoted in collaboration with the University of

Cantabria that, through its volunteer programme, offers university students the possibility of collaborating with the association in diverse activities such as the following: promoting the blood campaigns that are carried out, distributing information, helping to organize activities, sharing their testimonies in talks at primary and high schools and managing the association's presence on social media and the Internet.

Communication for Experienced Donors

As far as experienced donors (i.e. those over 30) are concerned, one measure that is reporting interesting benefits to the Blood Donor Association in terms of promotion and communication is the Sports and Solidarity Group, which is an open club that gives an opportunity for all participants to initiative activities. The Sports and Solidarity Group of Blood Donors of Cantabria has carried out various activities for the last 5 years. The club is mainly oriented to hiking, although activities have also been held in spelunking and bicycle rides. Through this club, the association appeals to the group feeling and to the emotional benefits that being part of a collective provides its members. To date, the Sports and Solidarity Group has sponsored more than 50 activities organized by the volunteers themselves, who promotes the Blood Donor Association by wearing promotional T-shirts of the association during the group's activities. A club mascot has also been created: Gotito (Fig. 4). The Blood Donor Association also participates in solidarity activities with other associations, such as Limones Solidarios (i.e. Solidarity Lemons), Esclerosis Múltiple (i.e. Multiple Sclerosis) and Buscando Sonrisas (i.e. Looking for Smiles),

Fig. 4 Gotito. Source: www.hdsc.org (2018)

Table 1 Conventional media that lend their support to the Blood Donor Association of Cantabria

Radio	Cadena Ser (Cantabria), Radio Nacional de España (Cantabria), COPE (Cantabria), Onda Cero (Cantabria), Onda Cantabria FM, Radio Valle del Buelna, Radio Camargo, Ser Castro Urdiales, Onda Cero Castro, Castro Punto Radio, Radio Cantabria Digital, Radio Laredo, Radio Meruelo, Radio Mix Selaya, Radio Onda Occidental, Radio Santoña, Radio Torrelavega Ser, Radio Tres Mares, Radio Intereconomía, Radio Foramontanos, Radio Distinta, Radio Dime, OID Gestiona Radio
Television	RTVE (Cantabria), Tele Bahía, Tele Costa, Televisión Reinosa Cable, Popular TV Santander
Newspapers	El Mundo Hoy (Cantabria), El Diario Montañés, Alerta, Gente, En Santander, Crónica de Cantabria, Ciudad Viva Santander, Jovenmanía, Faro Cantabria, Cantabria Económica, Valdecilla "La Salud" de Cantabria
Communication agencies	EFE, Europa Press

Source: Blood Donor Association of Cantabria (2014)

while it also takes advantage of national events to make itself known (e.g. World Book Day, International Human Rights Day and others).

For the market segment of experienced donors, other promotional activities include the regular publication of the magazine of the Blood Donor Association or collaboration with conventional media (i.e. TV, radio and newspapers) at the regional and local levels (Table 1). The magazine is distributed online through the association website and offline in waiting and consultation rooms at Marqués de Valdecilla University Hospital, at the blood bank and at the different mobile units that visit the region (e.g. at social centres, institutes, universities). The magazine is also available at a number of locations where volunteers are allowed to leave copies. The magazine is published quarterly and provides information on all the activities and collaborations in which the association has participated during each period. Each issue includes a section noting the association's sponsorship campaigns, whereby members who regularly donate blood accompany first-time donors to provide support and alleviate their possible apprehension to the process.

Solving Seasonal Issues

As for the second communication challenge of the Blood Donor Association (i.e. seasonal blood shortages), it is observed that in Cantabria, as in any other developed country, blood demand during the summer or Christmas holidays is usually high due to a greater number of accidents occurring to people who have got out of their daily routines and are engaging in new or different behaviour. However, donors may not be motivated during that time because their attention is diverted to other activities. This suggests an issue of maintaining awareness among donors of the ongoing need for blood donation (Solomon 2012). Relationship and services marketing techniques can be used in this context to raise awareness, overcome ignorance and generate loyalty among donors, as well as to reinforce benefits and demonstrate needs being met among end-users and customers (Grant 2010). Therefore, the communication efforts of the Blood Donor Association of Cantabria are always intensified during these periods of the year. In this regard, not only does the association make special appeals through social media, but when there are specific needs for donations due to blood shortages in Cantabria (or any other region of the country), the association sends out text messages that donors receive on their mobile phones, indicating the specific situation that requires help and the logistics for donating to the specific cause.

Conclusions

Blood is a source of life. Many people depend on the availability of safe blood supplies. Thus, donation, as a free and voluntary act, should be continually promoted. With regard to this, the case study has focused on the awareness actions carried out by the Blood Donor Association of Cantabria, paying special attention to the activities addressed to young people. According to the association, the blood needs of the Cantabria region have always been met up to now. However, it is important to keep working to attract new donors and retain existing ones. The segment of the population under 30 has much potential for growth, so the Blood Donor Association has designed awareness programmes at schools, activities with universities and social media communication, among other measures, whose results are expected to be seen in the short and medium term. With regard to existing donors, the actions are linked to maintain their commitment, with different actions in terms of public relations and advertising.

Discussion Questions

- Is there a blood donor association in your area? Describe the initiatives it carries out to promote blood donation.
- What blood donation figures have been reached in your area in recent years? Compare them with the figures shown in the case.
- What is the level of involvement of young people in blood donation in your area?
- What are some innovative initiatives that could be designed to improve the awareness and participation of young people in blood donation?

References

Aldamiz-Echevarría, C., & Aguirre-García, S. (2014). Modelo de comportamiento de los donantes de sangre y estrategias de marketing para retenerles y atraerles. *Revista Latino-Americana de Enfermagem, 22*(3), 467–475.
Beerli-Palacio, A., & Martín-Santana, J. (2008). How to increase blood donation by social marketing. *International Review of Public Nonprofit Marketing, 12*, 253–266.

Blood Donor Association of Cantabria (2014). *Memoria Anual 2014*. Cantabria: Blood Donor Association of Cantabria.

Gillespie, T., & Hillyer, C. (2002). Blood donors and factors impacting the blood donation decision. *Transfusion Medicine Reviews, 16*(2), 115–130.

Grant, D. B. (2010). Integration of supply and marketing for a blood service. *Management Research Review, 33*(2), 123–133.

Hermandad de Donantes de Sangre de Cantabria. (2014). *Memoria Anual 2014*. Cantabria: Hermandad de Donantes de Sangre de Cantabria.

Hupfer, M. E. (2006). Helping me, helping you: Self-referencing and gender roles in donor advertising. *Transfusion, 46*(6), 996–1005.

Kotler, P. (1994). *Marketing management, analysis, planning, implementation, and control*. Upper Saddle River, NJ: Prentice-Hall.

Lemmens, K., Abraham, C., Ruiter, R., Veldhuizen, I., Dehing, C., Boss, A., et al. (2009). Modelling antecedents of blood donation motivation among non-donors of varying age and education. *British Journal of Psychology, 100*, 71–90.

Misje, A., Bosnes, V., Gåsdal, O., & Heier, H. (2005). Motivation, recruitment and retention of voluntary nonremunerated blood donors: A survey-based questionnaire study. *Vox Sanguinis, 89*, 236–244.

Mowen, J. C., & Minor, M. (1998). *Consumer behaviour* (5th ed.). Upper Saddle River, NJ: Prentice-Hall.

National Transplant Organization. (2017). *Balance de actividad de la Organización Nacional de Trasplantes*. Available online http://www.ont.es/Documents/Datos20172018ENE11.pdf

Pentecost, R., Arli, R., & Thiele, S. (2017). It's my choice! Investigating barriers to pro-social blood donating behaviour. *Marketing Intelligence & Planning, 35*(2), 243–258.

Solomon, G. D. (2012). Segmentation and communications to solve the blood shortage: An exploration of the problem with recommendations. *Voluntas, 23*, 415–433.

Spanish Federation of Blood Donors. (2017). *Informe 2017 sobre la Donación de Sangre en España*. Available online http://www.donantesdesangre.es/menu.htm

World Health Organization. (2017). *Blood safety and availability*. Accessed January 25, 2018, from http://www.who.int/mediacentre/factsheets/fs279/en/

The Importance of Social Marketing in Global Health Emergencies: The Case of Zika Virus Infection

M. Mercedes Galan-Ladero and M. Angeles Galan-Ladero

Abstract At the beginning of 2016, the World Health Organization (WHO) declared the infection caused by Zika virus a global health emergency, what triggered alarms worldwide. Social marketing campaigns had a fundamental role to prevent transmission, raise awareness, and involve citizens in solving the problem.

In this paper, the application of social marketing in the case of this disease will be studied in depth. In order to do so, an exploratory study has been conducted. Images from 47 campaigns launched in 19 countries of the American continent have been analyzed.

These campaigns are characterized by being designed mainly with illustrative pictures and simple texts so as to reach the whole population. The message focuses on providing information about the Zika virus and on catching the attention of all the population in order to prevent the disease. Different tones have been used: imperative, informative, interrogative, and alarming (causing fear). All kinds of media were used to broadcast the message: radio, TV, the press, billboards, the Internet (websites, YouTube, social networks such as Facebook or Twitter), and different apps.

M. M. Galan-Ladero (✉)
University of Extremadura, Badajoz, Spain
e-mail: mgalan@unex.es

M. A. Galan-Ladero
Andalusian Health Service, Almeria, Spain

Learning Objectives
1. To deepen in the role played by social marketing and to learn how it is applied to the health field not only in general but also specifically in case of a global health emergency
2. To analyze the consequences a global health emergency caused by a specific virus can have (demographic, economic, technological, environmental, social, cultural, political, and/or legal consequences)
3. To show the wide variety of social marketing campaigns that can be carried out by different kinds of organizations, whether national or international organizations, as well as NGOs, or even firms, in case of a global health emergency
4. To analyze some social marketing campaigns launched in the case of the Zika virus health emergency and their different approaches and/or implementations in several countries
5. To study the population targets of those social marketing campaigns launched in the case of the Zika virus
6. To deepen in the study of some aspects of those campaigns (messages used, tone, purpose, etc.)

Introduction

The infection caused by Zika virus, though not a new one,[1] gained media attention and global relevance at the beginning of 2016, when the news of an unusual rise in the number of babies born with microcephaly that might be Zika-induced in Brazil was spread (Galan-Ladero and Galan-Ladero 2016).

Alarms triggered when the Centers for Disease Control (CDC) in the United States surprised the world with a travel advisory level 2, explicitly warning pregnant women and women of reproductive age against traveling to certain countries in Latin America; 1 week later, the World Health Organization (WHO) declared Zika a public health emergency (Forbes 2016).

The quick spread of the virus to new areas, the serious consequences of the disease (neurological disorders), the lack of information about the virus, the uncertainty about how it gets transmitted and the real scope of the problem (really, how many people were affected), together with the lack of availability of diagnosis tests that were considered accurate and reliable, and the fact that there was no vaccine or specific treatment available nor preventive therapy to protect the most vulnerable groups (mainly, pregnant women) caused international deep concern at all levels (health, political, and social).

---

[1]This virus was discovered in 1947 during surveillance studies of jungle yellow fever in rhesus monkeys in the Zika forest, in Uganda (Red Nacional de Vigilancia Epidemiologica 2016).

Nonetheless, Zika virus gained even more media attention worldwide when it was made public that many elite athletes were thinking about withdrawing from Olympic Games Rio 2016 over Zika virus fears (some of them actually did cancel their appearances at the Rio Olympics that summer), what increased concerned and fear to travel to Latin America (especially to Brazil), and even chaos in some of the affected areas.

Faced with this certain virus threat, and predicting the (sports and economic) Olympic Games success might get jeopardized, as well as the image of Brazil as a country facing an enormous sanitary challenge, several measures were taken, among them, significant social marketing campaigns that were launched in the country.

But having been declared a global health emergency, measures were also taken at global level: (1) *international measures* (it can be highlighted those taken by the World Health Organization (WHO), in collaboration with other organizations such as the Food and Agriculture Organization of the United Nations (FAO), the United Development Program (UNDP), the International Federation of Red Cross and Red Crescent Societies (IFRC), the Centers for Disease Control and Prevention (CDC) in the USA, the European Centre for Disease Prevention and Control (ECDC), the Community of Latin America and Caribbean States (CELAC), the South American Trade Bloc–Mercado Comun del Sur (MERCOSUR), the Pan American Health Organization (PAHO), etc.); (2) *national measures* (especially, in those countries hit by Zika virus, but also in countries where imported cases of the disease were detected); and (3) *local measures* (in the worst hit endemic areas).

Even though media attention is over nowadays and it is not a media issue anymore, Zika virus epidemic goes on being a risk to the population at a global level. New cases of people diagnosed with Zika have been reported in new regions and new countries all over the world (America, the Pacific, Africa, Southeast Asia, etc.), but it is true that figures have reduced significantly.[2] Nonetheless, more than 2000 million people live in places with risk of getting infected (Martinez and Sarukhan 2017).

Development of the Case

Zika Virus: Description of the Disease

Although at first it was believed that the disease was only Zika-induced by being bitten by *Aedes aegypti* mosquitoes (those that also transmit dengue fever, chikungunya, and yellow fever), other sources of transmission have been confirmed,

---

[2]For example, in Brazil, according to the data provided by the Ministry of Health (Secretaria de Vigilancia em Saude – Ministerio da Saude 2018), it has gone from 216,207 probable cases of Zika virus disease registered in 2016 to 17,594 probable cases in 2017. In the first five months of 2018, 2234 probable cases had been registered, of which only 677 had been subsequently confirmed.

such as vertical transmission (by mothers infected by Zika), blood transfusions, or sexual contact.

Zika virus infection is a minor clinical profile, characterized by a moderate fever, maculopapular rash often spreading from the face to the rest of the body, temporary arthritis or arthralgia (mainly small joints in feet and hands), conjunctival hyperemia or bilateral conjunctivitis, and other non-specific symptoms such as myalgia, tiredness, and cephalea (Red Nacional de Vigilancia Epidemiologica 2016, p. 2).

Asymptomatic infections are common, and it is estimated that only one out of four people infected with the virus actually have some symptoms (Red Nacional de Vigilancia Epidemiologica 2016). In general, the disease develops without serious complications, with low hospitalization rates. Besides, once exposed to the virus, patients develop long-lasting immunity (Red Nacional de Vigilancia Epidemiologica 2016). That means, it is little dangerous for the general population, and its symptoms are similar to those of any other infection (fever, general feeling of discomfort, pain), plus the abovementioned dermatological manifestation. There is no specific treatment, nor vaccine, but it heals spontaneously (De Benito 2016). The only specific treatment is symptomatic relief and supportive measures for severe cases (Perez and Chamorro 2018). Incubation period is short,[3] but it is enough for a person to travel anywhere before knowing he or she was infected by the virus, causing the disease to spread worldwide.

Consequences of Declaring Zika Virus a Global Health Emergency

The consequences of declaring Zika virus a global health emergency have been different in different countries, both in the short and in the long run. Among the most relevant ones, we can highlight sociodemographic, economic, technological, environmental, political, and legal consequences (Table 1).

Response Plan to the Epidemic of Zika Virus

There were very short-term proposals (very urgent), but also short, medium, and long-term proposals to respond to the Zika virus epidemic (Table 2).

Social Marketing and Zika Virus

One of the main measures taken to face the Zika epidemic was to raise people awareness so as to prevent the disease and to get the implication of local communities in solving the problem. In order to achieve it, social marketing campaigns have played a decisive role.

---

[3] Between 2 and 7 days (De Benito 2016)

Table 1 The most relevant consequences of declaring Zika virus a global health emergency

Consequences	Comments
Sociodemographic	Decrease in the birth rate in some affected Latin American countries[a]
Economic	Affected sectors:
	Negatively: tourism (international tourism, mainly) and health systems
	Positively: research centers, pharmaceuticals, disinsection services, medical services, biobanks, and other companies
Technological	New applications of existing technologies, new methods of biological control and development of new technologies
Environmental	Genetic manipulation of the mosquito (ethical problems)
	Effects of fumigations in risk areas and of the greater personal use of insecticides and repellents
Political—legal	Management of the epidemic: effect on the public image of the authorities, with the corresponding results in the polls
	The public health problems derived from Zika have been a major blow to the health policies of the most affected countries
	National responses against the virus in the Americas have revealed important deficiencies
	No new laws have appeared (with prohibitions or mandatory regulations), but there are declarations of health warning and recommendations to prevent contagion

Source: Own research, based on Galan-Ladero and Galan-Ladero (2016)
[a]Because of the recommendation of the health authorities to avoid pregnancies in those months and the increasing number of abortions

The global health emergency declared by the WHO in 2016 made us think, from a social marketing point of view, of what has been done up to now and what is still being done, what measures have been taken, and what Zika virus campaigns have been launched up to now or are currently being launched, both at an international and at a national or local level.

Exploratory research has been done by analyzing 47 campaigns launched in 19 countries within the Americas.

Methodology

Images of the different campaigns have been found by using Google and typing the key words "*campañas virus Zika*'/'*campanhas Zika virus*'/'*ZIKV campaigns*." Then, the specific web pages of those campaigns have been visited. Reports from official sources, informative dossiers from different organizations [WHO, Red Nacional de Vigilancia Epidemiologica (*National Network of Epidemiological Surveillance*) in Spain, etc.], and pieces of news published in international newspapers have been consulted.

Content analysis has been carried out, focusing on the following aspects: message of the campaign, tone used, purpose, graphic design, country, organization that promotes it, broadcasting media, and the target audience.

Table 2 Response plan to the epidemic of Zika virus

Term	Solutions
Very short term (very urgent)	Quickly isolation of the Zika virus (to see its characteristics and know the real dimension of the problem)
	Strengthening epidemiological surveillance and creation of laboratory capacity to detect the virus
	Making recommendations on the clinical care and follow-up of people infected with Zika virus
	Definition of the priority research areas on Zika virus disease and its possible complications
	New medical protocols to prevent and cure the disease
	International collaboration for the generation of knowledge through R&D for new technologies of diagnosis, treatment and prevention
	Sending updated information about the virus to all health personnel in the region
Short term	Vector control
	Intensification of personal and population measures for the control of mosquitoes[a]
	Involvement of local communities in local, regional and national preparedness and response strategies
	Test of new techniques: new applications of existing technologies, new biological control methods, and innovative technological solutions
	Greater collaboration between different sectors (governments, international organizations, universities, companies, local communities, etc.), to avoid the lack of coordination and fragmentation of the preventive measures programs, and for an adequate management of information
	Prevention campaigns
	Border controls
	Promotion of gender equality and sexual and reproductive health, so that the response to Zika virus is effective, as well as reducing social inequality and exclusion to promote health and development
	Government aid for families with limited resources to access prevention or treatment products against the virus
	Mechanisms for social protection and health care, suitable for all affected people (economic subsidies)
Medium term	Vaccine
Long term	Change of the urbanization model in Latin America: properly structured cities invest in improvements in water supply and sanitary conditions in cities
	Long-term government aid to assist those affected by microcephaly (they will require almost exclusive dedication and special medical, psychological, and educational attention throughout their lives)
	Additional financial resources for contingency plans, comprehensive health services, virus surveillance, etc.

Sources: Chan and Da Silva (2016), De Benito and Sahuquillo (2016), Moneo and Marshall (2016), Martinez (2016), UNDP (2017), and Periago (2016)

[a]For example, clothes to wear, safe use of repellents and insecticides, massive fumigations, water and waste treatment, elimination of mosquito breeding sites, etc

Results

In general, social marketing and campaigns on Zika virus have been different depending on the country where they were launched, and their effectiveness has been variable, too. Approaches and strategies have also been different, and campaigns have evolved over time (differences among the first campaigns and those launched a few months later can be noticed).

In the Zika virus case, several complementary social marketing approaches have been used. However, the most common ones are technological and informative approaches (Table 3).

There have been several target groups (Table 4). For example, WHO has used mainly an informative approach, focused on two target groups: health authorities and policy-makers. In those countries directly affected by Zika virus, different information has been provided with regard to prevention measures, detecting symptoms, and

Table 3 Complementary social marketing approaches

Approach	Characteristics
Legal approach	Unlike other diseases, there have been no mandatory laws or regulations (*e.g., prohibition to travel to a certain country*), although there are health warning statements and recommendations that should be followed (*e.g., avoid pregnancies, avoid standing water in homes and urban areas, avoid traveling to the affected areas*, etc.)
Technological approach	Medical tests have increased and more precise diagnostic tests have been developed for the detection of the virus in clinical laboratories; research has been intensified to obtain possible vaccines and specific drugs; the effectiveness of insect repellents has been improved; and banks of semen have also increased and improved their services to meet the demand for semen freezing. Genetic engineering has also acquired great importance in the case of the Zika virus. New techniques have been also tried
Economic approach	Free disinfection services have been provided, and insect repellents have been provided in poor areas, where people had no money to buy them; contingency plans have been made to address the epidemic; investments have been made in research and capacity building of clinical laboratories; epidemiological surveillance has been strengthened; and financial assistance has been given to affected families. Important amounts have also been allocated to develop the different campaigns and disseminate it in the different media
Informative approach	An official website has been created on this disease, news in the media has been generalized, and official information has been provided from the different involved ministries addressed to the affected local population, as well as to tourists who have traveled to the areas of risk
	For prevention, messages of public health, vector control at the community level, and to change people's attitude (active participation in the prevention and fight against the disease) have been disseminated (UNDP 2017). Information has also been provided on prevention measures, symptoms, and differentiation of other diseases
	On the other hand, an attempt was made to offer real-time information to health personnel, as well as new protocols for action

Source: Own elaboration

Table 4 Targets

Target	Measures and actions
Health personnel	Recommendations on clinical care and follow-up of people infected with Zika virus
	Active training to learn about the new action protocols to prevent and cure the disease and to know the new information (especially from WHO and the national epidemiological surveillance networks)
	Dispatch of updated information about the virus to all medical personnel in the region, especially virologists and pathologists (Colombia), pediatricians and neurologists (Brazil), and microbiologists (worldwide)
Citizens	Awareness, prevention, and involvement campaigns focus on general population. Aims:
	Intensification of personal and household measures for the mosquito control
	Information for immediate defense (habits of mosquitoes, appropriate clothing, doors and windows closed, mosquito nets, avoiding stagnant water, do not travel to the affected areas, and postpone trips, etc.).
	Safe use of insecticides (to avoid food contamination)
	Recommendation of mosquito-resistant repellents
	Information campaigns about the Zika virus and recommendations to prevent infections and identify the symptoms of the disease (and distinguish it from others with similar symptoms)
Health and public authorities	Advice on the control of the vector (mosquito)
	Advice on the safe use of insecticides (to avoid food contamination) and massive fumigations (water and waste treatment) to eliminate mosquito breeding sites, especially in large cities
	Promotion of greater collaboration between different sectors (governments, international organizations, universities, companies, etc.) to avoid lack of coordination and fragmentation of prevent measures programs
	Border control
	Aid management for the prevention and treatment of affected people (babies with microcephaly in particular)
	Recommendations to promote development programs to improve cities
	Dissemination of public health messages
	Raise awareness

Source: Own elaboration

how to distinguish this from other diseases. This information has been provided to medical staff and also to the population in general (pregnant women in particular). In countries on alert because of possible imported cases (e.g., Spain), there have been two target groups: medical staff and the common citizen. The flow of communication has been a key factor for the right information management (to support and reinforce prevention and response strategies and avoid reactions of exaggerated alarm)—Martinez and Sarukhan (2017).

Nonetheless, the campaigns analyzed in this research, those broadcast in the most important mass media, have focused on the potentially affected population. For other target groups, these media have not been used, but just the official informative channels (*e.g., circulars and regulations from different Ministries of Health, technical journals, educational and informative talks, etc.*).

With regard to the social marketing strategies used, complementarity is to be highlighted, combining, above all, reinforcement and inducement strategies (Table 5).

Messages are different, but they all focus mainly on (1) providing information on Zika virus (what it is, features, ways of transmission, symptoms, distinguishing this from other viruses, etc.); (2) identifying *Aedes aegypti* mosquito (transmitting mosquito, of this and other serious illnesses); (3) elimination of hatcheries (removal of materials); (4) preventing mosquito bites; (5) preventing self-medication; (6) calling for citizen joint action; (7) fight and combat (heroes, victory); and (8) avoiding rumors.

Different tones have also been used: imperative, informative, interrogative, alarming (inciting fear), positive (encouraging tone), and/or impressive (feeling guilty) tones.

Main purposes are preventing the disease, raising awareness, and/or calling for the mobilization of the citizens.

Campaigns have been promoted by the councils of the affected areas, by Ministries of Health of several countries, non-governmental organizations (NGOs) (such as the Red Cross, Save the Children, Ayuda en Accion), international institutions (lead by WHO: UNICEF, PAHO, etc.), and even enterprises. On many

Table 5 Social marketing strategies

Strategies	Characteristics
Reinforcement	They aim at people who have a positive attitude toward prevention and carry out the recommended behavior
	For example, remember the measures to be taken to avoid mosquito bites, reporting the symptoms of the disease (to identify it as soon as possible, avoid self-medication and go to the doctor, etc.)
Induction	They aim at people who have a positive attitude toward prevention and the recommendations of health authorities, but do not carry them out, for various reasons (e.g., ignorance, forgetfulness, etc.)
	For example, remember the hygiene measures to follow at home (especially in containers with water that can promote the breeding of mosquitoes) and the utility of having mosquito nets or windows closed
Rationalization	They aim at people who have a negative attitude, even if they finally carry out the desired behavior
	For example, awareness campaigns to inform people why certain behaviors are recommended (e.g., in trips, home, etc.)
Confrontation	They aim at people who have a negative attitude toward prevention and, in addition, do not carry out the recommended behaviors (e.g., traveling to affected areas, without taking special precautions)
	For example, awareness campaigns to show people the serious consequences of the disease (alarming campaigns)

Source: Own elaboration

occasions, the campaign was valid (appropriate) and common for dengue fever, chikungunya, and Zika since they are all caused by the same mosquito.

They were shown in different media: radio,[4] television, the press, billboards, the Internet (websites, YouTube), social networks (e.g., Facebook, Twitter), and apps. But also customized information ("door-to-door")[5] and "guerrilla actions" in the street were used. And with eye-catching designs, explanatory images and pictures can be highlighted as opposed to written texts so as to reach the population of all social classes.

Some Criticisms to the Campaigns That Have Been Carried Out so Far

Among the main criticisms to the campaigns carried out up to now, those gathered by the UNDP (2017) are the ones that stand out:

1. Criticism of the messages launched.

    For example, with regard to campaigns to convince women to postpone pregnancy, it seems that women of the highest socioeconomic status paid more attention to messages from the public health service. Therefore it has been affirmed that those messages were addressed to middle and upper classes and did not have the desired impact on the lower classes, the poorest ones, with no knowledge nor means to prevent pregnancy.[6]

2. Criticisms due to public institutions' contradictory messages.

    For example, with regard to sexual transmission of the disease. Contradictions were found due to cultural and/or religious issues, together with a lack of guidelines from international organizations on how to deal with pregnancy when infected by Zika virus (especially when the epidemic broke out).

3. Criticisms to the authorities involved because, in most cases, they just rose awareness among the population, they warned women against getting pregnant, and they looked for mosquito outbreaks in the streets. Besides, on some occasions, especially at the beginning, campaigns were launch separately and lacked coordination.

---

[4]Radio was the main mean chosen by UNESCO, IFRC, and WHO to develop the joint Zika virus prevention campaign in Latin America and the Caribbean, in 2016 (because of the proximity to the population and its low cost). International networks and broadcasting organizations (20,000 radio stations) transmitted informative and preventive spots against the spread of the virus in four languages of the region (English, French, Portuguese, and Spanish).

[5]For example, in Brazil: 220,000 members of the Army, the Navy, and the Air Force visited houses in 350 Brazilian cities to explain to the population how to stop mosquito breeding (Martin and De Oliveira 2016).

[6]The fall in the birth rate presents differences according to the socioeconomic level.

Conclusions

With regard to Zika virus, social marketing campaigns have played an essential role. They have been varied, presenting big differences, depending on the country where they have been launched. Their main features are eye-catching designs, big images and pictures with short texts in order to reach everyone, and the use of all kinds of media to spread the information and make it known to all the population. Messages have mainly focused on providing information on Zika virus, on preventing the population from getting infected, and on calling for joint action to eliminate hatcheries. Different tones have been used, from imperative to mere informative ones, even using fear and public alarm as instruments.

The main criticisms have to do with the lack of coordination, especially at the beginning, with the socioeconomic approach of the campaigns, with contradictory messages sent to the population, and with the lack of comprehensive actions remaining just as campaigns to raise awareness among the population and to look for mosquito hatcheries in the street.

Even though Zika virus epidemic goes on being a risk for all the population at a global level, the decrease in the number of cases detected in the Americas, together with the low incidence rate of the disease in other continents, such as Europe, for example (with just imported cases, without serious complications), has calmed down the public opinion, and it is rarely on the news now (its media impact is over).

Although the health staff have been actively trained and go on paying attention to the possibility of new cases been detected, Zika virus related social marketing campaigns addressed to citizens are hardly ever visible in the mass media nowadays.

It was a trendy topic and therefore widely broadcast in Latin America's mass media in 2017, but nowadays the situation has changed, and there are no longer some many Zika virus campaigns. Actually, they are really scarce, what makes the population think the situation is under control, especially in big cities, even if this is not absolutely true. The limited resources available and the outbreak of new diseases have overshadowed Zika virus (e.g., in Brazil, in 2018, the main concern has been yellow fever, and many campaigns on vaccination against it have been launched to alert the population of the extremely high mortality rate this disease presents).

Nevertheless, Zika virus campaigns are expected to be resumed in the rainy season, when mosquitoes proliferate, but not anymore as a specific campaign but as a general one to prevent mosquito bites, a common campaign to prevent dengue fever, chikungunya, and Zika.

This virus has brought to light the need to combine effort and resources in a multidisciplinary way, in order to guarantee faster and more effective responses against emerging and reemerging diseases (Martinez and Sarukhan 2017).

Discussion Questions

1. What do you think is the degree of concern about Zika virus at an international level nowadays?
2. Has any information related to Zika virus been provided in your country? If so, what kind of information has been provided? Where does the information come from (e.g., medical sources, governmental sources, the mass media, others)?
3. What social marketing campaigns related to Zika virus have been carried out in your country? How long did they last or have lasted so far? Is there any one on nowadays?
4. With regard to Zika virus, do you think Rio 2016 marked a turning point?
5. Assess the main consequences Zika virus has had since it was declared a public health emergency in 2016 (demographic, economic, social, environmental, cultural, technological, political, legal consequences, or of any other kind).

References

Chan, M., & Da Silva, J. G. (2016). *Controlar los mosquitos para detener el zika*. El País, 18/02/2016.
De Benito, E. (2016). *La UE desaconseja a las embarazadas viajar a zonas con virus zika*. El País, 22/01/2016.
De Benito, E., & Sahuquillo, M. R. (2016). *La OMS declara el virus del zika una emergencia global*. El País, 03/02/2016.
Forbes. (2016). Virus Zika, ¿una amenaza económica global? *Forbes México*. Accessed August 7, 2016, http://www.forbes.com.mx
Galan-Ladero, M. A., & Galan-Ladero, M. M. (2016). El papel del marketing social ante una emergencia sanitaria internacional. El caso de la infección por virus Zika. *8th International Congress of Teaching Cases on Public and Nonprofit Marketing*. Porto (Portugal).
Martin, M., & De Oliveira, A. (2016). *El 60% de las Fuerzas Armadas en Brasil salen a la calle a combatir el zika*. El País, 13/02/2016.
Martinez, M. (2016). *La CELAC y Mercosur se coordinan contra el virus zika*. El País, 04/02/2016.
Martinez, P., & Sarukhan, A. (2017). *El zika, un año después*. Planeta Futuro. El País, 30/01/2017.
Moneo, A., & Marshall, M. (2016). *Innovación abierta contra el zika*. Planeta Futuro. El País, 23/11/2016.
Perez, J. A., & Chamorro, S. (2018). Zika virus: An emerging player in the global scenario. *Enfermedades Infecciosas. Microbiología Clínica, 36*(1), 1–3.
Periago, R. (2016). *La solución pasa por eliminar el mosquito*. Planeta Futuro. El País, 30/11/2016.
Red Nacional de Vigilancia Epidemiologica. (2016). *Protocolo de vigilancia de la enfermedad por virus Zika*.
Secretaria de Vigilância em Saúde – Ministério da Saúde. (2018, May). Monitoramento dos casos de dengue, febre de chikungunya e doença aguda pelo vírus Zika até a Semana Epidemiológica 15 de 2018. *Boletim Epidemiológico, 49*.
United Nations Development Programme. (2017). *Los costes socioeconómicos del Zika podrían llegar hasta 18 mil millones de dólares en Latinoamérica y el Caribe*. Accessed May 7, 2018, from http://www.undp.org/content/undp/es/home/presscenter/pressreleases/2017/04/06/social-and-economic-costs-of-zika-can-reach-up-to-us-18-billion-in-latin-america-and-the-caribbean.html

Social Marketing Applied to HIV/AIDS Prevention: The Case of a Five-Year Governmental Response in Portugal

Beatriz Casais, João F. Proença, and Henrique Barros

Abstract

HIV infection has been a concerning health issue prioritised by health governmental institutions that has required the development of public health policies with an integrated social marketing intervention in an upstream dimension. A behaviour change strategy should invest in segmented communication for priority targets, in partnership with multiple stakeholders.

This case explores and discusses the integrated social marketing programme developed by the Portuguese Ministry of Health to prevent HIV/AIDS in the period 2006–2011 and its long-term evaluation in behaviour change, comparing data from 2005 and 2017. This case shows the initial diagnosis; the social marketing strategy developed for different targets in partnership with civil society organisations, following a variety of theoretical frameworks; and effectiveness evaluation in epidemic outcomes. A guide is provided with questions for discussion.

B. Casais (✉)
University of Minho, School of Economics and Management, Braga, Portugal

Polytechnic Institute of Cávado and Ave, Barcelos, Portugal

IPAM Porto – Universidade Europeia, Porto, Portugal
e-mail: bcasais@eeg.uminho.pt

J. F. Proença
Faculty of Economics, University of Porto, Porto, Portugal

ADVANCE/CSG, ISEG, University of Lisbon, Lisbon, Portugal
e-mail: jproenca@fep.up.pt

H. Barros
Institute of Public Health, University of Porto, Porto, Portugal
e-mail: hbarros@med.up.pt

© Springer Nature Switzerland AG 2019
M. M. Galan-Ladero, H. M. Alves (eds.), *Case Studies on Social Marketing*, Management for Professionals, https://doi.org/10.1007/978-3-030-04843-3_8

Learning Objectives
This case study illustrates and discusses a national social marketing intervention in public health policy. The case discusses the application of theoretical models in the implementation of an innovative social marketing strategy in HIV/AIDS prevention, considering the specificities of this epidemic in the infection's prevalence, stigma and discrimination. Briefly, the case discusses:

- The role of upstream social marketing and partnerships between governmental institutions and non-governmental organisations, in a downstream level
- Social marketing activities developed by public policy in partnership with business companies
- The use of targeting orientation in marketing practices
- The integrative marketing mix perspective of a social marketing strategy
- The application of the following social marketing theories: exchange theory, health belief model, protection motivation theory, cognitive dissonance and prototype-willingness model
- Celebrity endorsement in social marketing programmes

Introduction

Social marketing is an important strategic tool for public policy. It focuses on influencing attitude and behaviour change, and public health is one of the fields where social marketing is mostly applied to (Gordon et al. 2006; Grier and Bryant 2005; Truong 2014). A social marketing strategy should balance the upstream and downstream levels, considering the importance of a top-down intervention with policy direction, regulation and educational guidelines (Gordon 2013; MartinKey and Czaplewski 2017) but also the collaboration with civil society organisations that develop community-based work, adapt the programme to the specificities of the target (Milbourne 2009) and use relationship marketing to strengthen trust and self-confidence in behaviour change (Hastings 2003).

HIV was first diagnosed in 1981 in the United States, and AIDS rapidly became a worldwide major cause of death. Since 1996, with the discovery of effective treatment, HIV infection presented a chronic disease course. Because behaviours associated with the transmission of infection are stereotyped, people living with HIV have suffered from stigma and discrimination (Merson et al. 2008). This is why HIV prevention messages have to be adapted to the nature of the epidemic, the community and country contexts (Merson et al. 2008) and integrated in a social marketing strategy that requires audience research, segmenting, the use of marketing mix tools and the consciousness of competition of unhealthy behaviours in order to get behaviour change in an exchange process (McDermott et al. 2005). This means that theories applied to social marketing should be adapted correctly to the specificity of the desired behaviour change and the context of intervention.

This case study consists of a description and critical analysis of practices that can help readers understand how social theories can be applied (French et al. 2010) to HIV/AIDS prevention, an issue with communication constraints that should be addressed with an intervention adapted to its nature and contextual epidemic situation (Airhihenbuwa and Obregon 2000).

The evaluation of social marketing effectiveness is an important step of a social marketing strategy that is regularly forgotten in public policy (Silva and Silva 2012). The evaluation should analyse the integration of health messages and behaviour change by the target audiences but should also have a long-term perspective through monitoring the epidemic evolution (Wymer 2011). This case presents and discusses the Portuguese governmental social marketing response to HIV/AIDS in the period 2006–2011 and analyses its potential long-term impact following epidemic data until 2017.

Case Development

The leadership of the Portuguese governmental response to HIV/AIDS was attributed in the period 2005–2011 to the National Coordination for HIV/AIDS, under the umbrella of the Ministry of Health. An initial diagnosis was developed based on reports, epidemic data and the description of previous interventions and evaluation of their effectiveness. Among other documents, the diagnostic of the HIV/AIDS epidemic situation in Portugal published in the National Prevention Plan for HIV/AIDS infection control 2007–2010 was particularly important to identify the strategic potential for social marketing intervention.

SWOT Analysis

The Portuguese plan for HIV/AIDS 2007–2010 was developed under a situation of particular challenges. In 2005, Portugal was in an alarming situation of new HIV diagnosis, within Western European countries context. The National Health Plan considered fighting HIV and AIDS a priority, since the human, social, financial and economic implications of the epidemic for individuals and their families, as well as for society in general, were highly concerning.

In order to conduct a public policy strategy with the vision of preventing new HIV transmission cases and providing high standards of diagnosis, treatment and social support in a multisectoral response, there was a particular strategical potential that enabled a successful social marketing intervention.

Strengths

- Financial support from social lotteries, which prevented dependency from the state budget
- High institutional and cause awareness due to the mass media campaigns developed and targeted to the general population
- Interrelation with civil society activities through the development of a competitive project's funding scheme
- Innovative and successful intervention with the population of drug users through the needle exchange programme in pharmacies

Weaknesses

- Weak scientific data on knowledge, attitudes and behaviours related to HIV/AIDS
- Absence of effectiveness evaluation reports about communication campaigns
- Development of sporadic interventions, without an established strategy for intervention and control in priority settings
- Absence of specific communication especially targeted to the most vulnerable populations

Opportunities

- The prevalence of the epidemic was mainly concentrated in specific vulnerable populations—injection drug users and incarcerated people—and 16.5% of the heterosexual transmission occurred in migrants from countries with generalised epidemics. This fact helped identify the target audiences of the social marketing strategy.
- Residual mother-child transmission.

Threats

- The incidence of HIV infection in Portugal was the second highest in Europe.
- A high rate of non-diagnosed infected people, who did not know their serological state and may not contribute to prevent the transmission of the virus.
- High levels of misconceptions about HIV transmission and prevention methods in the community, along with discriminatory attitudes towards people living with the infection.
- A low rate of consistent condom use and high rates of risky behaviours in the population.

Partnerships

In order to establish an integrated response, the National Coordination for HIV/AIDS developed a leadership strategy, involving an inter-ministerial governmental strategy organised in a National Council. This was materialised with the development of a national contest in partnership with the Ministries of Health and Education with the purpose of students creating pedagogical materials for sexual education, under the supervision of teachers, and its national presentation in a touring exhibition for basic and secondary schools. Further, the partnership with the Ministry of Labour and ILO (International Labour Organization) allowed for the creation of a white book for non-discrimination in the labour context (see Fig. 1).

In international relations, cooperation with developing countries in Africa in public health strategies had the purpose of preventing the consequent effect of an epidemic in Portugal due to the phenomena of immigration. Governmental partnerships in upstream levels also included the development of pilot programmes for the implementation of rapid tests in health centres supporting drug users and for needle exchange in prisons.

This case presents a social marketing strategy both with upstream and downstream actions developed in partnership with non-governmental institutions. The funding programme to civil society, called ADIS, was optimised in order to prevent redundant responses and promote joint efforts between institutions with complimentary activities under the creation of a civil society forum. Also, the upstream guidelines, policies and campaigns were created based on a continuous involvement of civil society with community intervention on HIV prevention. As an example, the process of developing a media campaign started by including a focus group with (a) targeted people who participated in the brainstorming and pretest phases of communication campaigns in order to share their ideas and incorporate evidence in a bottom-up direction and (b) health professionals who contributed to national therapeutic and support guidelines. The syringe and needle exchange programme into community pharmacies was maintained, in cooperation with the National Pharmacy Association.

There were also partnerships with private business. In some cases, sharing costs in win–win advertising initiatives, such as the promotion of rapid tests that was co-financed by the pharmaceutical industry. Other cases were developed under the Corporate Social Responsibility (CSR) umbrella, such as the contribution of contents for CSR posters and pamphlets for a national retailer, for example, contents for the academy of a beauty care brand about safe procedures for hairdressers without discrimination in services (see Fig. 2).

Segmentation and Targeting

Social marketing involves the process of targeting actions to different audiences, and, in the case under analysis, mass orientation was replaced by particular attention to the most vulnerable populations to HIV infection: injection drug users,

Fig. 1 Poster developed for prevention in the labour context. Source: with kind permission by Portuguese National AIDS Coordination

Fig. 2 Technical contents developed for CSR of a retail brand and a beauty care brand. Source: with kind permission by Portuguese National AIDS Coordination, Sonae and L'Oreal

incarcerated population, migrants and ethnic and sexual minorities, sex workers, men who have sex with men (MSM), adolescents, women and heterosexual adults, both in established and casual relationships.

The difference between a mass and a segmented strategy consists on targeting messages, media and channels used in order to get a more effective behaviour change. Figure 3 shows an example of a targeted message to pregnant women.

The targeted marketing strategy was controversial, because of the connection of risky behaviours with vulnerable targets that could emphasise stigma and discrimination towards those populations. Figure 4 is an example of a particular controversial campaign, targeting MSM, instead of generalising the risk of infection to the general population. However, despite the universal risk of transmission, the communication strategy was focused on targeting different audiences in different risk contexts in order to increase the risk perception through a better identification with messages.

Instead of targeting the general population with general messages on condom use or testing or advertising the help line, the segmented strategy developed different

Fig. 3 Social advertising campaign targeting pregnant women. Source: with kind permission by Portuguese National AIDS Coordination

Fig. 4 MSM campaign for stable and casual partners. Source: with kind permission by Portuguese National AIDS Coordination

interventions for adolescents in schools, adolescents in informal settings, heterosexuals and MSM, both with stable and casual partners. Behaviour change activities also targeted migrants in Chinese and Ukrainian communities in Portugal with adapted contents (see Fig. 5).

Fig. 5 Informational pamphlets in Chinese and Ukrainian. Source: with kind permission by Portuguese National AIDS Coordination

Social Marketing Mix

A social marketing framework has the focus of promoting behaviour or attitude change in different target audiences through interconnected social marketing actions developed in joint partnerships. Exchange theory is an important dimension of that framework, since it considers the benefits and costs associated with social change, as well as behavioural competitors. Exchange theory is emphasised in this case with the social marketing benefit: (a) HIV transmission prevention as a benefit connected with a healthy life, through condom use and the nonsharing of needles by drug users or in tattooing; (b) the knowledge of serologic status using the free, rapid and confidential HIV test for the early-stage diagnosis of infection and prevention of transmission and infection progress (see Fig. 6 with an HIV detection campaign); (c) and the promotion of an inclusive and non-discriminating society for people living with HIV/AIDS.

The cost of that exchange is related with the cost of consistent preventive behaviours such as condom use (male or female) in sexual intercourses, with the economic, psychological and social costs it represents; the requirement of HIV testing after risk behaviours, with the cost of psychological anxiety and social discomfort of contacting health professionals for that purpose; and the cost of overcoming the fear of HIV transmission in social contact with people living with the infection. In order to decrease the price of condoms as social products, there was a negotiation with the Ministry of Health suppliers and the main national retailers in order to guarantee the existence of a first-price brand in the market without neglecting the quality and safe perception.

The free distribution of male and female condoms was intensified in health institutions, schools and social events, such as music festivals, and a special kit targeting MSM was produced. Female condoms were distributed in partnership with

Fig. 6 Poster promoting the HIV test. Source: with kind permission by Portuguese National AIDS Coordination

civil society organisations intervening particularly among sex workers, considering that the product was not available in commercial retailers. As distribution actions, the availability of sterilised needles free of charge for exchange in pharmacies was reinforced, and the intervention was introduced in jails. Access to the rapid test was intensified in intervention community teams, such as in drug users' support centres.

The communication strategy involves the development of advertising campaigns, designed with the inclusion of focus groups of targeted audiences—heterosexual population, MSM, sex workers, young people, pregnant women, drug users and migrants.

The health belief model and the protection motivation theory (PMT) are disease prevention models evidenced in this case study due to the intentional use of severity and threats to provide perceptions of risk and vulnerability to individuals, as well as self-efficacy to change behaviours with low costs (French et al. 2010). These models are present in advertisements using fear appeals to show the dangerous consequences of the disease but also use incentivising appeals to use healthy behaviours by copy-response of celebrity influencers. The use of copy-response social models follows the theory of the prototype-willingness model. A good example is the Portuguese campaign internationally awarded by the Germany government as the best European public HIV prevention advertising in 2009. The mentioned campaign integrated the cognitive dissonance theory by showing the five reasons mostly argued not to wear a condom but at the same time showing the negative faces of the disease, with the shocking report of an HIV-positive test, therapy adherence and terminal phase of AIDS with body wounds (see Fig. 7). Cognitive dissonance phenomena occur when people change their beliefs in order to adapt behaviours. As people commonly find excuses not to wear a condom, this campaign, acted by public figures, shows that it is

Fig. 7 Campaign '5 reasons not to wear a condom'.
Source: with kind permission by Portuguese National AIDS Coordination

worth it to wear or use a condom. This campaign was the most remembered in a joint evaluation in national surveys of five television campaigns developed in the same year (Casais 2008).

In fact, the value of celebrity endorsement in social marketing is known, especially in HIV prevention, both for awareness of the social cause and the marketing positioning of the celebrity brand, besides their conscious role as social influencers (Casais and Proenca 2012). The use of celebrity endorsement is also present in the campaign illustrated in Figs. 7 and 8.

Also, other communication strategies were used, such as product placement in a television fiction series targeted to adolescents through the content guide of a rapid test procedure in a health service for the main protagonists; public relations, with consistent participation in television contents, media coverage of institutional activities and epidemic outcomes discussion; the organisation of national contests for copywriting and exhibitions in schools; the development and distribution of merchandising highlighting the red ribbon to promote cause awareness; and the organisation of a workshop for journalists about technical contents of HIV and a

Fig. 8 'Angels' sex campaign. Source: with kind permission by Portuguese National AIDS Coordination

Fig. 9 Banner in the National Parliament. Source: with kind permission by Portuguese National AIDS Coordination

special journalism award to promote quality media coverage on the topic. Figure 9 shows outdoor banners in public institutions.

Evaluating Social Marketing Effectiveness

Behaviour change in social marketing should be monitored and evaluated in the long-term (Wymer 2011). A national barometer was implemented to determine population knowledge, attitudes and behaviours towards HIV/AIDS infection, although without significant results in the short term. The survey also tried to evaluate the awareness and acceptance of social advertising campaigns. The results showed a particular increase in HIV prevention campaigns spontaneous recognition and a higher suggested awareness for social advertising campaigns with celebrity endorsers (Casais 2008).

Besides awareness and recognition, as well as the acceptance of communication messages, the available metrics to evaluate social marketing effectiveness are epidemic data outcomes in a long-term perspective. In order to analyse this case in the long term, epidemic outcomes until 2017 were collected. Table 1 shows the evolution of newly diagnosed HIV infections in Portugal—rates per 100,000 population by year of diagnosis—although the results require the attention to notification delay of the most recent years.

Table 1 Incidence rate by year of diagnosis (rate per 100,000 population—2005–2016)

Country	2005	2006	2007	2008	2009	2010	2011	2012	2013	2014	2015	2016
Portugal	19.6	21.2	20.6	21.1	19.3	18.2	16.1	15.6	15.1	11.8	11.5	10.0

Source: authors, with data from HIV/AIDS surveillance in Europe 2012, 2015 and 2016 (ECDC and WHO 2013, 2016, 2017)

After the described social marketing strategy, Portugal went from the second country with highest incidence rate in 2005 to the fifth in 2016 in the same ranking (ECDC and WHO 2017).

Conclusions

This case study describes the particularities of a social marketing intervention in a stigmatised public health topic and the successful outcome of adapting social marketing frameworks directed to a target audience based on the populations most vulnerable to HIV/AIDS. This case shows integrated social marketing mix activities, with a particular emphasis on communication, combining incentives and fear appeals and celebrity endorsements. Finally, the effectiveness of social marketing policies is analysed with a long-term overview of the epidemic evolution, in terms of infection incidence. Although HIV infection is decreasing worldwide, responding to the wide access to treatment and the policies of early diagnosis and treatment, the observed national outcome might, at least partially, be a consequence of the social marketing response in the past. The temporal relation favours such an explanation.

Discussion Questions

1. What are the advantages and disadvantages of a social marketing strategy involving the partnership of public policy with business companies and other organisations?
2. What are benefits and risks of a segmented communication to the most vulnerable populations?
3. What other actions of the social marketing mix would you suggest for this health public policy strategy?
4. What are the assumptions of exchange theory, health belief model, protection motivation theory, cognitive dissonance and prototype-willingness model in this case?
5. Assuming the potential of digital media and the growing attention given to microcelebrities, who have a social influence in digital social media, what would you propose to activate behaviour change and generate electronic word of mouth?
6. What other indicators could be used to evaluate the social marketing effectiveness of HIV/AIDS prevention?

Acknowledgements Beatriz Casais was the social marketing manager of the Portuguese National AIDS Coordination during the period the case respects to. João F. Proença gratefully acknowledges financial support from FCT-Fundação para a Ciência e Tecnologia (Portugal), national funding through research grant UID/SOC/04521/2013. Henrique Barros was the Portuguese National AIDS Coordinator during the period the case respects to.

References

Airhihenbuwa, C. O., & Obregon, R. (2000). A critical assessment of theories/models used in health communication for HIV/AIDS. *Journal of Health Communication: International Perspectives, 5*, 5–15.

Casais, B. (2008). *Avaliação de campanhas televisivas de prevenção do VIH*. Paper presented at the II Congresso da CPLP sobre DST e AIDS, Rio de Janeiro.

Casais, B., & Proenca, J. F. (2012). Inhibitions and implications associated with celebrity participation in health-related social marketing: An exploratory research focused on HIV prevention in Portugal. *Health Marketing Quarterly, 29*(3), 206–222.

ECDC, & WHO. (2013). *HIV/AIDS surveillance in Europe 2012*. Stockholm: ECDC.

ECDC, & WHO. (2016). *HIV/AIDS surveillance in Europe 2015*. Stockholm: ECDC.

ECDC, & WHO. (2017). *HIV/AIDS surveillance in Europe 2016*. Stockholm: ECDC.

French, J., Blair-Stevens, C., McVey, D., & Merritt, R. (2010). *Social marketing and public health theory and practice*. New York: Oxford University Press.

Gordon, R. (2013). Unlocking the potential of upstream social marketing. *European Journal of Marketing, 47*(9), 1525–1547.

Gordon, R., McDermmot, L., Stead, M., & Angus, K. (2006). The effectiveness of social marketing interventions for health improvement: What's the evidence? *Public Health, 120*(12), 1113–1139.

Grier, S., & Bryant, C. A. (2005). Social marketing in public health. *Annual Review of Public Health, 26*, 319–339.

Hastings, G. (2003). Relational paradigms in social marketing. *Journal of Macromarketing, 23*(1), 6–15.

MartinKey, T., & Czaplewski, A. J. (2017). Upstream social marketing strategy: An integrated marketing communications approach. *Business Horizons, 60*(3), 325–333.

McDermott, L., Stead, M., & Hastings, G. (2005). What is and what is not social marketing: The challenge of reviewing the evidence. *Journal of Marketing Management, 21*(5–6), 545–553.

Merson, M. H., O'Malley, J., Serwadda, D., & Apisuk, C. (2008). The history and challenge of HIV prevention. *Lancet, 372*(9637), 475–488.

Milbourne, L. (2009). Remodelling the third sector: Advancing collaboration or competition in community-based initiatives? *Journal of Social Policy, 38*, 277–297.

Silva, S. C., & Silva, M. F. (2012). Failure is a stepping stone for success. *International Review on Public and Nonprofit Marketing, 9*(2), 153–179.

Truong, V. D. (2014). Social marketing: A systematic review of research 1998–2012. *Social Marketing Quarterly, 20*(1), 15–34.

Wymer, W. (2011). Developing more effective social marketing strategies. *Journal of Social Marketing, 1*(1), 17–31.

Social Knowledge in Public Health: Case Study on Substantiating and Instrumenting the Social Marketing Campaigns in Romania

Ani Matei and Corina-Georgiana Antonovici

Abstract Social marketing influences in a relevant manner the process of producing and disseminating social knowledge, thus asserting attitudes and approaches according to various objectives of social evolution.

The field literature reveals the fact that for the area of public health, the studies on social marketing are based both on improvement of specific social knowledge and strategic approaches for knowledge transfer towards the beneficiaries of public health policies, transfer designed to have impact on change of attitude and enhancement of social knowledge level.

The current chapter presents a case study concerning the social marketing campaign in the area of public health, "NO to randomly taken antibiotics", in Romania, aimed to promote adequate antibiotic use by informing the doctors and nonspecialized public concerning their risk of excessive and wrong use.

A. Matei (✉) · C.-G. Antonovici
National University of Political Studies and Public Administration, Bucharest, Romania
e-mail: amatei@snspa.ro; corina.antonovici@administratiepublica.eu

Learning Objectives
This chapter analyses the social marketing campaign in the public health area "NO to randomly taken antibiotics", developed by the Ministry of Health in Romania.
The study has the following objectives:

- Conceiving and developing a framework of analysis for the social marketing campaign in the public health area, substantiated on the importance, role and assertion of social knowledge, concerning the treatment with antibiotics of the Romanian citizens
- Identifying the types of strategies used in the implementation and delivery of the campaign in view of reaching its objectives, highlighting the marketing mix and the type of informational approach
- Presenting the campaign impact on the improvement of citizens' health, change of behaviour and attitude concerning the Romanians' treatment with antibiotics for simple diseases, by means of presenting the results of a questionnaire applied to citizens from Bucharest.

Introduction

Although there is no clear definition, at general level, social knowledge represents the body of collective knowledge produced by a community. The process of creating social knowledge involves the different participation of several actors, institutions and individuals. Thus, social knowledge becomes the outcome of the relationships and connections between the community members. Social behaviour definitely depends on the level of social knowledge in a certain community.

Girard and Girard (2011: XV) provide relevant theoretical frameworks "for improving the understanding of the scientific role of social knowledge in business, government, or non-profit sectors".

The theoretical frameworks based on researchers' outcomes and practitioners' best practices reveal the diversity and scientific importance of social knowledge, conceived for using social media in order "to create, transfer, and preserve organizational knowledge—past, present, and future—with a view to achieving the organizational vision" (Girard and Girard 2011: XIV).

The typology of knowledge as "different ways of knowing about a social issue" embodies (Bryant 2002):

- *Instrumental* or expert knowledge—usually created by "experts". It is perceived to be, like its creators, objective and systematically developed through "scientific"—usually quantitative—research methods.

- *Interactive* or lay knowledge—develops from lived experience and is exchanged among people in their daily lives.
- *Critical knowledge*, which is reflective knowledge. This knowledge considers the role of social structures and power relations in reinforcing inequalities and disempowering people. Critical knowledge considers questions of right and wrong, analyses existing social conditions and outlines what can be done to alter social conditions to improve quality of life.

Linking instrumental, interactive and critical knowledge can root policy ideas in the community within which health promotion programmes and public health policy are ultimately applied. The solicitation and use of interactive and critical knowledge are consistent with the principles of health promotion and democracy (Bryant 2002).

Narrowing the debate to the health area, it is necessary to start with Solar and Irwin's statement (2010: 4) that "complexity defines health".

In this context, the series *Debates, Policy and Practice, Case Studies* of the World Health Organization (WHO) describes the so-called social determinants of health, health being understood as a social phenomenon requiring multiple complex action forms and inter-sectoral policies.

Social knowledge will represent their support and reason, being continuously associated with learning, innovation or collaborative socialization of knowledge.

Social Marketing as Instrument of Social Knowledge

The field literature debates about "social production of health and disease", highlighting three important theoretical approaches:

- Psychosocial approaches
- Social productions of disease/political economy of health
- Eco-social frameworks (Solar and Irwin 2010: 4)

Social marketing in the health area belongs to the third approach.

Social marketing, the use of marketing to design and implement programmes to promote socially beneficial behavioural change, has grown in popularity and usage within the public health community (Grier and Bryant 2005).

Social marketing recognizes that what people know, and even people's attitudes, do not always impact their actual behaviour.

It seeks to understand people's motivations and needs, as well as to gain a better understanding of how the environments in which their actions take place influence behaviours (ECDC 2014: 5). Knowledge represents a factor influencing their behaviour.

The objectives of social marketing as instrument of social knowledge in the health area are described, even indirectly, by the WHO (1998). In this context, public health activities should:

- Enable individuals and communities to gain more power over the personal, socioeconomic and environmental factors that affect their health
- Involve those who are concerned about an issue in all stages of project planning, implementation and evaluation
- Be guided by a concern for equity and social justice

Achieving such goals will require collaboration between experts and community members, specifically by drawing upon community members' knowledge about their health and well-being. This knowledge should be complemented with critical analysis of how social and political structures affect health. It is also important to make explicit the various forces that influence whether different forms of knowledge are allowed to contribute to the policy development process or not (Bryant 2002).

Case Development

During 2012–2015, according to the statistics of the European Centre for Disease Prevention and Control, Romania was the second country in Europe (after Greece) concerning antibiotic consumption per 1000 inhabitants. In the hospitals participating in the data collection, the prescription of antibiotics seems exaggerated and/or wrong, while the measures for preventing the infections associated with medical assistance are insufficient/inefficient (CNEPSS 2017). According to the Romanian Health Observatory (2017), Romania is the EU Member State with the highest weight of antibiotic use without medical prescription. The evidence reveals a high level of resistance to antibiotics in Romania.

High European officials, such as the Director of the European Centre for Disease Prevention and Control, Dr. Marc Sprenger, have drawn attention since 2014 that Romania belongs to "the red area", and the solutions depend to a large extent on the "political will".[1]

The CARMIN study (2015) and the Romanian Health Observatory (2017) consider the following causes for the above situation:

- Insufficient information and/or wrong mentality of the population concerning the role, benefits and risks of antibiotics; guides for antibiotic therapy are not suitable or are ignored.
- Excessive and unjustified use of antibiotics, through excessive prescriptions, both in hospital and ambulatory, either at the patient's request or by doctors.
- Facile accessibility to antibiotics, without complying with the regulations.
- Collaboration of pharmaceutical companies with opinion leaders in view to disseminate messages favouring the excessive use of antibiotics.
- Low number of specialist doctors dedicated to solving the problem.

---

[1]Interview in Medical Life, 21 November 2014. http://www.viata-medicala.ro/Romania-are-unul-dincele-mai-mari-consumuri-de-antibiotice.html*articleID_9392-dArt.html

The statistics of the Ministry of Health in Romania indicate that more than half of the antibiotics sold are given on uncompensated prescription or even without prescription; half of this consumption is not justified, from the medical point of view. The Ministry of Health considers that the excessive consumption is generated by patients, distributors and doctors.

In view to support the above-mentioned issues, concerning the citizens' and doctors' behaviour, the Minister of Health in 2016 (Vlad Voiculescu), in a press conference, asserted: "On the one hand, the patients and their families ask the doctors or chemists to prescribe or release antibiotics without medical prescription. On the other hand, the prescribers recommend useless antibiotics for several reasons: lack of updated medical information, either at the patient's or his family's pressure, persuasion of pharmaceutical companies. (...)The above are confirmed by doctors and chemists".

Methodology

Research Design In order to achieve our research objectives, within the study, we used exploratory research. It was performed by means of an exploratory inquiry among the consumers of antibiotics, in the form of a questionnaire, and by analysing the social marketing campaign run in Romania, proving that this high consumption of antibiotics in our country is also the product of social knowledge.

Analysis of the Social Inquiry

Defining the Sample We used the non-probabilistic sampling technique, more precisely, convenience sampling. The questionnaire was applied to citizens in Bucharest, capital of Romania, 18 to 80 years of age (the City of Bucharest, in year 2018, according to the National Statistics Institute, had a population of 2,104,967 inhabitants).

Data Collection The questionnaire initially identified the sex and age of respondents. It comprised seven questions designed to determine the respondents' perception concerning the antibiotic consumption, aiming to identify the citizens' behaviour related to the consumption of drugs and the impact of the campaign developed by the Ministry of Health.

Data collection took place during the period 25 January–28 February 2018. All 235 online questionnaires were valid.

Results 73.8% of the respondents are female, and 26.2% are male. Concerning the age, 59.4% of the respondents are 18–30 years of age, 21.8% are 31–40 years of age, 13.7% are 41–50 years of age and 5.1% are over 51 years old.

Concerning the question "Have you consumed antibiotics in the last 5 years?", the responses were as follows: 65% of the respondents had consumed based on clear

Fig. 1 Have you heard about the campaign of the authorities: "NO to randomly taken antibiotics"? Source: Authors, based on data obtained from the questionnaire

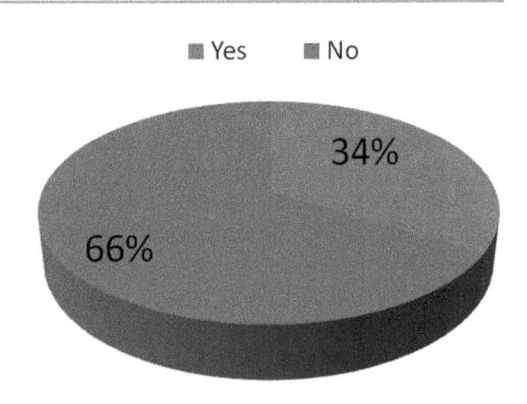

indications of a doctor, 24.8% without clear indications from a doctor and 10.3% did not consume.

At the same time, regarding the question "Have you consumed antibiotics without a doctor's prescription in the last year?", there were 23.5% affirmative answers. For the question "When you are sick, which is the first action that you do?", 20.9% of the respondents mentioned that they were taking the same treatment as the previous time, without seeing a doctor, 12.8% respondents were doing nothing, 5.1% were seeking the advice of a friend/parent, while 26.5% were asking the support of a chemist and only 34.6% were paying a visit to the doctor.

Concerning the question "Do you have antibiotics at home for the time being? (just in case)", 52.8% responded affirmative.

Taking into consideration the above answers, we notice that only a small part of the respondents have a doctor's advice centred behaviour, the others were taking treatment with antibiotics by themselves, sometimes prudently.

We shall analyse the questions related to the impact of the social marketing campaign "NO to randomly taken antibiotics!" from our questionnaire. For the question "Would you listen/follow the advice of a social campaign to consume antibiotics only based on a specialist doctor's recommendation?", 78.5% responded affirmative. For the question "Have you heard about the campaign of the authorities: "NO to randomly taken antibiotics"?", 66.2% of the respondents provided negative responses (see Fig. 1), while for the question related to the influence of that campaign on their behaviour, 72.5% provided negative responses, 12.9% affirmative responses, only with the doctor's recommendation, and 14.6% mentioned that they were going to consume less antibiotics (see Fig. 2).

Analysis of the "NO to Randomly Taken Antibiotics" Campaign

On 18 November 2016, the Ministry of Health launched the awareness campaign on the risk of useless antibiotic consumption, *NO to randomly taken antibiotics*, drawing attention to the fact that Romania is on the top of the European ranking

■ No

■ Yes, now I do not consume antibiotics without a doctor's prescription

■ Yes, I consume less antibiotics

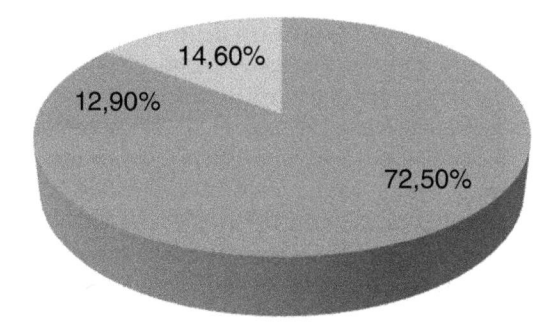

14,60%
12,90%
72,50%

Fig. 2 Has the "NO to randomly taken antibiotics" campaign influenced your behaviour? Source: Authors, based on data obtained from the questionnaire

concerning antibiotic consumption (above 90% of antibiotic consumption takes place outside the hospital, for infections treated at home).

The campaign "NO to randomly taken antibiotics" has aimed to increase the awareness on the adequate use of antibiotics by informing the doctor and public on the risk represented by inadequate and abusive use.

The campaign took place in the period 18 November–31 December 2016.

In the framework of the campaign "NO to random taken antibiotics!", several informational, educational and support materials were made (video spots, posters, flyers) for diverse target groups—patients, family doctors, specialist doctors in hospitals and drug producers, i.e. a combination of "types" and "forms" of customized interventions for each target segment. There are sets of instruments and messages for doctors in view to promote the adequate and responsible antibiotic use, as well as for informing the patients on the risks of resistance to antibiotics.

Analysing the materials of the campaign "NO to randomly taken antibiotics!", we notice that it has been based on knowledge development, information to enable behaviour change and to develop a new behaviour. The campaign addressed a target group with problematic behaviour, as well as the target group with positive behaviour, which should be encouraged and supported.

The strategy of the campaign "NO to randomly taken antibiotics!" was an induction one: the attitudes are positive, but socially desirable behaviour does not carry them out. The objective of the strategy is to try to induce the accomplishment of that behaviour (Santesmases 1999). Its actions aimed at education and information, in view to discourage the target group from recommending or taking treatment with antibiotics in useless cases.

In order to reduce the number of the people practicing self-medication, not as direct result of the campaign, the public authorities in Romania carry out controls in pharmacies to check the selling system of antibiotics (based only on prescription) and "punish" the pharmacies for releasing antibiotics without prescription.

The campaign uses the four Ps (Kotler et al. 2002): product, price, place and promotion. These key elements of social marketing are central to the planning and implementation of an integrated marketing strategy (Grier and Bryant 2005: 6.4).

The product, in social marketing, refers to the set of benefits associated with the desired behaviour or service use. In the field literature, there is a distinction between the main product (what the people obtain when adopting the behaviour, etc.) and the genuine product (desired behaviour) (Kotler et al. 2002). In the framework of the campaign "NO to randomly taken antibiotics!", the products are intangible—knowledge and information.

The price is represented by the cost of getting information in view to acquire knowledge to adopt the adequate behaviour related to behaviour change. The cost comprises intangible prices. It could be psychological (psychical discomfort associated with behavioural change, fear concerning the safety of treatment and healing) and social (risk to be perceived differently in the age group).

The place includes the location for developing the campaign but also includes intermediaries—organizations and people—who could provide information enabling the change process. The campaign "NO to randomly taken antibiotics!" has been developed in the places of interest visited usually for medical purpose, namely, the cabinets of family doctors, hospitals and channels of distribution such as television, press and website of the ministry.

The promotional activities of the campaign "NO to randomly taken antibiotics!" include advertisement on television channels, website, Facebook, printed materials and special events.

The following promotional materials and activities of the campaign "NO to randomly taken antibiotics!" were designed in view to facilitate the adoption of the desired behaviour:

- Broadcasting a TVspot, produced under the coordination of the Ministry of Health.
- Distributing boxes with pseudo-drugs, printed with the label "NO to randomly taken antibiotics!" and flyers. 12,000 boxes were distributed to family doctors, 13,000 boxes to doctors in hospitals and 25,000 boxes to patients, associations of students of the faculties of medicine and pharmacy.
- 10,000 posters were displayed in hospitals.
- Organization of the *European Antibiotic Awareness Day* on 18 November 2016, on the topic "Developing multidrug resistance to bacteria—severe threat for patients' safety and life", with the motto: "Red code for antibiotics: public information, careful prescription, rigorous hygiene in hospitals".

The European Centre for Disease Prevention and Control (ECDC) promotes and supports the prudent antibiotic use. Since 2008, ECDC coordinates the organization of the European Antibiotic Awareness Day, an initiative for public health, aimed to provide a platform and support for the national campaigns in this field. ECDC

Table 1 Trends in the consumption of antibiotics for systemic use in Romania, 2012–2016 (expressed as daily dose defined per 1000 inhabitants per day)

Country	2012	2013	2014	2015	2016	Trends in antimicrobial consumption, 2012–2016	Average annual change 2012–2016
Romania	30.4	31.6	31.2	33.3	29.5		0.00

Source: European Centre for Disease Prevention and Control, Summary of the latest data on antibiotic consumption in the European Union, ESAC-Net surveillance data, November 2017, p. 5

provides a series of materials and instruments of communication (video, posters, patients' stories, info graphics, key messages, etc.) in view to develop national campaigns concerning the danger represented by resistance to antibiotics for the public health.

The campaign has developed an integrated social marketing strategy, based on the four P in view to influence the target group behaviour.

The campaign used the informational approach (focused, above all, on persuasive information) (Santesmases 1999).

Based on the available information, it is quite burdensome to evaluate the efficiency of the analysed social marketing initiative. It has been also hard to identify the pertinent information, and we consider that the effects are rather "external" (self-reporting by respondents). Concluding, we dare to assert that the social marketing campaign had a positive impact.

In 2016, the statistics of the European Centre for Disease Prevention and Control ranked Romania the fourth country in Europe (after Greece, Cyprus and France), on a lower position compared to year 2015, concerning the antibiotic consumption per 1000 inhabitants, but the trend is to decrease the consumption. The evolution of the consumption of systemic use antibiotics in Romania in the period 2012–2016 (expressed as a daily dose defined per 1000 inhabitants, per day) can be seen in Table 1.

Conclusions

The social marketing campaign "NO to random taken antibiotics!" has focused both on the target group behaviour (individual behaviour) and on understanding the warning from the messages and the social and environmental causes.

For the time being, in Romania, the antibiotic use continues to be excessive. A major role is played by target group awareness and education on antibiotic consumption, counteracting causes such as insufficient information and/or wrong mentality of general population concerning the role, benefits and risks of antibiotics; excessive prescriptions both in hospitals and ambulatory; still easy accessibility to antibiotics; and infringement of the regulations for releasing them only based on prescriptions. The future measures refer to surveillance, control and illegal release of antibiotics in pharmacies (CNEPSS 2017).

For the future, in view to counteract the above-mentioned causes and to increase the impact of social marketing campaigns, the cooperation between various actors (public institutions/authorities, NGOs, companies) should be strengthened. At the same time, joint actions could have a greater impact.

Discussion Questions

1. Argument the role and importance of social knowledge in the impact of the results of the social marketing campaigns.
2. In the absence of solid proof of official assessment of the efficiency of the social marketing campaign "NO to randomly taken antibiotics!", can we speak of a "real" positive impact on the population?
3. What other measures meant to counteract causes such as insufficient information/lack of knowledge of the population, regarding the role, benefits and risks of antibiotic administration and excessive prescription, would you recommend in order to rectify this critical situation in Romania? What improvements would you bring to the measures already taken by Romania?

References

Bryant, T. (2002). Role of knowledge in public health and health promotion policy change. *Health Promote International, 17*(1), 89–98. https://academic.oup.com/heapro/article/17/1/89/550102

European Antibiotics Awareness Day. (2013). http://dspb.ro/diverse/20131105-zeia.pdf

European Centre for Disease Prevention and Control (ECDC). *An agency of the European Union. European Antibiotics Awareness Day. A European Health Initiative.* https://antibiotic.ecdc.europa.eu/en/about

European Centre for Disease Prevention and Control (ECDC). (2014). *Social marketing guide for public health managers and practitioners*. Stockholm: ECDC.

European Centre for Disease Prevention and Control (ECDC). (2017, November). *Summary of the latest data on antibiotic consumption in the European Union, ESAC-Net surveillance data.*

Girard, J. P., & Girard, J. L. (Eds.). (2011). *Social knowledge: Using social media to know what you know*. Hershey: Information Science Reference.

Grier, S., & Bryant, C. A. (2005). Social marketing in public health. *Annual Review of Public Health, 26*, 6.1–6.21.

Interview in Medical Life. (2014, November 21). http://www.viata-medicala.ro/Romania-are-unul-dincele-mai-mari-consumuri-de-antibiotics.html*articleID_9392-dArt.html

Kotler, P., Roberto, N., & Lee, N. (2002). *Social marketing, improving the quality of life* (2nd ed.). London: Sage.

Ministry of Health in Romania. http://www.ms.ro/antibiotics/

National Centre for Health Evaluation and Promotion (CNEPSS) – ZEIA Analysis. (2017). http://insp.gov.ro/sites/cnepss/wp-content/uploads/2017/10/2-Analiza-de-situatie-ZEIA-2017-final.pdf

National Institute of Public Health and National Centre for Transmissible Disease Surveillance and Control. (2017). *Analysis of the evolution of transmissible diseases under surveillance*. Report for 2016, Bucharest.

Romanian Health Observatory. (2017). *Romania, EU top country in antibiotic consumption. The authorities neglect the situation.* http://health-observatory.ro/wp-content/uploads/2017/11/Raport_alerta_ORS_antibiotics_nov_2017.pdf

Santesmases, M. M. (1999). *Marketing. Conceptos y Estrategias.* Madrid: Piramide.

Solar, O., & Irwin, A. (2010). *A conceptual framework for action on the social determinants of health.* Social Determinants of Health Discussion, Paper 2 (Policy and Practice). World Health Organization (WHO).

World Health Organization (WHO). (1998). http://www.who.int/en/

Vidyasagar Institute of Mental Health: Bringing People Together for a Cause

Deep Shree, Shiksha Kushwah, and Mahim Sagar

Abstract

Mental health and related issues have lately emerged as a crisis engulfing the global population. Despite the recent surge in awareness and acknowledgment of mental health crisis, these problems have received scant attention from low- and middle-income countries, barriers being lack of funding due to diversion of funds to existing public health programs, government's priorities, scarcity of trained professionals, and the difficulties in delivering mental health-care services in primary health-care centers.

Vidyasagar Institute of Mental Health and Neuro Sciences (VIMHANS) started as a mental health and rehabilitation institution in 1983. But, with sources of donations drying up, the stigma associated with mental health issues and lack of interest of the government in mental health-care sector, it is increasingly becoming difficult to run the organization.

The case examines whether the conscious use of social marketing for awareness and community engagement can result in better performance of the hospital and help it in garnering the requisite support.

D. Shree (✉) · S. Kushwah · M. Sagar
Department of Management Studies, Indian Institute of Technology Delhi, Hauz Khas, Delhi, India
e-mail: deepshree@dtu.ac.in; smz148414@dms.iitd.ac.in; mahim@dms.iitd.ac.in

© Springer Nature Switzerland AG 2019
M. M. Galan-Ladero, H. M. Alves (eds.), *Case Studies on Social Marketing*, Management for Professionals, https://doi.org/10.1007/978-3-030-04843-3_10

Learning Objectives
1. To gain an insight into the issues associated with running a charitable mental health-care facility in a developing nation
2. To elucidate the challenges faced in the implementation of social marketing strategies by charitable organizations in emerging economies
3. To analyze how a charitable organization can leverage the social cause it is promoting by using a well-designed social marketing campaign
4. To explore how VIMHANS can develop a successful awareness campaign for making mental health care accessible

Introduction

Mental health and related issues have lately emerged as a crisis engulfing the global population, which is further accentuated by the extremely low pace of developments in the field, the stigma associated with it and crippling lack of infrastructure to facilitate early diagnosis and treatment of mental illnesses. Mental health issues are increasingly becoming common, affecting 20–25% of all people at some time during their life (Prince et al. 2007).

Although mental illness affects a large population across the globe, people often tend to ignore this fact. Hence, resulting in a scenario where individuals who can get this support at an affordable price are denied the much-needed help and support from the community as well as the medical fraternity. This further generates a vicious cycle of misinformation, ignorance, and suffering. In addition, in the case of most of the developing nations, the priority of governments is lopsided toward physical health, and hence resources are diverted in that direction. In addition, out of the many individuals (nearly 7.5% in India) who suffer from a mental disorder, a very small percentage are able to actually afford the treatment.

Hence, to fill this gap in the provision of mental health care, several not-for-profit organizations have come to the fore. Even these organizations are struggling for funds, and it seems that spreading awareness about mental illnesses can not only help in better reporting of problems but will also breathe a new life in these organizations grappling with the scarcity of funds. Vidyasagar Institute of Mental Health and Neuro Sciences is one such not-for-profit organization working tirelessly toward providing treatment and care for mental health issues.

Of late, the need for mental health care has led to initiatives from government, nonprofits, and commercial organizations, but the stigma attached to mental health problems often nullifies the efforts taken by these institutions. The nongovernment organizations often find themselves struggling to attract attention and contributions for their cause.

Starting from 1971, when Kotler and Zaltman coined the term social marketing, it has continuously been adopted and applied by organizations for bringing in social changes. The use of social marketing as a tool for awareness and community engagement can result in better performance of the nonprofits and help them in garnering the requisite funds for survival. As these institutions cannot solely depend on the revenue earned from patients, they need to reach out to masses, make them aware of the impending dangers of mental illness, and ask them for support so that the collective voice reaches out to the government and local authorities. There have been numerous calls for invoking political will, for enhancing advocacy, and for galvanizing community participation, all with scant improvement in outcomes. Thus, it becomes now opportune to explore the paradigm of mental health awareness as a means of combating stigma, enhancing prevention, ensuring early recognition, and also stimulating simple and practical interventions within the community.

The main aim of VIMHANS is to create awareness for the cause of mental health, especially cater to the middle-income groups, and to generate enough funds to be able to subsidize the services at the hospital. This case study provides an overview of the social marketing initiatives undertaken by VIMHANS by providing a background of the change agent, i.e., VIMHANS, its competitors, and the barriers faced by service providers operating in this domain and the social marketing campaign launched by the hospital to increase awareness about mental health. Increased awareness will, in turn, lead to behavioral changes toward mental health care, and above all, it will help in attracting the attention of government for bringing in the necessary policy changes. It analyzes how the hospital intends to overcome the social barrier faced by mental illnesses in general, the taboo associated with it, the financial, and infrastructural issues the hospital has to face by launching a social marketing campaign with an intention to increase awareness and acceptance of mental health and related issues.

Mental Health in India: The Tough Reality

Despite the recent surge in awareness and acknowledgment of mental health crisis, these problems have received scant attention from low- and middle-income countries, barriers being lack of funding due to diversion of funds to existing public health programs, government's priorities, scarcity of trained professionals, and the difficulties in delivering mental health-care services in primary health-care centers (Saraceno et al. 2007).

As per the data provided by WHO, it was reported that India has one of the lowest numbers of mental health-care professionals in the world with only three psychiatrists per 10 lakh individuals and five psychologists per 10 million individuals (WHO 2011). The situation has been further worsened by the fact that owing to the lower number of trained professionals, they are in very high demand and hence their availability is limited by high-paying hospitals and urban areas, which leaves most of the rural areas unserved and at the mercy of quacks.

This challenge cannot be dealt with unless there is extensive support from the community. The community will extend its support and will ultimately channelize resources in the direction of mental health only when they are aware of mental health issues. Generating health awareness and improving health literacy are two sides of the same coin; the stigma attached to mental health and the discrimination meted out to patients is the manifestation of ignorance among the masses (Pinfold 2003).

Vidyasagar Institute of Mental Health (VIMHANS): The Social Change Agent

Inspired by the missionary zeal of Dr. Vidya Sagar, Vidyasagar Institute of Mental Health and Neuro Sciences (VIMHANS) was started by his family members to pay homage to him after his demise in 1978. Starting from a paltry sum of US$564 left by Dr. Vidya Sagar and another US$338 received as donations, this hospital has slowly emerged as a center of excellence in the much-needed field of mental health care. Vidyasagar Institute of Mental Health and Neuro Sciences (VIMHANS) started as a mental health and rehabilitation institution in 1983. From the original field of mental health, the hospital has expanded into a multispecialty institute. It offers outpatient, inpatient, and rehabilitation programs managed with the 40 consultants and professionals from various mental health disciplines—psychiatry, psychology, physical rehabilitation (physiotherapy, speech therapy, occupational therapy), special educators, integrated arts therapists, and nursing professionals. They run a 21-bedded ICU along with 40 beds for the departments of neurosciences and orthopedics—looked after by a separate set of consultants, paramedical staffs, and nursing staffs. VIMHANS has three outreach centers in different parts of North India. It is the leader for mental health in North India and is the only nongovernment institute to provide inpatient facilities, approximately 60 beds dedicated, for individuals diagnosed with moderate to severe mental illness.

The clients come from all over India as well as neighboring countries like Afghanistan, Pakistan, Myanmar, Sri Lanka, Bhutan, Bangladesh, UAE, Kenya, etc. The hospital has updated a range of medical technology and in addition, also has an active social outlook.

VIMHANS is planning to start several satellite centers in remote areas in few years, but they are facing several issues as starting new satellite centers entails several costs such as land buying costs, infrastructure development cost, and cost of running the hospital. All of this must be done while maintaining its high quality and low cost. The funding/donations have to increase and also the patient flow; the only solution seems to be increased awareness of mental health and related issues among the patients as well as the donors.

The Social Marketing Campaign

Social marketing campaigns are launched to change people's attitude and behavior with an intention to bring positive change in the society (Kotler and Roberto 1989). The social marketing movement which started with a focus on products offered for bringing in social change has evolved a lot in the last few decades. Researchers now agree that the motive of social marketing is not the promotion of an idea as initially suggested but to influence behavior for achieving a greater good (Andreasen 2004). Hence, the focus of VIMHANS's social marketing initiative is to increase awareness about mental health and thus remove the stigma attached to it so that people start accepting mental health issues like any other health issue and seek professional advice for it.

Toward the achievement of this end, VIMHANS has launched a social marketing campaign for creating impact in by improving the mental well-being of the society as a whole. The following sections detail out the various components of social marketing initiatives of VIMHANS.

Marketing Mix

Not-for-profit organizations need to bring in more creativity in marketing mix elements as there is very less scope to alter/modify the product/offering to bring it more attractive to the target audience.

Product

Firstly, the hospital aims to create awareness about various mental health issues. VIMHANS is not targeting any specific issue or any age group in particular but intends to make people aware of the various facets of mental health problems.

Also, it might not always be feasible for individuals to identify that someone is suffering from mental health issues and needs professional advice, hence VIMHANS works in collaboration with schools to spread awareness starting from early years, and it also organizes workshops (paid as well as free) for diverse segments where individuals are encouraged to talk about such issues and offered guidance on identifying the early diagnostic indicators. This encourages people to open to these problems thus reducing the stigma attached to it.

Price

VIMHANS is a not-for-profit organization which aims to provide affordable mental health-care facilities. They need to remain profitable to cover the costs and unlike other issues of social concern, mental health has not been able to attract funds from donors or the government. That's why they have to charge the fee from the patients, though they also provide free treatment in accordance with government regulations. A nominal fee is charged for consultation, which might go on for even an hour. The fee is not dependent on the time spent but is constant for each patient. Despite increasing costs, the hospital has not been able to increase the consultation fee as the patients may not be able to afford it. Even this nominal fee charged from patients acts as a barrier as unlike in developed countries where therapies, consultation, and medication are covered by insurance, in most of the developing countries, the insurance companies do not cover the costs even when the patient has to be admitted for mental illness. Thus, the family has to bear the cost of consultation and treatment, which might go on for long or even for lifetime in case of mental illness. VIMHANS also collaborates with several other nonprofit organizations for providing a free consultation. The major sources of earning are income from consultations, from rents received from outsourced departments and from collaborative agreements with other organizations.

Place

For a health-care facility, accessibility is one of the most important attributes and VIMHANS has the benefit in this respect. It is located in one of the prime locations of Delhi. For the purpose of spreading awareness and reaching out to people, the hospital organizes several workshops and training programs. Many such outreach activities are held within the hospital premises itself, while several such programs are also organized in schools, colleges, refugee settlements, other NGOs, and other organizations. For example, owing to increased cases of depression and anxiety among schoolchildren, the hospital has entered into collaborative agreements with several schools in Delhi wherein counselors from the hospital visit the school and counsel the students and parents about such issues. In addition, schools are encouraged to send their students to the hospital wherein they are engaged in activities like art therapy sessions and movie sessions and get chance to interact with mentally challenged individuals for increasing awareness and sensitivity toward mental health issues. Also, its outreach activities are carried out at different locations within the city and nearby areas, and it is also helping in carrying out operations in several satellite centers in North India by providing with guidance and necessary support and expertise. But, the hospital lags behind in online presence. It is not active on different social media platforms and lacks active communication with target segments outside the concrete walls. Increased awareness often leads to increased curiosity, and in today's digital era, people often tend to turn toward online portals in search for answers. The absence from social media and other online platform often results in a communication gap.

Promotion

The focus point of all these social marketing activities is to spread awareness about mental health and work on reducing the stigma associated with it as all these activities are undertaken without charging anything from the beneficiaries in most of the cases.

A. *For Children*

To spread awareness about mental health in children, the hospital has collaborated with several schools in Delhi NCR, and they often organize hospital visits for students and an interactive session with parents. These activities have opened a new spectrum of pursuing the world of mental health for these young minds as career options and helped the kids and their families in grasping the fact that mental health and well-being are as important as physical health and there is no shame in visiting a mental health-care facility. The hospital is also providing counseling services and life skill enhancement program for school children for early detection of academic and behavioral issues.

B. *For Teenagers and Adults*

The hospital is providing guidance and counseling to youths struggling with substance abuse, psychosis, and mood disorders through self-help groups and family groups. A structured outreach program is also being implemented in collaboration with another nonprofit Don Bosco since 2006, for international refugees. Most importantly, the hospital has been organizing awareness programs for young adults and their family members at India Habitat Centre. Also, the mental health department of the hospital has started a unique initiative of interacting with family physicians through continuing medical education programs, where mental health issues are discussed with physicians as they are the first point of interaction for most of the patients and are in regular touch with them. So, if they are well-informed, they may detect issues at an early stage and can also convince the patient and/or his/her family to visit a mental health-care facility.

C. *For Elderlies*

The hospital has been organizing awareness lecture series for "Issues concerning the Elderly." The outreach program is a comprehensive program that goes beyond mental health-care concerns and also includes social and financial assistance, legal advice, assisted living, and many more. VIMHANS is also collaborating with Ashiana Group which provides residential facilities for elderlies for a better quality of life experience. The hospital provides preventive medical screening, rehabilitation support, training and placement support for caregivers, specialty medical camps and consultation, etc.

VIMHANS also organizes several paid workshops for awareness and therapy round the year for interested individuals.

In Pursuance of the Goal

All social marketing initiatives are undertaken with the goal to create impact in the society by bringing together stakeholders for the cause they intend to pursue. Impact, in this case, can be defined as "the net effect of an activity on a community and the well-being of individuals and families. It is outcome-led adaptive thinking and action taken by businesses, government, social purpose organizations and knowledge creators that contribute in creating a positive, meaningful and sustainable change for the benefit of society and particularly those at disadvantage as a result of systemic, long-term problems" (Home | CSI 2016).

Social marketing initiatives can go a long way as an instrument of community awareness, engagement, intervention, and empowerment. VIMHANS intends to act as a carrier for creating impact by acting as a catalyst for bringing change and thus helping the community in combating the menace of mental health issues. The various steps in impact creation are summarized in Fig. 1.

Hence while taking several initiatives, VIMHANS spreads awareness by organizing workshops and outreach activities with youths, elderlies, and students

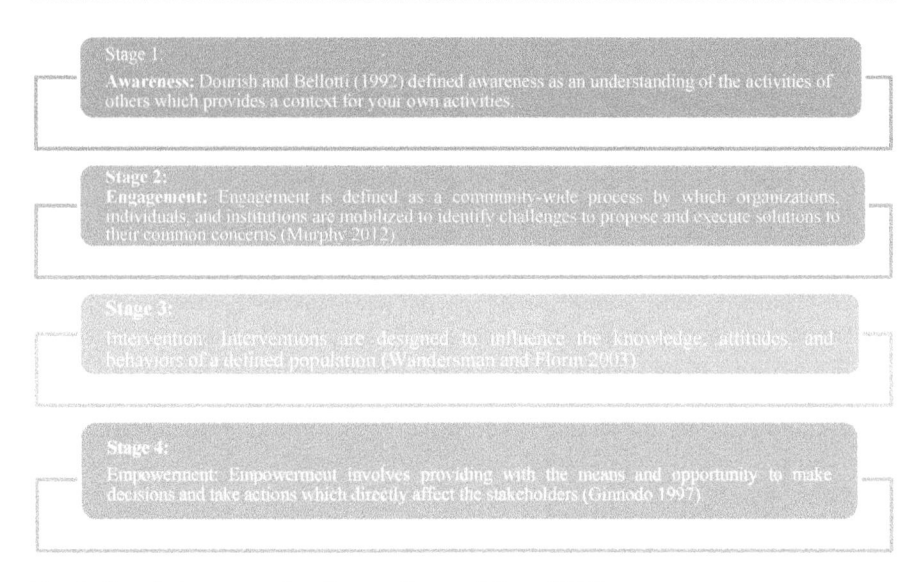

Stage 1:
Awareness: Dourish and Bellotti (1992) defined awareness as an understanding of the activities of others which provides a context for your own activities.

Stage 2:
Engagement: Engagement is defined as a community-wide process by which organizations, individuals, and institutions are mobilized to identify challenges to propose and execute solutions to their common concerns (Murphy 2012).

Stage 3:
Intervention: Interventions are designed to influence the knowledge, attitudes, and behaviors of a defined population (Wandersman and Florin 2003).

Stage 4:
Empowerment: Empowerment involves providing with the means and opportunity to make decisions and take actions which directly affect the stakeholders (Ginnodo 1997).

Fig. 1 Steps in impact creation. Source: Shree and Sagar (2016)

in schools and colleges and also with the general public. The next phase of response involves active engagement of different stakeholders including local community for carrying out initiatives, while recognizing the need to address the challenges faced by the cause, it also demands interventions from the organization at different levels. The last phase involves empowering the community so that they are able to carry forward the cause on their own. Several of the patients, who received treatment from VIMHANS, have started centers for treatment of mental health issues in different parts of the country under the guidance received from the hospital.

Awareness of the cause is the only effective way in which one can bring about mass participation. Hence, any social initiative is successful only when the general public has some awareness about the cause. Capacity building, preparedness, and awareness campaigns are key components of a proactive approach. Immediate family is often the first responder and also the primary caregiver in case of mental health. If they are properly sensitized about the precautions and preventive actions to be taken, the damages can be drastically reduced.

Conclusion

Mental health-care institutions suffer from a distinct set of issues in comparison to health-care institutions engaged in treating patients with physical disorders or problems. The first and foremost is the stigma attached to mental illness which has resulted in an extremely low number of patient turnouts even in case of developed nations with more awareness and better resources at their disposal. Also, owing to the unique issues faced by them in developing country like India marred with issues like malnutrition, high infant, and maternal mortality and other such health issues affecting its teeming millions, government is siphoning most of its fund toward physical health, thus pushing mental health further down the priority list. One of the most fundamental premises of not-for-profit marketing entails marketing the cause the organization supports rather than just marketing the organization. Even not-for-profit organizations need revenue for sustenance, and once people are aware of the cause, they start looking up to the organization for interventions and solutions. The case of VIMHANS strives to find a solution to such organizations struggling for funds in developing economies.

Awareness generated from the use of social marketing tools can be very effective in not only improving the revenue generated which is required for the sustenance of the hospital, but it also significantly affects community's attitude toward mental health-related issues. With rising awareness, it can be expected that early recognition and access to treatment will follow, as will the adoption of preventive measures. It can also be expected that with enlarging awareness in a democratic society, advocacy, leveraging of political will, funding, and cross-synergies shall follow. The case of VIMHANS suggests some interesting methods for spreading awareness among masses, and these methods have so far helped the hospital in not only increasing awareness about the cause, i.e., mental health and well-being, but also about the hospital and its service offerings. It further reiterates that social marketing initiatives are quintessential for plugging the gaping hole in the mental health-care system.

Discussion Questions

1. Critically analyze the decision of VIMHANS to target all the segments instead of focusing on one particular segment.
2. Is the strategy of the creation of awareness first and caring for sustenance next an appropriate one? Why/Why not?
3. What steps should be taken by VIMHANS to improve its social marketing activities?
4. What changes should be brought in the marketing mix, to make the cause more appealing to youths?

References

Andreasen, A. R. (2004). A social marketing approach to changing mental health practices directed at youth and adolescents. *Health Marketing Quarterly, 21*(4), 51–75.

Dourish, P., & Bellotti, V. (1992, December). Awareness and coordination in shared workspaces. In *Proceedings of the 1992 ACM conference on computer-supported cooperative work* (pp. 107–114). Toronto: ACM.

Ginnodo, B. (Ed.). (1997). *The power of empowerment: What the experts say and 16 actionable case studies*. Arlington Heights, IL: Pride.

Home | CSI. (2016). Retrieved from https://www.csi.edu.au/

Kotler, P., & Roberto, E. L. (1989). *Social marketing. Strategies for changing public behavior.* New York: Free Press.

Murphy, F. (Ed.). (2012). *Community engagement, organization, and development for public health practice.* New York: Springer.

Pinfold, V. (2003). *How can we make mental health education work? Example of successful local mental health awareness programme challenging stigma and discrimination.* London: Rethink Publications.

Prince, M., Patel, V., Saxena, S., Maj, M., Maselko, J., Phillips, M. R., et al. (2007). No health without mental health. *The Lancet, 370*(9590), 859–877.

Saraceno, B., van Ommeren, M., Batniji, R., Cohen, A., Gureje, O., Mahoney, J., et al. (2007). Barriers to improvement of mental health services in low-income and middle-income countries. *The Lancet, 370*(9593), 1164–1174.

Shree, D., & Sagar, M. (2016). *Using awareness, engagement and intervention for community empowerment for creating a public sector brand: A case study of NDRF.* [online] thecasecentre. org. Accessed August 31, 2018, from https://www.thecasecentre.org/educators/products/view?id=138811

Wandersman, A., & Florin, P. (2003). Community interventions and effective prevention. *American Psychologist, 58*(6–7), 441.

WHO. (2011). *Mental health in India.* Retrieved from http://www.searo.who.int/india/topics/mental_health/about_mentalhealth/en/

How to Encourage the Consumption of Tap Water: A Case Study on Águas do Porto

Ana J. Almeida, Ana P. Ribeiro, Rute D. Martins, Marisa R. Ferreira, and João F. Proença

Abstract This study aims to describe and analyze the social marketing campaign undertaken by the Portuguese public company AdP—Águas do Porto, E.M.—since March 2015. This campaign focuses on the incentive of promoting new habits of drinking water consumption and has been a pioneer in the water distribution sector, establishing a trend followed by other public companies in the country.

The AdP case discusses the contribution of social marketing in the changing of rooted and generalized consumption habits, the benefits of consuming tap water instead of bottled water for the individual and the society, and the strategy of the campaign and its linkage to the global city brand "Porto Ponto."

A. J. Almeida · A. P. Ribeiro · R. D. Martins
Porto Business School, Porto, Portugal

M. R. Ferreira (✉)
School of Management and Technology, CIICESI, Porto Polytechnic Institute, Porto, Portugal
e-mail: mferreira@estg.ipp.pt

J. F. Proença
Faculty of Economics, University of Porto, Porto, Portugal

ADVANCE/CSG, ISEG, University of Lisbon, Lisbon, Portugal
e-mail: jproenca@fep.up.pt

© Springer Nature Switzerland AG 2019
M. M. Galan-Ladero, H. M. Alves (eds.), *Case Studies on Social Marketing*, Management for Professionals, https://doi.org/10.1007/978-3-030-04843-3_11

> **Learning Objectives**
> - To discuss social marketing: concept, stages, consequences
> - To verify the real benefits of tap water consumption
> - To look behind scenes of the desired behavioral change
> - To explain the symbiotic relationship between two brands: Porto and Águas do Porto

Introduction

AdP—Águas do Porto—is a Portuguese public company founded in October 2006 that was established to replace the Municipal Water and Sanitation Services of the Porto City Council. Nowadays, AdP focuses mainly on the treatment and supply of high-quality water to the Porto community and is one of the biggest water suppliers in the country, having more than 153,821 customers, which is the equivalent of 370,000 inhabitants (Águas do Porto 2016). Please note that the urban area of Porto has a population of less than two million people and the city itself around 240,000 people.

In the last 20 years, there has been a significant improvement in the water quality distributed to Portuguese citizens and its distribution process—more people have access to excellent tap water, which places Portugal at the same level as the most developed countries in the world (Pordata 2016).

AdP, conscious of, on one hand, the need to rethink their medium-/long-term strategy and, on the other hand, the inseparability between the organization, the society, and the environment, introduced in 2014 a new strategy with a redefined mission, vision, and values. Despite having always contributed to Porto and its community's growth, this new strategy focuses on sustainability and social responsibility, with the clear intention of contributing to the global creation of economic and social value.

As a commodity company, AdP's new strategy and marketing plan are innovative. The ultimate goal is to transform water, seen as a utility or a commodity, into a brand. In order to do this, AdP has undertaken a social marketing campaign named "Beba Água do Porto. É boa todos os dias!" (In English: Drink Porto's Water. It's good every day!) that intends to encourage the consumption of tap water through behavioral change (Lowe et al. 2015). AdP has reinforced and proved the safety conditions of tap water consumption to the Portuguese that still prefer to consume bottled water (and this is a growing consumption). Água do Porto is water of excellent quality and very healthy since it is balanced in terms of minerals and diversified, eco-friendly, and available anytime or anywhere in the Porto area (Lowe et al. 2015). As such, there are only benefits in consuming it: benefits for the individual, for the society, and for the environment.

Social Marketing

Social marketing can be considered as (Kotler and Lee 2004) "the use of marketing techniques and principles to influence a specific public that voluntary accepts, rejects, modifies or abandons behavior for the benefit of individuals, groups or society as a whole." Choosing the right goal for a social marketing campaign is a critical point, since there is a wide range of possible objectives. We may be trying to change people's perspectives, values, actions, or behaviors. Also, when we are planning a social marketing campaign, it is important to follow many of the same steps used for traditional products and services (Kotler and Keller 2012). According to the same authors, the essential steps are:

1. Where are we?
   – Define the program focus.
   – Identify the campaign purpose.
   – Conduct a SWOT analysis.
   – Review past and similar efforts.
2. Where do we want to go?
   – Select target audiences.
   – Set objectives and goals.
   – Analyze target audiences and competition.
3. How will we get there?
   – Product: design the market offering.
   – Price: manage costs of behavior change.
   – Distribution: make the product available.
   – Communication: create messages and choose media.
4. How will we stay on course?
   – Develop a plan for evaluation and monitoring.
   – Establish budgets and find funding sources.
   – Complete an implementation plan.

The Real Benefits of Tap Water Consumption

Access to drinkable water is a fundamental human right, which is at the heart of a crisis of scarcity of resources that affects millions of people around the world. Water is a necessity of life. In this world there are still too many people having to trek miles every day to fetch their water from the nearest stream, but that is not the case for European countries such as Portugal, for example. Portuguese are very lucky to live in a country where clean, safe water is available at the turn of a tap.

So why are Portuguese consuming more and more bottled water if the tap water is more than safe? Portuguese consumers are becoming increasingly conscious of health and well-being issues (which is positive), but it means that they consider bottled water the most natural soft drink and the ideal way to rehydrate as part of a healthy and balanced nutrition. This trend together with signs of economic recovery has encouraged Portuguese consumers to buy bottled water instead of drinking tap water. In Porto Council, this national trend is replicated: merely 37.6% of Porto's population consumes only tap water (Universidade Católica do Porto 2015), with a low consumption of tap water opposed to a generalized increase in the consumption of bottled water. In fact, in Portugal bottled water consumption increased by 6% in off-trade volume and 4% in off-trade value to stand at sales of 898 million liters and 226 million euros in 2016 and looks set to continue to see an interesting performance over the 2016–2021 forecast period (Euromonitor International 2017).

The domestic consumption of bottled water leads us to one of the great mysteries of capitalism: the packaging and sale or purchase of products for which we already have free access—"manufactured demand" (Queiroz et al. 2012). The consumerism generalization and advertising are pointed out as the reason for the purchase, sometimes at high prices, of branded water, although this is not always synonymous with superior quality (Queiroz et al. 2012). Capitalism, marketing, fashion, and the cultural, economic, and political trends greatly encourage the consumption of bottled water (Royte 2011). Bottled water has become a status symbol, which communicates a lifestyle and conveys feelings of belonging to a real or desired group (Queiroz et al. 2012). A Portuguese family of four, for example, who consumes tap water daily, spends around 2.50 € a year, while if it consumes bottled water will spend around 590.00 € a year. Tap water is 450 times cheaper than bottled water (Queiroz et al. 2012).

However, we are not suggesting that drinking bottled water is always a bad idea. For instance, when a flood or a broken pipe interrupts the local water supply, bottled water can be a literal lifesaver. Similarly, if you are out at a concert or a ball game and you need to buy a drink, choosing a bottle of water instead of a bottle of soda is definitely the right choice for your health. However, when you have a choice between bottled water and tap water, either filtered or unfiltered, drinking from the tap is a better choice for your wallet and for the planet since there is no evidence bottled water is better for us, and it actually might be less safe than tap water. There are a lot of myths related to tap water and bottled water. Here are the top three debunked myths (Torres 2018):

1. Is bottled water better than tap water?

    Thanks to decades of myth-building, the common belief is that bottled water is better than tap water. This is not true. In Western Europe about 99% of public tap water is potable (drinkable according to EU and WHO guidelines). The only drawback in some places is poor taste and smell, mainly due to hardness, minerals, and higher concentration of chlorine (used for disinfection purposes). There is no scientific proof that bottled water is healthier than tap water.
2. Is bottled water safer than tap water?

    Tap water is strictly regulated. AdP, for example, is very strict regarding their tap water quality with more than 47,000 tests done every year. Porto tap water is analyzed daily in physicochemical and bacteriological terms, with results above 99.9% in compliance with the criteria. There is once again no scientific evidence

that bottled water is safer. Actually, studies show that, in 100 different brands of bottled water, 30% will have some type of problem or anomaly, just as tap water does (Queiroz et al. 2012).
3. Is it fine to drink bottled water as long as the bottles are recycled?
The issue is not just the plastic waste but the entire value chain of water bottles. From production to distribution, the process of generating bottled water in plastic is unsustainable: 3 L of water is needed on average to produce 1 L of bottled water when including production of plastic, transportation, filtering, and filling up the bottles; the plastic used in the water bottles is made of oil and natural gas, both nonrenewable resources; and the distribution of bottled water contributes to global warming, since land transport, for example, is very polluting. This situation is exacerbated when 25% of all bottled water is marketed and consumed outside the country of production (Queiroz et al. 2012).

Behind the Scenes of the Desired Behavioral Change

The main reason for this generalized consumption behavior has not yet been identified, but studies and research point to the gap between the perceived quality and the real quality of tap water. AdP, being aware of the quality and excellence of their tap water, decided to investigate further and launched a campaign on World Water Day 2015, to change this perception and induce the desired behavior—that is, increase the consumption of tap water. By conducting a SWOT analysis, AdP realized the following (Table 1):

Clearly, there are more strengths and opportunities than weaknesses and threats, and AdP was willing to work hard on the weaknesses and overcome the threats (Almeida et al. 2016). AdP designed a social marketing campaign to inform, educate, and induce the public to stimulate the wanted behavioral change, a change wanted not only by AdP but by the city of Porto and society in general (Almeida et al. 2016). AdP wanted first to inform the public that Porto Council tap water was safe to consume, the quality was very high, and it was trustworthy; second, to raise

Table 1 SWOT analysis

Strengths	*Opportunities*
– Quality	– Financial and economic context
– Convenience	– Increasing concern with health and sustainability
– Health benefits	– Environmental awareness
– Economic benefits	– Media
Weaknesses	*Threats*
– Wrong perception of tap water quality	– Strong presence and competition of bottled water brands
– Taste and smell	– Status
– Lack of status from consuming it	– The increasing mobility of people
– Lack of portability	– Media

Source: Dias (2015)

public awareness in order to generate a behavior change; and finally, increase tap water consumption. Challenging negative stereotypes is essential to improving the perception of reliability and credibility (Means et al. 2002).

One of the priority targets of the campaign has been the X and Y generation, the trendsetters. This target has a recognized social, economic, and cultural role in society and has generalized access to information. Their power of choice, allied to the search, creation, and dissemination of content, elevated them to the status of one of the most influential groups when we refer to consumption trends (Figueiredo 2012).

However, the other groups that are a part of Porto's population could not be forgotten, since they are the followers. They follow the trendsetters; they follow the media. Studies reveal that, for the most part, the perception of consumers can be positively influenced by communication campaigns and that the absence of information considerably impairs their perception. Thus, communication campaigns that respond directly to the expectations of consumers in relation to water have had very positive effects on the value understood by the public and consequently on the consumption of tap water (Means et al. 2002). Just like the trendsetters, the followers highly defend the environment as a way to protect not only their quality of life but of future generations as well. For the priority target, AdP developed activities that focused on tap water quality, sustainability, convenience, and finally the very cheap price.

As secondary targets, AdP singled out students, from the first grade to university. Children, as consumers, have the power to influence their parents' decisions on what to buy (Figueiredo 2012). Young people who have been born and raised during the last two decades are a constituent part of a generation that is not deceived easily and is eagerly searching for more authenticity and seriousness (van Hooowijk 2009). HORECA channel (hotels, restaurant, and café), public institutions, private companies, AdP and Porto Council's internal public, and tourists were also aimed at as secondary targets.

For the secondary targets, AdP developed activities that focused on the environment, the feelings of belonging, the sustainability, the price, the promotion of Porto City brand, and the social responsibility.

AdP included health professionals as their targets because they actually have a say regarding consumer health habits. There was a great effort from AdP on disseminating this social marketing campaign, being that their approach strategy divided into three categories: the portability, the price, and the accessibility:

- As mentioned before, one of the downsides of consuming tap water instead of bottled water is the lack of portability. So AdP designed bottles for anyone to be able to drink from and carry their "Água do Porto" anywhere. For the HORECA channel, glass bottles were designed, and for the general public, aluminum ones were designed.
- The price, the very cheap price.
- And what if you are walking in a park on a sunny day and you need water? AdP will create access points for tap water, throughout the city, making it available

outside the home. Public water fountains placed in strategic places such as parks, gyms, council schools, universities, underground and train stations, etc.

The Symbiotic Relationship Between "Porto Ponto" and Águas do Porto

With this social marketing strategy, AdP wanted to build the brand Águas do Porto. This new brand should convey an attitude, and should appeal to the consumer's emotional side, so that it brings to the consumer feelings of belonging, emotional benefits, and status. It is not by chance that the statement "Beba Água do Porto. É boa todos os dias!" (In English: Drink Porto's Water. It's good every day!) was developed based on a popular expression, closely linked to the way of being shared by Porto people.

As a social marketing campaign, it is undeniable that there has been a strong informative component throughout the whole campaign, but the emotional tone is what has prevailed at all times, especially during the activities undertaken. Both merchandising (T-shirts, bottles, mugs) and offline mix (outdoors, mupis, radio, press, etc.) with Porto's popular sayings, such as "É da Bica, por isso é que o Porto ganha ao Benfica" (in English: It is tap water, that is why Porto wins over Benfica); slogans that demonstrate feelings of belonging, like "Sou 70% Água do Porto" (in English: I am 70% of water from Porto); and stickers called "The manifesto for Águas do Porto." We can see some of these examples in Fig. 1, e.g., one of the sayings mentioned "É da torneira, amiga do ambiente e da carteira" (in English: it is tap water, environmentally and wallet friendly).

Another distinctive factor is the timing and social context of this whole campaign. Porto has been known by its port wine for centuries; however, more recently, it has also been recognized by its city brand. "Porto Ponto" came to life after the realization of the need to represent Porto as a global city. The success of "Porto Ponto" is indisputable, incomparable, and unforgettable (Aires 2017).

AdP, aware of the strength, popularity, and reputation that Porto enjoys as a city and a brand (winner of the Best European Destination Award in 2012, 2014, and 2017), replicates this vitality and quality in their campaign, incorporating the values underlying the "Porto Ponto" brand, trying to create a coherent brand, perceived as

Fig. 1 Examples of merchandising and offline mix. Source: authors

reliable, trendy, and cool, in order to facilitate and promote the desired behavioral change—that is, increase tap water consumption.

Thus, conditions are created for a symbiotic relationship in which both parties benefit—AdP and Porto City. The entire campaign has involved many sectors and especially the participation of all the partners and public of Porto. The goal has been to engage them in different ways, inviting them to be the brand ambassadors and information vehicles themselves, ultimately promoting the image that Porto wants to convey. The involvement between citizens and public companies (developing a relationship and creating familiarity with their roles) has been important for building trust (Means et al. 2002). Therefore, in return, AdP gets to be represented in Porto public entities, social, and tourist structures, thus providing a clear leverage to disseminate their message of acceptance and behavioral change.

Conclusion

This AdP campaign has revealed an innovative and creative spirit in adding value to a product that had only been seen as a commodity for decades. Now consumers of "Água do Porto" have a chance to better understand the benefit that comes with the consumption of tap water not only for themselves but for the environment and for the world. This is in addition to perceiving it as a distinctive product of excellent quality that can compete with bottled water brands.

As a social marketing campaign, it has applied concepts and marketing strategies in order to change people's behavior that would ultimately result in benefits not only for the individuals but the whole community, thus conducing to a generalized social well-being. Since the whole plan has followed the steps that have been proved effective and efficient in past social marketing programs, it is expected that the desired results will be achieved.

Discussion Questions

Considering the specific characteristics inherent to this case, it seems adequate and suitable for a deeper and detailed discussion about social marketing, namely, some essential concepts associated with social marketing such as campaign purpose or marketing mix. The case also allows us to discuss and present how a social marketing plan can be formulated.

1. What are the main impacts/consequences of this campaign?

    There are still no results to assess the real impact of this social marketing campaign, which has turned out to be for us the main point of discussion. According to AdP, there is an inquiry planned for the campaign follow-up, but the current absence of monitoring and control has prevented any comparison with the figures presented by Universidade Católica do Porto in March 2015 before the start of the program. In this diagnosis, 73% of the respondents already recognized

the high quality of tap water, 37.6% affirmed to always drink tap water at home, while 12.1% affirmed to never drink it. In the same study, 70% of the 1853 respondents referred that they would drink or drink more tap water, if they had the assurance from the supplier that the excellent quality was guaranteed. As to the preferred water to drink, 33% affirmed that they preferred tap water, 30% preferred bottled water, and 36% showed indifference when choosing a type of water to drink. Also, 64% of the respondents argued that they would start consuming more tap water to protect the environment.
2. Are the results of the campaign in line with the planned strategy?

The new evaluation is planned to be done with a similar inquiry, with identical questions, in order to be able to compare results. Looking at the strategy of the marketing campaign, it would be expectable that the spread of the information and the efforts done to create awareness about the quality of tap water would lead to an increased percentage of people that recognize the excellent quality of the product and consequently would choose to consume it. As the figures show, the target audience is already aware of Água do Porto's quality of excellence, but does this awareness necessarily mean that the desired behavior change will occur? Were the promotional efforts adequate to achieve the established goals?

In our point of view, statistically speaking, the inquired sample used in the study of 2015 is not a representative of a community of more than 300,000 people. How can AdP, a local public company, even backed up by the well-known Porto City brand, induce and change a behavior that is spread all over the country and generalized in Europe and most of the developed countries? Will any social marketing campaign be powerful enough to beat bottled water marketing campaigns?

Acknowledgments João F. Proença gratefully acknowledges financial support from FCT-Fundação para a Ciencia e Tecnologia (Portugal), national funding through research grant UID/SOC/04521/2013.

References

Águas do Porto. (2016). *Relatório e Contas 2016*. Porto. Retrieved from http://www.aguasdoporto. pt/assets/misc/PDF'S/RelatórioeContas/RC2016_ROC.pdf
Aires, E. (2017). *Porto. Manual de Identidade Visual*. Porto. Retrieved from http://www.cm-porto. pt/assets/misc/documentos/Logos/01_Manual_14_digital_2017.pdf
Almeida, A., Ribeiro, A. P., Pereira, L., Martins, R., Ferreira, M. R., & Proença, J. F. (2016). Novos Hábitos de Consumo: Um estudo de caso sobre a Águas do Porto, E.M. In *VIII Congresso Internacional de Casos Docentes em Marketing Público e Não Lucrativo*. Porto.
Dias, A. S. M. (2015). *O simbólico como estratégia para a alteração comportamental: o caso Águas do Porto*. Braga: Universidade do Minho.
Euromonitor International. (2017). *Bottled water in Portugal – Country report*. Retrieved from http://www.euromonitor.com/bottled-water-in-portugal/report
Figueiredo, I. M. M. (2012). *Perceções e atitudes dos jovens sobre a água: Um contributo para planear a comunicação da empresa Águas do Noroeste*. Braga: Universidade do Minho.
Kotler, P., & Keller, K. L. (2012). *Marketing management* (14th ed.). London: Pearson Education.

Kotler, P., & Lee, N. (2004). *Corporate social responsibility: Doing the most good for your company and your cause*. Hoboken, NJ: Wiley.

Lowe, B., Lynch, D., & Lowe, J. (2015). Reducing household water consumption: A social marketing approach. *Journal of Marketing Management, 31*(3–4), 378–408. https://doi.org/10.1080/0267257X.2014.971044.

Means, E. G., Brueck, T., Dixon, L., Manning, A., Miles, J., & Patrick, R. (2002). Drinking water quality in the new millennium: The risk of underestimating public perception. *Journal of American Water Works Association, 94*(8), 28. pp. 30–32, 34.

PORDATA. (2016). Qualidade da água para consumo humano. Retrieved from https://www.pordata.pt/Municipios/Qualidade+da+água+para+consumo+humano-8

Queiroz, J. T. M., Rosenberg, M. W., Heller, L., Zhouri, A. L. M., & Silva, S. R. (2012). News about tap and bottled water: Can this influence people's choices? *Journal of Environmental Protection, 3*(4), 324–333. https://doi.org/10.4236/jep.2012.34041.

Royte, E. (2011). *Bottlemania – Big business, local springs, and the battle over America's drinking water* (1st ed.). New York: Bloomsbury.

Torres, P. (2018). Bottled water vs. tap water: Rethink what you drink. *Reader's Digest*. Retrieved from https://www.rd.com/health/diet-weight-loss/rethink-what-you-drink/

Universidade Católica do Porto. (2015). *Beba a Água do Porto - Estudo sobre o hábito de consumo de água da torneira da Estudo sobre o hábito de consumo de água da torneira da população da cidade do Porto*. Porto.

van Heeswijk, J. (2009). Young & sustainable – Young people, sustainable development and education. *Hiteq*. Retrieved from https://www.duurzaamdoor.nl/sites/default/files/hiteq_young_and_sustainable_tcm24-290908.pdf

Part III

Social Marketing Cases: Society, Culture and Education

The Role of Social Marketing in a Controversial Cause: The Eradication of Child Marriage

Francisco I. Vega-Gomez and M. Mercedes Galan-Ladero

Abstract This case focuses on the application of social marketing to a controversial cause: the eradication of child marriage, which is a common cultural practice in many countries.

Our aim is to study this problem from a social marketing perspective. Thus, we examine different projects carried out by different nonprofit organizations (NPOs) that deal with this issue, and we focus on a campaign: Thea's Blog, by Plan International.

We conclude that causes that foster child marriage are clearly identified: they have a sociocultural and economic nature. Thus, actions for the eradication of this phenomenon should be focused on these two areas: sociocultural (tradition, religion, and superstitions) and economic (poverty and inequality).

Campaigns such as Thea's Blog have helped to become aware of this problem in Western countries. Now, child marriage practice has a global dimension and there is a higher international pressure to eradicate it.

F. I. Vega-Gomez · M. M. Galan-Ladero (✉)
University of Extremadura, Badajoz, Spain
e-mail: fvegagomez@unex.es; mgalan@unex.es

Learning Objectives
We propose as main learning objectives to achieve the following ones:

- To know more about the practice of child marriage in the world and study the current situation, especially in underdeveloped and developing countries
- To analyze the causes and effects/consequences of child marriage
- To understand the link between child marriage and the lack of opportunities for women (higher female poverty and lower literacy rates)
- To discover the usefulness of social marketing as a tool for changing undesirable or inappropriate attitudes and behaviors, specifically in the case of child marriage
- To explore what NPOs are focused on fighting against child marriage and what social marketing campaigns have been developed (and are being developed currently)
- To foster critical thinking and stimulate discussion related child marriage and justify the need to eradicate it

Introduction

Child marriage can be defined as "the union of two people, at least one of them being under 18 years of age (usually, the woman), and in which there are social, economic, and family pressures for its execution" (Nour 2009).

This phenomenon, among others, has prevented the achievement of the millennium development goals (Table 1), which had been proposed by the United Nations to be achieved by 2015 (United Nations 2018).

Child marriage also involves the violation of international agreements and conventions, such as (Nour 2006, 2009; Gaffney-Rhys 2011; Nguyen and Wodon 2012):

Table 1 The eight millennium development goals

Goals	Content
1	Eradicate extreme poverty and hunger
2	Achieve universal primary education
3	Promote gender equality and empower women
4	Reduce child mortality
5	Improve maternal health
6	Combat HIV/AIDS, malaria, and other diseases
7	Ensure environmental sustainability
8	Global partnership for development

Source: United Nations (2018)

Table 2 Convention on Consent to Marriage, Minimum Age for Marriage, and Registration of Marriages

Article	Content
1	No marriage shall be legally entered into without the full and free consent of both parties
2	States shall take legislative action to specify a minimum age for marriage
3	All marriages shall be registered in an appropriate official register by the competent authority

Source: United Nations Human Rights. Office of the High Commissioner (2018)

Table 3 Convention on the Elimination of All Forms of Discrimination Against Women

Article 16
1. States parties shall take all appropriate measures to eliminate discrimination against women in all matters relating to marriage and family relations and shall ensure, on a basis of equality of men and women
2. The betrothal and the marriage of a child shall have no legal effect, and all necessary action, including legislation, shall be taken to specify a minimum age for marriage and to make the registration of marriages in an official registry compulsory

Source: United Nations (1979)

Table 4 Convention on the Rights of the Child (1989)

Art. 24.3
"... States Parties shall take all effective and appropriate measures with a view to abolishing traditional practices prejudicial to the health of children"

Source: United Nations (1989)

1. *Convention on Consent to Marriage, Minimum Age for Marriage, and Registration of Marriages* (1962): in particular, Articles 1, 2, and 3 (Table 2).
2. *The Convention on the Elimination of All Forms of Discrimination against Women (1979)*: specifically, Article 16 (Table 3).
3. *Convention on the Rights of the Child (1989)*, promoted by the United Nations: Although it does not explicitly refer to child marriage, it does propose to abolish traditional practices that are harmful to the children's health in Article 24.3 (Table 4).
4. *International Conference on Population and Development (1994)*: It refers to child marriage in some chapters (Table 5).
5. *Universal Declaration of Human Rights (1948)*: It also referred to marriage in Article 16 (Table 6).

Many of these forced child marriages specially affect girls (Gangoli et al. 2009), since they get married to older men. The gender ratio is clearly negative, so there is an important discrimination according to sex. This ratio is, for example, 72:1 in Mali (i.e., for every man under 18 years of age who gets married in the country, 72 girls do

Table 5 Some chapters related to child marriage—International Conference on Population and Development (1994)

* Chapter 2
Principle 9: "... Marriage must be entered into with the free consent of the intending spouses, and husband and wife should be equal partners"
* Chapter 4
4.21 Governments should strictly enforce laws to ensure that marriage is entered into only with the free and full consent of the intending spouses
In addition, governments should strictly enforce laws concerning the minimum legal age of consent and the minimum age at marriage and should raise the minimum age at marriage where necessary. Governments and nongovernmental organizations should generate social support for the enforcement of laws on the minimum legal age at marriage, in particular by providing educational and employment opportunities
* Chapter 5
5.5 ... Measures should be adopted and enforced to eliminate child marriages...
* Chapter 6
6.7. (c) To encourage children, adolescents, and youth, particularly young women, to continue their education in order to equip them for a better life, to increase their human potential, to help prevent early marriages and high-risk childbearing, and to reduce associated mortality and morbidity
6.11 Countries should create a socioeconomic environment conducive to the elimination of all child marriages and other unions as a matter of urgency and should discourage early marriage...
* Chapter 7
7.41 Overall for young women, early marriage and early motherhood can severely curtail educational and employment opportunities and are likely to have a long-term, adverse impact on their and their children's quality of life

Fuente: United Nations Population Information Network (1994)

Table 6 Universal Declaration of Human Rights

Article 16 of the Universal Declaration of Human Rights states that
(1) Men and women of full age, without any limitation due to race, nationality or religion, have the right to marry and to fund a family. They are entitled to equal rights as to marriage, during marriage, and at its dissolution
(2) Marriage shall be entered into only with the free and full consent of the intending spouses

Source: United Nations (1948)

it) or Kenya, with a ratio of 21:1, compared with the 8:1 of the USA. This means that girls are two to eight times more likely to get HIV/AIDS (Nour 2006).

According to UNICEF (2017), around 25,000 girls are forced to get married every day, most of them in Africa and Asia, although this practice also exists in other areas. Thus, between 2010 and 2016, 82.3% of Bangladeshi marriages were celebrated with girls under the age of 18: 77.9% in Niger, 71.8% in Chad, or 69.4% in Guinea (Fig. 1); in countries such as Nepal, 7% of girls got married before their tenth birthday.

In 2017, the countries with highest ratios in child marriage were Niger (76%); Chad and the Central African Republic (68%); Bangladesh (59%); Guinea, Burkina

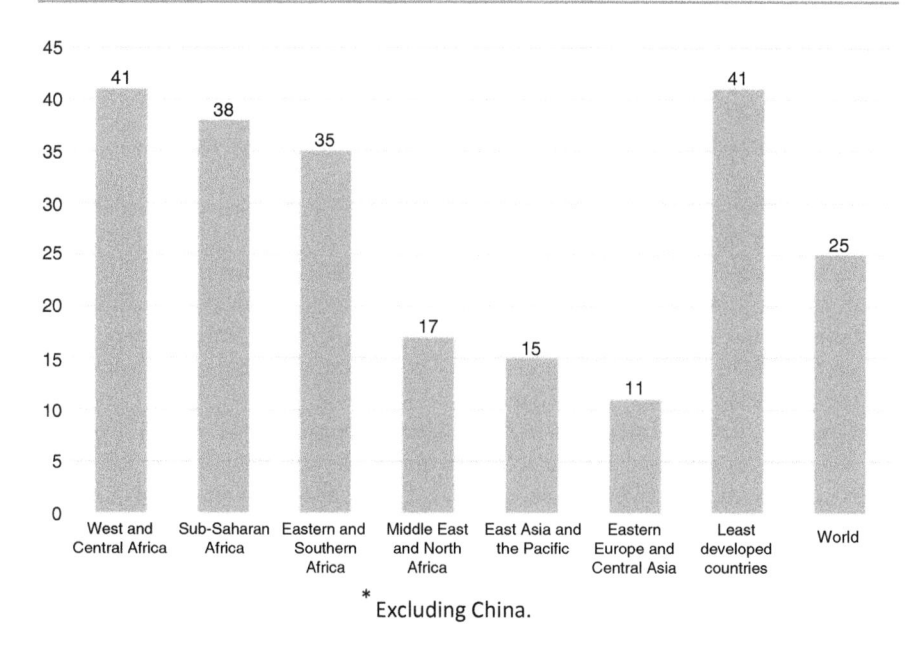

Fig. 1 Percentage of child marriages over the total by region (excluding China) (2010–2016). Source: own elaboration, according to UNICEF (2017)

Faso, Mali, and South Sudan (52%); Mozambique (48%); and India (47%)—Efevbera et al. (2018) and Raj et al. (2018).

Some news had special coverage in the international media. For example:

- About Rawan, an 8-year-old Yemeni girl who got married to a 40-year-old man died on the wedding night. It caused a deep international commotion. Although news about her death was denied later by Yemeni authorities (but it was confirmed by local sources and human rights activists) (El Pais 2013), strong international pressure continued. The result was a law proposal to establish the legal age of marriage in 16 years in Yemen. However, it was finally rejected because it was considered anti-Islamic.
- About the historical decision of the Supreme Court of India, it dictated that "sex with a minor in marriage is a violation," in 2017. However, this decision may have a reduced impact in practice because, although it is illegal since 2006, child marriage is deeply rooted in India (El Pais 2017).

Currently, child marriage is a real problem that usually arises from underdevelopment, poverty, and poor educational training (Murphy-Graham and Leal 2014), as well as wars.[1] Many parents give their daughters in marriage for socioeconomic

---

[1] Save the Children has documented an increase in child marriage for Syrian refugee girls in Jordan (Garcia 2014).

conveniences (e.g., family agreements, search for a better social position, etc.) and to save their lives, thus protecting them from sexual violence (Chowdhury 2004; Kyari and Ayodele 2014).

Child marriage has important consequences and effects, such as:

- The abandonment of education: the married girl is forced to leave school and take care of her husband and children.
- Health problems: pregnancies at very young ages (Raj and Boehmer 2013; Handa et al. 2015) increase the probability of dying (during pregnancy or childbirth), both for the mother and the baby, and also suffering infections, septicemia, postpartum hemorrhages, eclampsia, HIV contagion, and other sexually transmitted diseases, as well as uterus cancer.
- Gender violence (Kidman 2016): the husband considers the girl as a product which he has paid for and must submit to him. If she does not allow him and/or he is not pleased, she can be beaten, mistreated and raped, and even killed due to her adult husband's brutality (Mikhail 2002; Raj et al. 2009; Hampton 2010; Kyari and Ayodele 2014; Kamal et al. 2015; Murphy-Graham and Leal 2014). She can also be murdered because of the so-called honor killing, which can be ordered by her own family if she abandons her husband or even refuses to get married to whom her family has chosen for her.

Several nonprofit organizations, NPOs, many of them with an international scope, have echoed this problem and are working in these countries. They develop projects focused on the attitude change toward this common and culturally accepted practice.

But also, recently, some of these NPOs have wanted to raise awareness about this situation in developed countries (e.g., European ones). Child marriage is exceptional in these countries, so it is an unknown topic for a large part of the population. That is why NPOs have been developing campaigns to raise awareness and sensitize citizens about this common practice in other countries, reporting effects and consequences of child marriage (Table 7). Thus, NPOs are getting donations and resources to finance and develop their programs in the affected countries.

Case Development: Thea's Blog

Thea's Blog was a campaign developed by the non-governmental organization (NGO) "Plan International" in Norway, in 2014 (Galan-Ladero and Vega-Gomez, 2015). Three steps were followed:

First Step: Creation of Thea's Blog—Dissemination Through the Internet and Social Networks

Thea, a 12-year-old girl, opened a blog on the Internet to tell the details of her upcoming wedding, which would take place on October 11, 2014. Her parents had just communicated to her, 1 month before the celebration. Her mother had decided who her future husband would be: Geir, a 37-year-old man.

Table 7 Some NPOs that work to eradicate child marriage

NPO	Campaigns
ACNUR	"Ayuda a evitar el matrimonio infantil entre niñas refugiadas" [*Help prevent child marriage among refugee girls*] (2018)—website, YouTube, and social media
Ayuda en Accion	"No quiero" [*I don't want*] (2017)—website "Stop child marriages. Give us books, not husbands" (2018)—website
Breakthrough India	"Elimination of early marriage" (2015)—website "Ending Early ("Child") Marriage: Gang of Stars (Taaron ki Toli)" (2018)—YouTube
CARE	"Vows of Poverty" (2018)—website
Egyptian Foundation for Advancement of the Childhood Condition	Child Marriage (2012 and 2014)—website
Forum for African Women Educationalists (FAWE)	"Stop Child Marriages" (2018)—website
Forward	"No girl should be a child bride" (2014)—website
Fundación Vicente Ferrer	Información sobre el matrimonio infantil [*Information about child marriage*] (2015)—website
Girls Not Brides	"Toward an end to child marriage" (2018)—website, mass media, social media, apps
Girls Up	"Ending Child Marriage" (2016)—website
Humanium	Child Marriage (2011)—website
International Center for Research on Women (ICRW)	Child Marriage (2018)—website
Misiones Salesianas	Matrimonio infantil [*Child marriage*] (2017)—website
ONU	Información sobre el matrimonio infantil [*Information about child marriage*] (2016)—website
Plan International	Thea's Blog (2014)—blog in the Internet and social media #Habla ahora o calla para siempre [*Speak now, or shut up forever*] (2017)—social media ¡Mueve un dedo contra el matrimonio infantil! [*Move a finger against child marriage*] (2018)—website and social media
Saarthi Trust	Child Marriage Annulment (2018)—website and social media
Save the Children	Información sobre el matrimonio infantil [*Information about child marriage*]—website and reports
Seyaj Childhood Protection	Child Marriage (2018)—website, YouTube, theatre play
The Coexist Initiative	"I am a girl child. Do not make me a child mother"—website
The Knowledge Hub on Child Marriage	Child Marriage (2018)—website and posters
United Nations Population Fund (UNFPA)	#DONT (2018)—in YouTube

(continued)

Table 7 (continued)

NPO	Campaigns
UNICEF	"A Storybook Wedding—Except For One Thing" (2016)—in YouTube and Social Media "La Peor Novela" [*The Worst Story*] (2017)—website "Poner fin al matrimonio infantil es posible" [*Ending child marriage is possible*] (2018)—website
World Vision	"Marriage Later/Studies First Programme" (2013)—website

Source: Own elaboration, from Olson (2013)

Thea told her life and her feelings in this blog. She detailed, step by step, the preparation of the event. The blog was written as a 12-year-old girl would really do it (with misspellings and syntax errors, emoticons, specific expressions, etc.). She included several photos of her and her wedding dresses, the wedding invitations, the lingerie for the honeymoon, the bridal cake, etc. Some of the most commented posts by the target audience are in Table 8.

This ad hoc blog was launched on the Internet, being accessible from anywhere (although it was written in Norwegian, so it was only readable by those who could understand this language). Despite the fact that no promotional campaign was carried out, it was promoted by the blog readers themselves, through their comments and sharing them on Facebook and Twitter.

The citizens became outraged, scandalized, or unbelievers, when they read on the blog what marriage was like from a girl's perspective, still in her childhood stage: her doubts and her fears, her confidence, her respect and blind obedience in her parents' decisions, etc.

This viral promotion achieved spectacular results (Plan International Norge 2018):

- In just a few hours, 78,000 comments were written on Twitter, tens of thousands of comments on Facebook, and hundreds of comments on the blog itself, which had more than 500,000 visits on its first day (Thea's wedding blog became Norway's most read blog during the course of the first day).
- Dozens of people called the police to report the case and stop the upcoming wedding. Groups were actually created on social networks asking that this wedding never took place. Some Norwegians even went to police stations and contacted social services (child welfare service) to take custody of their parents. Thousands of people also discussed the subject on social media.

Second Step: Dissemination in the Media

The media (national and foreign ones) echoed the enormous popularity that this initiative had and spread news and the results achieved.

Table 8 Some of the most commented posts by the target audience

Post	Content
Post 1	Thea introduces herself: how old she is, where she lives, the school she goes to, and who her parents are. She also comments on the news that she has just received: she is getting married next month
Post 2	Thea tells her feelings about the wedding, her confusion, and the results of her search on the Internet about what and how a wedding is
Post 3	Thea tests the wedding dress—four different models (*her mother did not let her choose the pink dress, because it was too childish*). She seemed more like a girl who was going to celebrate her first communion than a bride
Post 4	Thea writes about the wedding ring she would like to have and uploads several photos of her favorite ones (*but they will have to be adapted, because they are for adult women and none fits her small fine fingers*)
Post 5	The visit of her future husband was one of the most commented posts, especially when she discovers that he is a man much older than her (Gear was 37 years old, 25 years older than her)
Post 6	The problems begin: her mother forbids her to invite her friends and schoolmates to the wedding, even though she had already created his children's invitations for the event She is happy because she will not have to go to school anymore, but she is also sad because she has to be a woman and will not be able to see her friends again
Post 7	The honeymoon Her mother has chosen the honeymoon. Thea will go to Paris (she is very happy because Disneyland is there, and she loves it) Many readers got angry because Thea was not going to Paris as a child, but as a wife (there is a big difference between a honeymoon and an amusement park for children)
Post 8	The wedding cakes Thea chooses cakes with dolls, like wedding cake
Post 9	The wedding night It was the most controversial post. Thea expresses her doubts about sexuality and wonders if she should buy the lingerie that the models wear online (although she prefers her pajamas)
Post 10	This post is about her future. Thea wanted to be a veterinarian, but now, she cannot be because she must leave school. Her mother has told her that she will not have to work, because she will take care of her children and her home
Post 11	It refers to the music of the ceremony. Thea would like Marion Ravn to be at her wedding, because she is a friend of her future husband's friend, and she will attend

Source: Adapted from Thea's wedding blog (2014)

Third Step: Video on YouTube

The third way to distribute the campaign was through a video on YouTube, which showed each step followed to prepare Thea for the wedding (makeup, hairdressing, dress, etc.). The wedding was also simulated: Thea entered the church for the celebration of the event, accompanied by hundreds of people. The video ended with the scene in which Thea answered "no" to the priest's question, receiving a round of applause, and with a final warning about the thousands of girls forced to marry each year.

Results

According to Plan International Norge (2018), the main results were:

1. Thea's Blog was a revolution for the Norwegians, because of the topic, its repercussion in the media (it was featured 402 times in Norwegian media), and its consequences and also, for other Western countries, because the campaign received massive attention worldwide (thousands of international media covered the wedding).
2. The goal of this NGO was to increase awareness, knowledge, and engagement in the fight against child marriage. This goal was achieved successfully: campaign awareness among the Norwegian population reached 82%, and 9 out of 10 thought Norway should take an international lead in the fight against child marriage.
3. Through the campaign, Plan International offered Norwegian citizens:
    The opportunity to participate in social pressure to eradicate this brutal and anachronistic practice
    The opportunity to become a member, to collaborate with the NGO to carry out their programs against child marriage, and in favor of children's rights and the improvement of their lives
4. The campaign recruited thousands of new child sponsors for Plan International Norway (and in other countries). Many companies contacted with this NGO to collaborate in the fight against child marriage, and the Government of Norway took an international lead against child marriage.
5. Plan International Norway's campaign #stopthewedding reached people all over the world and received numerous awards. The blog was read by 2.5 million people, and the campaign generated 30 million views on Twitter, Instagram, and Facebook. Some world celebrities picked up and shared in social media, several hundred thousand people shared the campaign on their personal social media pages, and the wedding movie was seen by 4.4 million people on YouTube.

Conclusions

The causes that foster child marriage are clearly identified. They have a socioeconomic nature so that the spectrum of action for the eradication of this phenomenon should focus on these two specific aspects:

1. *Sociocultural Aspect (Tradition, Religion, and Superstitions)*
    Child marriages are derived from the tradition of some geographical areas in which these types of marriages are socially well-considered. Moreover, it is perceived negatively if it does not do so.
    In many communities, it is a great dishonor for families that girls become pregnant without being married. Through early marriage, it is believed that rapes will be prevented.

In other cases, getting married the daughters at an early age is incited by the religious leaders of some communities (it is believed that the family will receive blessings and will be enriched). In addition, they defend the idea that it is better women to get married when they are girls because they are more docile, more controllable, and more subject to their husbands.

In some areas of Africa, where men have high HIV ratio and polygamy exists, the idea that getting married a virgin girl cures AIDS has even spread. So many carriers of this disease pay high amounts to get married girls that will be also infected with the virus. Furthermore, some specific causes, such as wars, make child marriage to worsen and prevail. Thus, for example, there are an increasing number of child marriages in Syrian refugee camps in Jordan (Bartels et al. 2018).

2. *Economic Aspect*

The other cause of these marriages is economic. Many families marry off their daughters at a very early age to get rid of them, to avoid the costs of maintaining them, and to educate them (Efevbera et al. 2017), because they have a high number of children. These parents consider that, thanks to these arranged marriages, they will get their daughters to have a more comfortable life and, in addition, they obtain financial resources to alleviate their poverty.

Thus, a clear profile of the socioeconomic situation that fosters child marriage can be created (Kamal et al. 2015):

1. *Rural Scope*

    It is the area with the highest incidence (especially those places furthest away from the large urban centers).

2. *Low Educational Level*

    The lower the educational level is, the greater the probability of being married at a young age. And the fact of being married at an early age prevents, especially women, to continue their education.

3. *Religion*

    The religious aspect has been revealed as a determining condition. The majority of child marriages occur in Muslim communities.

4. *Poverty*

    The majority of married girls come from poor families. This leads to the chronification, inheritance, and feminization of poverty.

Child marriages can have serious consequences, especially for women, and place major obstacles to achieving gender equality. Campaigns such as Thea's Blog have helped to "discover" and become aware of this problem in Western countries, where it is not a usual practice and, therefore, was not paid attention to it. But currently, it has acquired a global dimension (despite being geographically located), and an increasing international pressure tries to eradicate this practice.

The success of the Thea's Blog campaign and the media impact obtained allowed the NGO "Plan International" to achieve two fundamental objectives:

1. To increase Norwegians' awareness about one of the most serious problems affecting children in less developed countries, such as forced child marriage
2. To obtain greater "brand" awareness as an organization that fights for the children's rights in the world, being named by thousands of people in their personal profiles of social networks, and by the media, obtaining an important free promotion, both in terms of temporary space and in terms of economic costs

Social marketing has become a key tool to raise awareness about this problem and change the attitudes and behaviors toward child marriage in those communities that still practice it.

Discussion Questions

1. Do you consider that child marriage is a located and exclusive problem of poor countries? How can it affect the world economy?
2. Do you consider that it is an ethical practice to marry off the daughters to assure them a maintenance and protection that, otherwise, the parents cannot offer them?
    Discuss these two specific cases: marriages of Syrian girls in refugee camps in Jordan and marriages of Rohingya girls in Bangladesh.
3. Do you consider that the tradition, culture, and/or religious practices that support child marriage should be respected in any case?
4. What can be done to avoid these practices of marriages between girls and older men, who they do not even choose?
5. What social marketing campaigns could be developed to eradicate child marriage? What approach could be better? What kind of strategy would you choose?
    What do you think would be more appropriate campaigns for developed countries and for the less developed ones?

References

Bartels, S. A., Michael, S., Roupetz, S., Garbern, S., Kilzar, L., Bergquist, H., & Bunting, A. (2018). Making sense of child, early and forced marriage among Syrian refugee girls: A mixed methods study in Lebanon. *BMJ Global Health, 3*(1), e000509.
Chowdhury, F. D. (2004). The socio-cultural context of child marriage in a Bangladeshi village. *International Journal of Social Welfare, 13*(3), 244–253.
Efevbera, Y., Bhabha, J., Farmer, P. E., & Fink, G. (2017). Girl child marriage as a risk factor for early childhood development and stunting. *Social Science & Medicine, 185*, 91–101.
Efevbera, Y., Bhabha, J., Farmer, P., & Fink, G. (2018). Child marriage and underweight in sub-Saharan Africa: A 35 country cross-national study. *Journal of Adolescent Health, 62*(2), S25–S26.
El Pais. (2013). Una niña yemení de 8 años muere en su noche de bodas por lesiones sexuales. *El País. Sociedad,* 9 de Septiembre.
El Pais. (2017). El Supremo de India dicta que el sexo con una menor en el matrimonio es violación. *El País. Internacional,* 11 de Octubre.

Gaffney-Rhys, R. (2011). International law as an instrument to combat child marriage. *The International Journal of Human Rights, 15*(3), 359–373.

Galan-Ladero, M. M., & Vega-Gomez, F. I. (2015). Marketing Social en Internet: Análisis de la Campaña 'El Blog de Thea'. *Revista de Casos de Marketing Público y No Lucrativo, 2*, 85–93.

Gangoli, G., McCarry, M., & Razak, A. (2009). Child marriage or forced marriage? South Asian communities in north east England. *Children & Society, 23*(6), 418–429.

Garcia, A. (2014, October 7). Matrimonio infantil, cómo apoyar para evitarlo. *Eroski Consumer.*

Hampton, T. (2010). Child marriage threatens girls' health. *JAMA, 304*(5), 509–510.

Handa, S., Peterman, A., Huang, C., Halpern, C., Pettifor, A., & Thirumurthy, H. (2015). Impact of the Kenya cash transfer for orphans and vulnerable children on early pregnancy and marriage of adolescent girls. *Social Science & Medicine, 141*, 36–45.

Kamal, S. M., Hassan, C. H., Alam, G. M., & Ying, Y. (2015). Child marriage in Bangladesh: Trends and determinants. *Journal of biosocial Science, 47*(1), 120–139.

Kidman, R. (2016). Child marriage and intimate partner violence: A comparative study of 34 countries. *International Journal of Epidemiology, 46*(2), 662–675.

Kyari, G. V., & Ayodele, J. (2014). The socio-economic effect of early marriage in North Western Nigeria. *Mediterranean Journal of Social Sciences, 5*(14), 582.

Mikhail, S. L. B. (2002). Child marriage and child prostitution: Two forms of sexual exploitation. *Gender & Development, 10*(1), 43–49.

Murphy-Graham, E., & Leal, G. (2014). Child marriage, agency, and schooling in rural Honduras. *Comparative Education Review, 59*(1), 24–49.

Naciones Unidas. (1948). *Declaración Universal de Derechos Humanos*. Accessed August 3, 2018, from https://www.ohchr.org/EN/UDHR/Documents/UDHR_Translations/spn.pdf

Nguyen, M. C., & Wodon, Q. (2012). *Global trends in child marriage*. Washington, DC: World Bank.

Nour, N. M. (2006). Health consequences of child marriage in Africa. *Emerging Infectious Diseases, 12*(11), 1644.

Nour, N. M. (2009). Child marriage: A silent health and human rights issue. *Reviews in Obstetrics and Gynecology, 2*(1), 51.

Olson, C. (2013). 16 Organisations working to stop child marriage. *The Pixel Project's "16 for 16" Campaign*. Accessed August 3, 2018, from http://16days.thepixelproject.net/16-organisations-working-to-stop-child-marriage/

Plan International Norge. (2018). *12-year-old Thea's wedding to 37-year-old Geir*. Accessed August 3, 2018, from https://www.youtube.com/watch?v=CrPkpa-NL1I

Plan International Norwey. (2014). *Stop the wedding*. Accessed August 3, 2018, from https://www.plan-norge.no/english/stop-wedding

Raj, A., & Boehmer, U. (2013). Girl child marriage and its association with national rates of HIV, maternal health, and infant mortality across 97 countries. *Violence Against Women, 19*(4), 536–551.

Raj, A., Saggurti, N., Balaiah, D., & Silverman, J. G. (2009). Prevalence of child marriage and its effect on fertility and fertility-control outcomes of young women in India: A cross-sectional, observational study. *The Lancet, 373*(9678), 1883–1889.

Raj, A., Jackson, E., & Dunham, S. (2018). Girl child marriage: A persistent global women's health and human rights violation. In S. Choudhury, J. T. Erausquin, & M. Withers (Eds.), *Global perspectives on women's sexual and reproductive health across the lifecourse* (pp. 3–19). Cham: Springer.

Thea's Wedding Blog [Theas Bryllupsblogg]. (2014). *Stopp Bryllupet*. Accessed August 3, 2018, from http://theasbryllup.blogg.no

United Nations. (1979). *Convention on the elimination of all forms of discrimination against women*. Accessed August 4, 2018, from http://www.un.org/womenwatch/daw/cedaw/text/econvention.htm#article16

United Nations. (1989). *Convention on the rights of the child*. Accessed August 4, 2018, from https://www.ohchr.org/en/professionalinterest/pages/crc.aspx

United Nations. (1994). *A/CONF. 171/13*. Accessed August 1, 2018, from http://www.un.org/en/development/desa/population/migration/generalassembly/docs/globalcompact/A_CONF.171_13.pdf

United Nations. (2018). *Millennium development goals*. Accessed August 3, 2018, from http://www.un.org/millenniumgoals/

United Nations – Human Rights – Office of the High Commissioner. (1962). *Convention on consent to marriage, minimum age for marriage and registration of marriages*. Accessed August 3, 2018, from http://www.ohchr.org/EN/ProfessionalInterest/Pages/MinimumAgeForMarriage.aspx

UNICEF. (2017). *Child marriage*. Accessed August 1, 2018, from https://data.unicef.org/topic/child-protection/child-marriage/

A Successful Festival for Kids in Győr

Ida Ercsey

Abstract

The Győr Kids Festival was established to be a free outdoor festival for socially disadvantaged children. The organizers later expanded the festival so it would be longer than 1 day and children could participate in all kinds of programmes including sports, culture, arts and crafts. The festival's primary target audience were the parents of children 3–14 years old.

The product was designed to create access to cultural events, and due to subsequent behavioural changes, such as starting or increasing the participation in cultural activities, the families could experience the benefits of an improved well-being. In order to achieve the realization of the desired behaviour, the Vaskakas Puppet Theatre (VPT), as the main organizer, should coordinate different complementary approaches, namely, an economic, a technological and an informational one. In this case two major strategies can be followed: a reinforcement and an induction. In 2015, the VPT launched a development in the marketing mix to reduce the barriers of participation in the Györkőc Festival. This festival has increased the number of visitors every year, and now it is the largest free outdoor children's festival in Hungary with 26,000 registered children and approximately 50,000 visitors.

I. Ercsey (✉)
Széchenyi István University Győr, Győr, Hungary
e-mail: ercsey@sze.hu

> **Learning Objectives**
> - The learning objectives of this case study provide students with the opportunity to:
> - Identify and describe the four complementary approaches, namely, a legal, an economic, a technological and an informational one with the purpose of behavioural change.
> - Explain the process of segmentation and the benefits of segmenting a target audience.
> - Describe with examples different variables that can be used to segment a target audience.
> - Describe the criteria that should be considered when selecting a segment to target with a behavioural change intervention.
> - Understand and apply the four major strategies in social marketing: reinforcement, induction, rationalization and confrontation strategies.
> - Use the 4Ps of marketing tools to create the social marketing programme.
> - Identify the specialities of services and develop methods to make the intangible tangible; manage the quality of service, the service capacity and the production of service with consumer.

Introduction

Social marketing is important in improving people's well-being and positively influencing individual's behaviour. Comprehending the theoretical aspects of social marketing and the execution of knowledge obtained provides a better understanding of the consumers' behaviour and implementation of the successful marketing strategy. In order to achieve the realization of the desired behaviour, the social marketers should coordinate different complementary approaches, namely, a legal, an economic, a technological and an informational (Santesmases 1999).

Since social marketing is customer centred, all strategic planning begins with understanding the target audience behaviour. Four major strategies can be followed: a reinforcement, an induction, a rationalization and a confrontation (Santesmases 1999). The social marketing programme pays attention not only to communication but also to the value proposition that it costs to the target audience members and the channels through which it is made available. It empowers students to carefully integrate communication promotion with the other 3Ps of the marketing mix elements.

Most non-profit organizations are primarily in the service market. The services can be delivered by people, places and objects. Services are especially difficult to manage because they are typically intangible, inseparable from the producer, variable in characteristics and perishable and involve the target audience in their production (Andreasen and Kotler 2008). The researchers focus increasingly on the examination of experience marketing in the service sector. Recently companies have begun to systematically design and manage the consumer experience as an added value to their primary service in order to differentiate their offering from competitors (Pine and Gilmore 1998; Wolf 1999). In this case study, the students can study the implementation of innovative services with tangible and intangible elements that affect consumers.

Overall life satisfaction did not change significantly between 2013 and 2016 in Hungary: it was 6.11 in 2013 and 6.10 in 2016 (on a scale of 0–10) (KSH 2017a). According to the Eurostat (EU-SILC3) survey in 2013, Hungary was at the end of the EU ranking and only ahead of Bulgaria. In Hungary, where households had a higher share of leisure expenditure (3.6%) than in some EU member states, residents rated their satisfaction with time use at only 6.3. Household expenditure on leisure reflects the cultural attitudes, the availability of leisure and cultural events and their price. Culture and entertainment are important activities, which contribute to an individual's quality of life. In Hungary, households with children had to make spending reductions because price is the second main barrier in accessing culture, after lack of time (EUROSTAT 2015). There is still a marked difference between the consumption of households in the worst and in the best financial situation. In 2015, the monthly consumption expenditure of households for culture in the top income quintile was 10.8 times as high as that of families in the lowest quintile (KSH 2016). The consumption of households with children increased in each consumption group except for transport and recreation and culture. In 2015, the proportion of expenditures on recreation and culture was 6.6%, and the rate of expenditures on communication equalled 7.2% (KSH 2017a).

There were various trends in demand for cultural services. On the whole the number of visitors fell in public cultural institutes over the past 20 years, and the rate of cultural activities is moderately low in families with children. In the case of theatres, the urbanization inclination was most noticeable, as half of performances were held in the capital. The geographical distance of families' residencies can make accessing cultural programme a bit difficult.

At the same time, the appearance of the Internet has fundamentally changed media consumption and cultural activities; the most up-to-date technical solutions and devices also support the use of online cultural products. The increase in the number of Internet users did not break the hegemony of television in Hungary; it has continued to be the most significant media in the country. This is due to the fact that television is readily available and relatively inexpensive and it allows information and entertainment programmes instantly available.

In regard to the conditions of poor families, they do not have a chance to visit cultural events, but they may have the need or mood to do so. In their spare time, they like to relax at home and they rarely go out. If they do go out, then they go to the cinema but this happens only annually. In their leisure time, they prefer to stay at home and rest by watching TV but prefer to surf on the channels as a bounty hunter, too (Illés 2017).

Győr as the county seat is located in the northwest of Hungary. The town has a developed economy, a good infrastructure and progressive tourism. In Győr there are about 129,000 people; furthermore in the Győr-Moson-Sopron County, the resident population is 447,985, and of them 43,281 are children aged 0 year to 9 years (KSH 2017b). For 26 years the Vaskakas Puppet Theatre has offered puppet performances for the children of this town. The number of performances and children has increased year by year, and the number of season tickets is at 7500. It is important that children can experience theatre or puppet theatre and hence may become conscious cultural consumers. In 2008 the Vaskakas Puppet Theatre (VPT) from Győr first organized the Győrkőc Festival[1] for children on the first weekend in July. The idea of the Győr Kids Festival was to establish a free outdoor festival for socially disadvantaged children. The organizers later expanded the festival so it would be longer than 1 day and children could participate in all kinds of programmes including sports, culture, arts and crafts.

Initially this festival satisfied the wants of local families, but the organizers could reach the target group of the Vaskakas Puppet Theatre. The VPT did not succeed in its original objective, as a moderately few socially disadvantaged children were involved in programmes of the Györkőc Festival. Within 4 years about half of the participants came from other cities and villages, but most of the visitors only came for 1 day to the festival. In order to change the behaviour of families with children, the organizers had to work out and implement additional marketing tools to use the appropriate approaches and strategies of social marketing.

Case Development

Target Audience

The festival's primary target audience were the parents of children ages 3–14 years in the region. These children had little opportunity to spend time on leisure activities. One of these activities is the children's day that offers different sport activities on the last Sunday of May in every settlement. However this popular event for children was held for only 1 day, and there is basically one line of programmes. Hungarian children have distinct wants, and there are some mutual values that Györkőc Festival provides that coincide with these wants.

Values for participants are that:

- Participation in all programmes is for free.
- There are programmes over 3 days.
- Many types of programmes are in several locations.
- The main organizer of the Győr Kids Festival is the Vaskakas Puppet Theatre, which has experience in the organization of performances and events.

---

[1]Győrkőc is a slang term for 'child' or 'kid'; the festival organizers use the term 'kid' as a translation.

The festival's secondary target audience consists of the local and regional enterprises. This festival is a very good opportunity to showcase their products and services. People from the region can meet them and buy from them. The festival also gives an opportunity for local and regional NGOs to have a booth and promote their activities.

In addition this festival has a significant value for the society in that it amplifies the importance of family.

Campaign Objectives: Behaviour Objectives

The children are accompanied by their parents, and the child-centric festival in Győr shows that this type of event can also be a good relaxing programme for the adults, not just the children. The family members can have a good time together at the festival. Participation in different indoor or outdoor programmes was a competing behaviour for children and parents because of the time, cost or convenience.

For the festival organizers, there were more objectives:

- To enhance the numbers of socially disadvantaged children in attendance at festival programmes
- To increase the participation time of children to 2 or 3 days
- To expand the attraction zone from a local event to a more regional one
- To reinforce the active behaviour of local children in order for them to return to the next Györkőc Festival

In order to achieve the realization of the desired behaviour, the VPT, as the main organizer, should coordinate different complementary approaches, namely, an economic, a technological and an informational one. Two major strategies may be suitable to achieve the objectives: a reinforcement and an induction.

Campaign Strategies

The VPT, the main organizer, has run an annual campaign promoting the Győr Kids Festival since 2008. The idea was originated by one of the artists in Vaskakas Puppet Theatre, and she was encouraged by the team of the VPT (23 artists and assistants). They are competent and have a lot of experience in the organization and realization of programmes and events for children. Initially the organizers could only reach those that had season tickets for the performances of the VPT; therefore most of visitors of the festival came from the town Győr and nearby countryside of Győr.

A survey was conducted on the opinions of attendance. In general the participants were satisfied with the level of programmes in the Györkőc Festival. At the same time, there were negative opinions regarding crowds in some locations and the level of infrastructure, for example, missing shielding in squares, and lack of hygienic conditions, such as mobile toilets for children. In addition, there was not an adequate flow of information to the different locations. In 2015, the VPT developed the marketing mix to reduce the barriers of participation in the Györkőc Festival. The festival has had an increase in the number of visitors over the years, and it is now the largest free outdoor children's festival in Hungary with 26,000 registered children and approximately 50,000 visitors.

Product Strategy
The social marketing product's goal is to access the cultural events to improve the individual and societal welfare. It is particularly important to change behaviour in socially disadvantaged families and enhance their cultural activities. The basic idea is that a problematic behaviour is exchanged for perceived individual benefit when an alternative behaviour is adopted.

In 2015, the VPT had to focus on developing and launching new offerings in the value proposition of Győr Kids Festival, and it has increased the number of its locations, thematic sites, games and performances. The organizers added new offerings that were relatively dissimilar to their present offerings, and they put emphasis on existing consumers and new consumers, too. In July the water games (water slide, jumping castle, small pedal boats, water dodgem and water cylinders) provided a wonderful experience for children. The Kids Eco Park delivered further new and great adventures with the exhibition of the Danube Museum so the children could gain knowledge on the relationship between human and natural environments in a family-friendly form. The festival also offered cultural and intellectual activities, which were very entertaining and memorable: Mátrai Wood, logic games; Tudor Game Family, unique strategic board games, the Arrabona Chess School, and Poem-Play-Ground. The value proposition of the festival is service, and the extensive involvement of the target audience is an integral part in the production of that service. Many children from 3 to 14 years old are involved in the exciting sport and means of transport in the vehicle park, e.g. canoe races, racetrack, tricky bikes, flying scouts, road traffic track and railway obstacle course. Special attention is given to the atmospherics of the different locations. Győr is the town of three rivers; hence the beach of Danube and the Raba Island give a fabulous natural environment for the programmes. Furthermore, the squares and streets in the city ensured extra special spaces, e.g. buildings with treasured baroque architecture and the gunnery near the castle. Figure 1 shows the map of all locations at the Györkőc Festival in 2015.

The Győr Kids Festival was complemented by the International Győr Kids Olympics in which organizers awaited teams from around the country and abroad. The teams competed in eight different sports (e.g. swimming, athletics, street basketball, soccer, tennis, beach volleyball, wrestling, water polo) in several sport centres in the town.

Price Strategy
Győr was transformed into a playground where children could participate in every programme with a wristband received free of charge in return for a photograph of

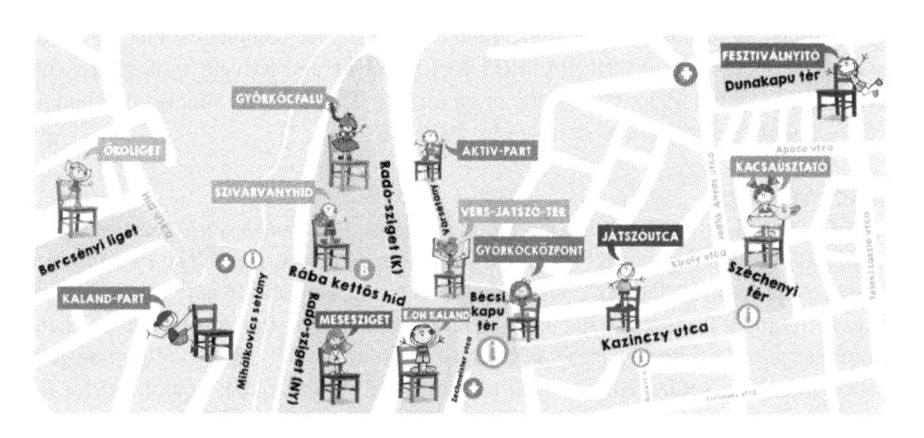

Fig. 1 Map of locations at the Györkőc Festival. Source: http://2015.gyorkoc.hu/en/programs

them smiling. The concept of the Győr Kids Festival was to establish a free outdoor festival for socially disadvantaged children. This goal was supported by different price discounts offered by local service organizations, e.g. Rába Quelle Spa, Thermal and Adventure Bath, Xantus Janos Zoo and other cultural organizations in Győr. The cultural programmes were very popular for families: free visitation to the Bishop's Castle and Saint Laszlo Visitors' Centre. The Mobilis Interactive Exhibition Centre was open to visitors with performances that included exciting and breathtaking experiments; the entry was free with a wristband. Many children enjoyed the Kids Raft Program, which was an adventurous cruise down the Rába and the Danube rivers. Children with Győr Kids wristbands could travel for free. In order to extend the time of children's participation to 2 or 3 days and to expand the attraction zone from a local event to a more regional one, the national railway company (MÁV-Start Ltd.) provided a free train trip home from Győr to children (aged 6–14) who participated in the Győr Kids Festival. During the Győrkőc Festival in many hotels, a child with a wristband could use the facilities for free if an adult had booked a room, and in several restaurants two children with wristbands could receive a free meal if an adult ordered a meal.

The consumers perceived nonmonetary costs in terms of effort, time, physical energy, or psychic costs. For poor families, however, such costs could be very significant: they could worry asking for time off from work, fear that they would be tired, potential embarrassment in that participation in the festival would be costly and worry about giving up current behaviour, which was simple and comfortable to them. These nonmonetary costs were minimized by an informational approach and an induction strategy.

In order to offer all programmes of the Györkőc Festival free of charge to children, event organizers were responsible for generating funds. With respect to the financial sources of the VPT, renting out property for enterprises produced some revenue. The VPT was satisfied that a number of food-beverage providers and arts-crafts vendors continuously increased. This festival was supported by the local government of Győr, the citizens, municipalities and companies that provided special services (e.g. EON, PATENT-SECURITY) and private individuals that collaborated in the realization of the programmes. Thanks to all support, the budget of the Györkőc Festival has doubled by 2015.

Place Strategy

The Györkőc Festival has attracted more attendees; therefore several locations were added along with the motto 'Thousand programmes on ten sites'. The management ensured that certain factors complied into creating an ideal event, specifically in regard to time it takes place in the convenience of summer and in regard to place the convenience of using the spaces in the city centre of Győr, and providing transportation to remote settlements, as well as providing infrastructural equipment for the hygienic services offered to the children. This was seen through the target audience members' repeated participation behaviour and positive word-of-mouth (WOM) because their expectations were met with the perceived benefit-cost. Figure 2 presents the opening ceremony in the city.

Every year the organization of the Györkőc Festival was incumbent on the VPT that employs 23 staff members, so it was necessary to have the cooperation of the stakeholders of town. During the festival the volunteers had important roles because they directly met with the consumers. They helped solve problems, shared in families' pleasure and made the programmes more memorable with their presence. Over the years there was increase in the volunteers, especially students. The website of the festival and the VPT was used to recruit persons for volunteering. Additional channels of volunteer promotion and information dissemination were done through schools and the university, using targeted, tailored information.

Fig. 2 Opening ceremony in Dunakapu Square. Source: http://2015.gyorkoc.hu/en/news

Marketing Communication Strategy

The organizers proposed to reinforce the awareness and popularity of the festival in the town and to enhance the numbers of participants and patrons in the region. Furthermore, the VPT would enhance the attractiveness of the Győr Kids Festival to children from other towns and villages in Hungary.

The festival maintains a website[2] and online presence on social networking sites (Facebook, Instagram and Twitter) in order to promote the programmes and encourage the children and their parents to visit the events. In the festival smiling volunteers await the smiling kids and parents and a photograph, which was the entrance fee to the festival. These smiling photos were uploaded to the website and social media.

In carrying out communication to its target audiences, the VPT used three main tools: paid advertising, joint advertising and publicity. The marketing adviser assisted in the planning and implementing of the marketing communication campaign. More theoretical background (AIDA, 5M models) was applied to perform an efficient campaign to change and maintain the target group's behaviour (Lewis 1903; Kotler 2002).

In order to change the behaviour of the socially disadvantaged children in attendance at the festival programmes, the managers of campaign used an induction strategy. Message focused on the awareness of festival programmes, the perceived economic and social benefits of behaviour and some important details regarding the accessibility of participation. According to the media consumption of the target group, they decided several mediums. The local families were reached by the regional daily newspaper (Kisalföld), local radio and Internet, which was the most preferred informational source. Two sponsors from the media industry (Kisalföld newspaper and Győr+MEDIA) continuously published actual information about the festival in the form of advertising materials and publicity by using printed and online communication. Some sponsors posted their special programmes on their web sites, e.g. GyőrSZOL, a waste management non-profit organization, promoted the Eco Park programme.

Advertising and publicity in social media and on the different cultural, tourist and thematic web sites contributed to the increase in the length of time of families' participation and also to the extension of the attraction zone to a more regional one.

In order to reinforce the active behaviour of local children, the VPT developed web components; they created well-designed and attractive web sites that encouraged the enhancement of online communication and advocated the campaign message.

---

[2] www.gyorkoc.hu

Conclusions

Given the significant growth demand, the Györkőc Festival is in a great position to continually increase its popularity, while providing a unique, varied and valuable programme for families with children.

The VPT keeps track of the number of children based on the wristbands received for a photograph of them smiling. In 2015, the Györkőc Festival registered 22,000 children from ages 3 to 5 in July, which represents a 15% rise in the number of children from 2014. The size of families was similar to the nuclear family model with a mean value 3.67 persons per family. According to age little ones and pupils found suitable activities in the festival, too. Enhancing the exposure was partly due to consistently offering free and exciting programmes in a fabulous environment. In addition, the dispersion of participants significantly changed, families from more than 50 km away successfully were reached (68%) and some consumers came from settlements abroad near the border (5%). A remarkable result is that many children who lived in villages and smaller towns participated in cultural programmes and special games in the vehicle park. They arrived consciously to spend more time with innovative services in different locations. At the same time, the local families spent more money in restaurants and hospitalities.

Many citizens had a desire to contribute towards making Győr a better place to live; more people were interested in volunteering. Online marketing communication resulted in more than 7000 followers in Facebook and plenty likes to the smiling photos in social media.

The success of the Győr Kids Festival is shown by the fact that it has already won the title of Excellent Quality Festival twice after a thorough examination by the Hungarian Festival Association. The festival has also received the Diamond Award of City Marketing, as well as the title of EFFE from the European Festival Association.

Discussion Questions

1. How are the stages of change of behaviour involved in the decision-making process of families in regards to the Györkőc Festival?
2. Explain the levels of the concept of product to the Györkőc Festival.
3. What can the VPT do to further increase the number of families participating in the festival programmes?
4. Which marketing research methods can be useful to get to know the attitude and behaviour of target attendance at the festival?
5. Do you have suggestions for improving their connection to sponsors and partners?
6. What are the relative strengths and weaknesses of media types used in the campaign?
7. How would you measure the effectiveness of the campaign of the Györkőc Festival?

References

Andreasen, A. R., & Kotler, P. (2008). *Strategic marketing for nonprofit organizations*. London: Pearson.
Illés, G. B. (2017). *The color TV the changes that took place both in our society and in the cultural needs of our country as consequences of the appearance of commercial TV industry, also in view of it's regional setting*. Theses of doctoral dissertation. University of Debrecen.
Kotler, P. (2002). *Marketing menedzsment*. Budapest: KIJK KERSZÖV.
Lewis, E. S. E. (1903). Catch-line and argument. *The Book-Keeper, 15*.
Pine, B. J., & Gilmore, J. H. (1998). Welcome to the experience economy. *Harvard Business Review, 76*(4), 97–105.
Santesmases, M. (1999). *Marketing. Conceptos y Estrategias*. Madrid: Piramide.
Wolf, M. (1999). *The entertainment economy*. New York: Random House.

Online Sources

EUROSTAT. (2015). *Quality of life in Europe – Facts and views – Leisure and social relations*. Accessed January 23, 2018, from http://ec.europa.eu/eurostat/statisticsexplained/
Györkőcfesztival. (2012). Accessed March 2, 2018, from www.gyorkoc.hu
Györkőcfesztival. (2013). Accessed March 2, 2018, from www.gyorkoc.hu
Györkőcfesztival. (2014). Accessed March 2, 2018, from www.gyorkoc.hu
Györkőcfesztivál. (2015a). Accessed March 2, 2018, from http://2015.gyorkoc.hu/en/programs
Györkőcfesztivál. (2015b). Accessed March 2, 2018, from www.gyorkoc.hu
KSH. (2016). *A háztartások fogyasztása, 2015. Statisztikai Tükör*. Accessed June 17, 2017, from http://www.ksh.hu/docs/hun/xftp/stattukor/haztfogy/haztfogy1512.pdf
KSH. (2017a). *Hungary, 2016*. Accessed January 20, 2018, from https://www.ksh.hu/docs/hun/xftp/idoszaki/mo/hungary2016.pdf
KSH. (2017b). *Magyarország közigazgatási helynévkönyve (Gazetteer of Hungary)*. Accessed January 20, 2018, from http://www.ksh.hu/docs/hun/hnk/hnk_2017.pdf

Social Marketing for Social Innovation: The Employment Plan of the Spanish Red Cross as a Case Study

Marta Rey-García and Vanessa Mato-Santiso

Abstract Social innovation consists of developing and implementing new ideas to meet social needs and create new social relationships or collaborations. Social marketing can contribute to achieving socially desirable outcomes or impacts, including those originating from new solutions to social problems. The goal of this chapter is to understand how the application of commercial marketing to influence the ideas and voluntary behavior of target audiences can contribute to the development and implementation of innovative solutions to social problems. Our case study focuses on work integration as a relevant social challenge globally and analyzes the social marketing campaign undertaken by the Spanish Red Cross to promote equal opportunities and treatment in the labor market for the most vulnerable citizens. Findings suggest social marketing may not only be a key strategy to promote socially innovative initiatives for work integration but also become a social innovation of the marketing type in its own right.

M. Rey-García · V. Mato-Santiso (✉)
School of Economics and Business, University of A Coruña, A Coruña, Spain
e-mail: martarey@udc.es; vanessa.mato@udc.es

> **Learning Objectives**
> 1. To examine the conceptual relationship between social marketing and social innovation
> 2. To understand how social marketing can contribute in practice to the development and implementation of innovative solutions to social problems through a case study on work integration
> 3. To analyze a social marketing campaign that innovatively addresses the challenge of promoting the equality of opportunities and treatment of the most vulnerable groups in the labor market, with the ultimate goal of integrating them into work

Introduction

Social innovation is defined as the development and implementation of new ideas (products, services, and models) to meet social needs and create new social relationships or collaborations. Social innovation as an impact can be attributed to a great extent to the nonprofit or third sector (Anheier et al. 2014) and includes those products, processes, and initiatives that profoundly challenge the system which created the problem they seek to address (Westley and Antadze 2010). The Oslo Manual (OECD and Eurostat 2005) distinguishes between four types of innovation that can be easily transposed to the realm of social challenges and goals: (1) product innovations, i.e., new or significantly improved products, services, activities, projects, or programs with respect to their characteristics or intended uses; (2) process innovations, that is, new or significantly improved planning, implementation and delivery, and evaluation methods; (3) marketing innovations, or new forms of communicating and managing the relationships with customers, beneficiaries, funders, partners, and other relevant stakeholders; and (4) organizational innovations, particularly the implementation of new organizational structures, the emergence of new types of actors, and the configuration of new institutional settings.

Social innovation thus entails new responses to pressing social demands, which in turn affect the process of social interactions. Furthermore, social innovations are innovations "that are not only good for society but also enhance individuals' capacity to act" (European Commission 2013: 6). Therefore, for social innovation to be fruitful, new ideas and behaviors must take root at both an individual and a collective level. This is precisely where social marketing comes into the picture. Its goal is to influence ideas or voluntary behaviors of a particular target or group through the application of marketing tools and strategies in order to increase individual, group, and overall well-being (Andreasen 2011; Lee and Kotler 2011). On the one hand, social marketing can be used as a tool to support socially innovative goals, processes, outputs, outcomes, or impacts, facilitating the development and implementation of new ways of tackling social challenges and improving the well-being of communities. On the other hand, social marketing strategies and campaigns can become themselves social innovations of the marketing type.

Coming up next, we will analyze the concrete social marketing strategies used and actions undertaken by a large nonprofit organization in Spain in order to achieve a social innovation impact in the field of work integration. We use a case study design (Yin 1994) based on documentary analysis from multiple sources, including one in-depth interview with a key decision-maker about his/her expert knowledge, experiences, attitudes, thoughts, beliefs, and routine actions (Dana and Dana 2005). The use of these different methods and sources, or triangulation, is a strategy that "reflects an attempt to secure an in-depth understanding of the phenomenon in question" (Denzin 2012: 82). Thus, it is possible to achieve coherent conclusions obtained with similar information from several independent sources (Dana and Dana 2005). Finally, we summarize the main conclusions and suggest three questions for discussion.

Case Development

The Global Challenge of Work Integration

The social challenge of work integration refers to the need to enhance the (re) employment and (re)incorporation of individuals to the regular labor market, particularly those belonging to population groups with compounding situations of unemployment, poverty, and/or social exclusion. These groups are considered vulnerable toward employment, as they present additional difficulties to access the standard labor market due to their low qualification and skills, disabilities, family constraints, or lack of cultural or social capital. Some examples would be low-skilled jobseekers, young people with difficulties in finding a first job, long-term unemployed, female victims of domestic violence, immigrants, refugees, minorities, former convicts and drug addicts, and disabled or chronically ill people, among others (Spanish Red Cross 2016). The problem of work integration of the most vulnerable citizens has a global dimension and demands innovative solutions from public agencies, nonprofit organizations, or work integration social enterprises (WISEs) (Rey-García and Mato-Santiso 2017).

Vulnerability Toward Employment in Spain

In the case of Spain, the recent economic crisis increased the challenge of work integration, as it contributed to increased unemployment, reduced income levels in real terms, raised inequality, and ultimately broadened the population segments in situation of vulnerability toward employment (Rey-García et al. 2018). According to a recent study quantifying and characterizing these segments, 1,800,000 Spaniards have a high probability of remaining jobless in the short term, and 2,400,000 have a high probability of living in poverty despite having a job. 31.9% of people who are vulnerable toward employment are young (between 25 and 34 years old), 60% only have primary or secondary education, 58% are women, and 40.4% do not receive any benefits and are not formally registered as jobseekers (FEDEA 2017).

The scale and scope of this challenge clearly exceed the capacity of WISEs—the traditional tool to address work integration in Spain. In 2014, the 204 WISEs existing in Spain employed a total of 2750 vulnerable people. Among the 714 vulnerable employees who ended their customized work integration itineraries during that year, only 50.42% were inserted in the regular labor market (FAEDEI 2015).

The Spanish Red Cross and its Employment Plan as a Social Innovation

In this context, the Spanish Red Cross carries out different social marketing actions in order to offer new responses to the pressing but as yet unresolved problem of work integration. The Spanish Red Cross is a humanitarian nonprofit organization that relies on 202,490 specialized volunteers, 10,700 paid professionals, and over 1,300,000 members to fulfil its mission of providing comprehensive responses to the needs of vulnerable people with a human development perspective. Its goal is to be closer to the vulnerable groups at national and international levels through integrated actions, carried out by volunteers and with broad social support. In 2016, over 35% of its total income (575 million euros) came from private sources: members contributed over 134 million euros, 56 million came from the sale of lotteries—of which 33 million through the Gold Grand Prize Lottery—and 32 million euros came from private donations. Additionally, more than 155 million euros were obtained from public subsidies (Spanish Red Cross 2016).

The evolution of the Spanish Red Cross has always been constantly adapting to changing social needs and problems. In 2000, it launched its employment plan, aimed at promoting the employment of the most vulnerable segments of population, in order to achieve their inclusion in society through labor opportunities. This employment plan is designed so that vulnerable people can improve, through orientation and training services, their opportunities of getting a job. It involves public entities, universities, other nonprofit organizations, and businesses. In 2016, it assisted 89,013 vulnerable people: 43,620 people improved their employability through basic, transversal, and technical competencies, and 17,983 found a job (Spanish Red Cross 2016). In addition, the employment plan provides services for the shelter and work orientation of these groups and the design of a customized path of work integration for each individual. This path integrates a training plan, an individualized accompaniment to socio-professional work integration, access strategies for employment and entrepreneurship, and finally, strategies to keep one's job.

The number of participants in the Spanish Red Cross employment plan has doubled since the beginning of the crisis, from 45,000 people assisted in 2008 (45,665) to nearly 90,000 in 2016 (89,013) (see Fig. 1). Red Cross has assisted more than 650,000 vulnerable people between 2008 and 2016. During this period,

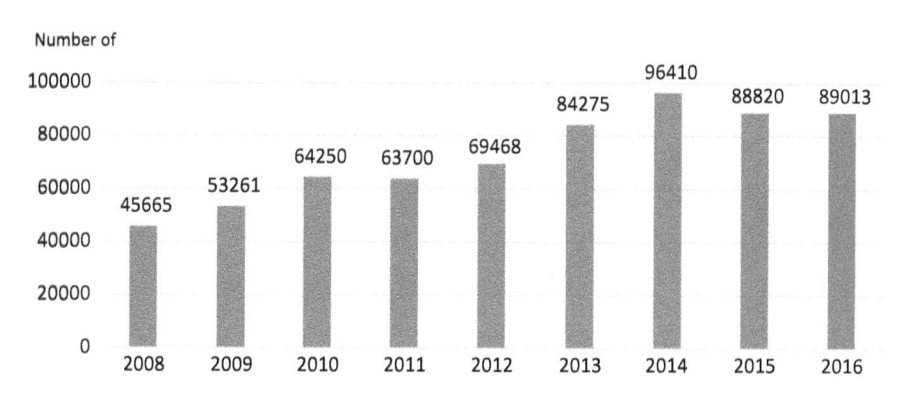

Fig. 1 People assisted by the employment plan of Spanish Red Cross (2008–2016). Source: Author's own elaboration with information retrieved from Spanish Red Cross (2018)

not only the employment needs of vulnerable segments of population expanded and deepened, but also the risk of social exclusion increased, particularly among the long-term unemployed.

The "En realidad no tiene gracia" [It Really Is Not Funny] Social Marketing Campaign

The Spanish Red Cross launched the "En realidad no tiene gracia" [It really is not funny] campaign in 2010 with the goal of supporting the development of the service delivery dimension of its employment plan. The main objective of this social marketing campaign is to mobilize society as a whole (it was labelled as a 360° campaign, aimed toward all types of target audiences), and especially companies, in favor of the equality of opportunities and treatment of people who are vulnerable toward employment, and to support the management of the resulting diversity in the workplace. This campaign uses humor, irony, and celebrity endorsements to structure multichannel contents (both online and offline) that contribute to the visibility of inequality and vulnerability toward employment, advocate the need of work integration, and ultimately improve the impact of the employment plan. It has been endorsed by famous people such as the actor Mariano Peña (Mauricio Colmenero in the TV series "Aida") and Pepe Rodríguez (Spanish renowned chef and judge in the program "MasterChef Spain"), among other celebrities. It includes a wide range of social marketing actions, including social media, audios and online series, interviews, publications, events, and workshops. In Table 1, we describe some illustrative examples of actions carried out within the framework of this social marketing campaign.

Table 1 Social marketing actions of the "En realidad no tiene gracia" [It really is not funny] campaign

Type of social marketing actions	Examples	Description
Initiatives through social media	"Caras raras por la igualdad" Project	The aim is to identify and eliminate some inappropriate situations involving jobseekers—such as when an employer asks a woman candidate if she plans to become pregnant—using humor and irony. For this initiative it is only necessary to post a tweet with one photo of a surprised face, with the hashtag #EstaCaraSeMeQueda and the phrase that represents that inadequate situation
	Concurso de fotografía Social "Mundo Diverso" [Social photography Competition "Diverse World"]	This project consists of people posting photos on twitter and sharing their vision of a more diverse and rich society, in order to give greater visibility to cultural diversity
Short audios and online series	Short audios with famous comedians and actors	Short audios with a joke about immigration, diversity, and work integration, lasting between 30 and 40 s, then saying the following sentence, "It really is not funny", and then seriously explaining the importance of the work integration challenge
	"Recetas para la integración laboral" ["Recipes for work integration"]	Web series of seven chapters starred by Pepe Rodriguez, judge of the TV show MasterChef. In each of these videos, important issues such as gender equality, cultural diversity, the influence of age, and motivation and talent management are discussed, among others (each of these issues is an "ingredient")
Interviews with opinion leaders and publications	Interviews with recognized professionals and celebrities	Telling personal stories and reflection over different themes, such as the benefits of diversity management, how diversity can enrich the company and society; how to eliminate employment barriers with enthusiasm, energy, and commitment; and how to overcome prejudice and stereotypes that persist in the workplace
	Publication of articles	For instance, the publication entitled "Without words there are no facts" approaches the challenges of the labor market in terms of diversity, integration, and equality of opportunities and treatment
Events and workshops	Dialogue roundtables	An area of joint work and co-creation, based on collaborative work and exchange. From these round tables, reflections and other contributions emerge that seek to promote the employment and work integration of vulnerable people and to assess how diversity should be managed in practice
	Cartoons and caricatures	Based on real cases, they raise interesting reflections about the role played by the prejudice that many people face in the labor market. The purpose of this activity is to eliminate the stereotypes and prejudice in the labor market and to remove barriers such as gender, age, and belonging to a different culture, among others

Source: Author's own elaboration with information retrieved from En realidad no tiene gracia (2018)

Social Marketing Strategies used in the "En realidad no tiene gracia" Campaign

Unlike traditional commercial marketing, social marketing highlights two main paradoxes: (1) in general, goods or a service are not sold in a social marketing campaign; and (2) the objectives of this type of campaign are long-term, and the benefits are of a social nature (Santesmases Mestre 1999). This campaign aims at changing the negative attitudes and behavior of business employers and of society in general toward vulnerable citizens, so that they become more supportive of the equality of opportunities and treatment in the employment field. Therefore this campaign uses a *confrontational strategy*, which consists of conducting awareness actions and advocacy to attempt to change the attitude and behavior of people, because they are contrary to socially desirable behavior (Santesmases Mestre 1999: 948).

It should be noted that abundant coercive regulatory measures are already in place in Spain to prevent or sanction undesirable behavior regarding discrimination in the labor market due to gender, age, nationality, disabilities, etc. or to promote diversity in the workplace, e.g., Royal Decree 364/2005, of April 8, which regulates the exceptional measures alternative to complying with the reserve quota in favor of employees with disabilities that has been compulsory for all Spanish organizations with over 50 employees since 1982; the recent Royal Decree-law 18/2017, of November 24, modifying the Commercial Code, the consolidated text of the Capital Companies Law approved by Royal Legislative Decree 1/2010, of July 2; and the Law 22/2015, of July 20, on Audit of Accounts, regarding nonfinancial information and diversity in large corporations, to name just a few.

However, the "It really is not funny" campaign goes beyond advocating corporate compliance and is rather focused on creating awareness about individual attitudes and day-to-day behaviors and routines in the workplace. It is based on an innovative mix of celebrity-based persuasion, a corrosive sense of humor and information and communication technology. It uses a direct and even aggressive style to put target audiences in front of a mirror, so that they are confronted their own prejudice and misbehavior toward vulnerable jobseekers. It also identifies positive practices that remove barriers against their work integration or promote diversity in the workplace and leverages the awareness effects through online interactive channels, particularly social media. The goal is to cause a voluntary change of attitude and behavior among potential business employers (the main source of mainstream jobs in the country) and society in general.

This type of social marketing strategy is essential to complement service delivery by WISEs and TSOs and supportive legislation on the side of regulators, because these alone are necessary but not sufficient conditions to achieve a socially desirable change. Apart from delivering services to vulnerable jobseekers and coercively preventing or sanctioning uncompliant behavior by (potential) employers, it is also indispensable to broadly stimulate social adoption of positive attitudes and behavior consistent with the socially desirable goal, i.e., finding solutions to the problem of unequal opportunities and treatment in the labor market.

Additionally, it is important to underline the pivotal role played by Spanish Red Cross as promoter of this social campaign, based on its volunteer nature, strength at service delivery, and broad social support. The messages originating from a legitimate advocate generate more empathy toward those affected and increased annoyance toward the perceived injustice, motivating intent to take action (Summers and Summers 2017).

Conclusions

In order to reach its goal of promoting equality and diversity for vulnerable jobseekers in the regular labor market, the employment plan of the Spanish Red Cross combines service provision—customized orientation and training for beneficiaries—with advocacy through its "It really is not funny" campaign. This campaign develops a wide range of innovative social marketing actions to raise awareness (change attitudes) and to stimulate actions (change behavior) among mainstream employers and society in general. The campaign aims at identifying and eliminating the practical barriers suffered by vulnerable people in the labor market in an innovative way. This campaign adopts a realistic approach to the human aspects and daily practice of corporate compliance with work integration and diversity regulations. It uses a direct language based on humor, irony, and critique as a vehicle for companies and citizens to confront their own stereotypes and prejudices regarding vulnerable people and to reflect on the role that they play as barriers to equality of access and treatment in the labor market. Diffusion of the effects of this confrontational strategy on people and organization is leveraged by digital communication technologies.

Thus, this social marketing campaign not only supports the implementation of the employment plan of the Spanish Red Cross as an innovative solution to the problem of work integration in Spain, but it is also a social marketing innovation per se. Little societal awareness exists about traditional work integration mechanisms prevailing in the country (e.g., WISEs) that rather rely upon ad hoc regulations and organizational formulas outside the standard labor market. By contrast, this campaign mainly targets mainstream companies and their employees, as they are the main source of jobs in the regular labor market, but may also become the main barrier when it comes to integrating vulnerable citizens.

This case study suggests a fruitful scenario to discuss the twofold relevance of social marketing in the realm of social innovation. On the one hand, it may be an effective tool to support the implementation of social innovation, contributing to initiatives mitigating or solving global social challenges at a local level in new, creative ways. On the other hand, the new ways in which the Spanish Red Cross' campaign confronts target audiences in order to change their attitudes and behavior toward vulnerable jobseekers suggest that innovative social marketing strategies may help joint redefinition of social problems with relevant stakeholders, bring into existence new forms of communicating and managing the relationships with them, or co-create new social relationships, becoming a social innovation in their own right. This twofold potential of social marketing is especially relevant in a context of economic strains and pressing problems, where effective service delivery and regulatory frameworks fall short on achieving sustainable social change by themselves.

Discussion Questions

Once the case study was analyzed, and after presenting the main conclusions, we suggest some questions for discussion.

1. The main objective of "It really is not funny" campaign, within the employment plan of Spanish Red Cross, is to promote the equality of opportunities and treatment for the most vulnerable citizens in the labor market and to better manage the resulting diversity. Which indicators should be used to measure its success as a social marketing campaign from the perspective of its socially innovative impact?
2. What are the main reasons why social marketing can become a key strategy to encourage social innovation? Illustrate with examples from your own country context.
3. The Spanish Red Cross is the largest volunteer organization in Spain. How can this feature of being a volunteer-based organization influence the effects of social marketing campaigns on the development of the employment plan as a social innovation?

Acknowledgments The authors acknowledge funding provided by the ITSSOIN (Impact of the Third Sector as SOcial INnovation) project for making the presentation of this paper possible in the VII International Congress on Teaching Cases related to Public and Nonprofit Marketing. ITSSOIN (www.itssoin.eu) is a research project funded under the European Commission's 7th Framework Programme responding to a call to investigate "The impact of the third sector on socio-economic development in Europe".

References

Andreasen, A. R. (2011). Opportunities and challenges in social marketing. In R. P. Bagozzi & A. A. Ruvio (Eds.), *Wiley international encyclopedia of marketing*. Chichester: Wiley.

Anheier, H. K., Krlev, G., Preuss, S., Mildenberger, G., Bekkers, R., Mensink, W., et al. (2014). *Social innovation as impact of the third sector*. Deliverable 1.1 of the project: "Impact of the Third Sector as Social Innovation" (ITSSOIN), European Commission – 7th Framework Programme. Brussels: European Commission, DG Research.

Dana, L. P., & Dana, T. E. (2005). Expanding the scope of methodologies used in entrepreneurship research. *International Journal of Entrepreneurship and Small Business, 2*(1), 79–88.

Denzin, N. K. (2012). Triangulation 2.0. *Journal of Mixed Methods Research, 6*(2), 80–88.

En realidad no tiene gracia. (2018). *Official website of the campaign*. Accessed February 26, 2018, from http://www.enrealidadnotienegracia.org

European Commission. (2013). *Guide to social innovation*. Accessed January 20, 2018, from http://ec.europa.eu/

FEDEA. (2017). *Población especialmente vulnerable ante el empleo en España*. Accessed January 29, 2018, from https://juntosporelempleo.cclearning.accenture.com/

Federación de Asociaciones Empresariales de Empresas de Inserción (FAEDEI). (2015). *Memoria Social 2014: Empresas de Inserción Laboral*. Accessed March 08, 2018, from www.faedei.org/images/docs/documento62.pdf

Lee, N. R., & Kotler, P. (2011). *Social marketing: Influencing behaviors for good* (4th ed.). London: Sage.

OECD, & Eurostat. (2005). *Oslo manual: Guidelines for collecting and interpreting innovation data. The measurement of scientific and technological activities* (3rd ed.). Paris: OECD Publishing. https://doi.org/10.1787/9789264013100-en.

Rey-García, M., Calvo, N., & Mato-Santiso, V. (2018). Collective social enterprises for social innovation: Understanding the potential and limitations of cross-sector partnerships in the field of work integration. *Management Decision.* https://doi.org/10.1108/MD-01-2017-0091.

Rey-García, M., & Mato-Santiso, V. (2017). Business-led social innovation in the work integration field: The role of large firms and corporate foundations. *Business and Management Research, 6* (1), 1–12.

Royal Decree 364/2005, of April 8, which regulates the alternative exceptional compliance with the reserve quota in favor of employees with disabilities.

Royal Decree-law 18/2017, of November 24, by which the Commercial Code, the consolidated text of the Capital Companies Law approved by Royal Legislative Decree 1/2010, of July 2, and the Law 22/2015, of July 20, on Audit of Accounts, regarding non-financial information and diversity are modified.

Santesmases Mestre, M. (1999). *Marketing. Conceptos y Estrategias.* Madrid: Piramide.

Spanish Red Cross. (2016). Annual report 2016. Accessed February 03, 2018, from http://www.cruzroja.es/

Spanish Red Cross. (2018). Official website of the organization. Annual reports. Accessed February 25, 2018, from http://www.cruzroja.es/

Summers, J., & Summers, J. (2017). Motivating intention to take action on behalf of an out-group: Implications for the use of advocacy messages in social marketing strategies. *Journal of Marketing Management, 33*(11–12), 973–1002.

Westley, F., & Antadze, N. (2010). Strategies for scaling social innovation for greater impact. *The Innovation Journal: The Public Sector Innovation Journal, 15*(2), Article 2, 1–19.

Yin, R. (1994). *Case study research: Design and methods.* Beverly Hills, CA: Sage.

The Role of Civil Society Organizations in Social Innovation as an Example of the New Social Marketing

Begoña Álvarez-García, Luis Ignacio Álvarez-González, Marta Rey-García, Noelia Salido-Andrés, and María José Sanzo-Pérez

Abstract The objective of the present case study is to describe to what extent the design and implementation of socially innovative activities and projects by Civil Society Organizations take into consideration the principles and tools of social marketing. With this objective, REAS (a Spanish Network of Alternative and Solidarity Economy Networks), and its online financial education platform economiasolidaria.org, has been selected as unit of analysis of the case. The empirical study developed reveals how REAS is effectively a nonprofit organization very oriented to the market, in the sense of adopting the concept of marketing, and how marketing-mix variables (fundamentally, the variables product, place, and promotion) have been very important in the design, implementation, and dissemination of its online platform.

B. Álvarez-García · M. Rey-García · N. Salido-Andrés
University of A Coruña, A Coruña, Spain
e-mail: balvarez@udc.es; marta.reyg@udc.es; noelia.sandres@udc.es

L. I. Álvarez-González (✉) · M. J. Sanzo-Pérez
University of Oviedo, Oviedo, Spain
e-mail: alvarezg@uniovi.es; mjsanzo@uniovi.es

Learning Objectives
- Identify the key dimensions of social innovation activities or projects.
- Determine how a civil society organization can promote social innovations in the nonprofit sector.
- Describe how the principles and values that underlie the marketing strategy are very important to implement and sustain a social innovation.
- Design social innovation activities or projects from the marketing standpoint.
- Develop a management plan to implement and to disseminate a social innovation activity or project through online marketing channels.

Introduction

The evolution of the concept of marketing has been characterized by its continuous expansion toward the social scope, in such a way that the social dimension plays a key role in the current conceptualization of marketing which primarily focuses on customer satisfaction and the needs of society (AMA 2013). In this context, the research on social innovation (SI) has grown rapidly (Phillips et al. 2015; Van der Have and Rubalcaba 2016), as this kind of innovation has become extremely popular as a way to tackle the growing social problems with dwindling resources (Borzaga and Bodini 2012). One of the basic dimensions of SI activities is their collaborative nature, as SI practices are deployed through new forms of collaboration and "involve a higher degree of bottom-up and grass-roots involvement than technological innovation" (Krlev et al. 2019: 19). In this sense, social alliances, understood as voluntary efforts of actors from two or more sectors that involve at least one civil society organization (CSO) and cooperatively pursue an objective aiming at improving social welfare (Sakarya et al. 2012), achieve particular importance.

From the perspective of social marketing, CSOs can play an outstanding role in promoting social innovations to the extent that they accomplish several requirements. First, CSOs participate in the definition of the social problem. Second, the entrepreneurial process is collective rather than individualistic. Third, the SI must be contextualized in terms of specific institutional/policy conditions, and investments in human/social capital are needed. Fourth, the phase of diffusion is particularly challenging, with evidence of scaling and replication failures in SI developed by CSOs (Spear 2012).

Under this scenario, the objective of our case study is to describe, from the perspective of the strategic and operational dimensions of the social marketing, how REAS (Red de Redes de Economía Alternativa y Solidaria/Network of Alternative and Solidarity Economy Networks, in English), a network of networks of civil society and social economy organizations, has developed and consolidated an online platform, economiasolidaria.org, with the aim at enhancing the consumer protection and literacy in the field of financial services through an online financial education initiatives.

The platform is implemented in a moment of time in which Spain has undergone several radical changes related to financial markets and products. After 2009 Spain underwent the largest restructuring of the banking sector in its history. At the root of these changes is a generalized social distrust of banks due to a series of irresponsible behaviors in relation to credit concession, the disclosure of generous compensation schemes for directors of banks under public rescue plans, and a broad perception of opacity and moral hazard (Anheier et al. 2015). It was a time when there seems to be rather low involvement of the Spanish government in the field but a strong demand on the part of the citizens for more empowerment. So, we refer to a time when innovative solutions in this field were required.

Case Development[1]

REAS is a nonprofit organization that, as a network of networks, encourages and coordinates 14 regional and 4 sectorial networks that are committed to solidarity-based economy in the Spanish State (www.reasred.org). In practice, REAS includes more than 500 organizations, mainly nonprofit associations, but also cooperatives or companies. REAS is present in the Intercontinental Network for the Promotion of Social Solidarity Economy (RIPESS) and in the Spanish Business Confederation of Social Economy (CEPES). REAS also collaborates directly with about 20 networks and sectorial associations (e.g., "Network of Alternative Finance" or "Association of Networks of Social Market"). Therefore, REAS is a CSO created with the objective of being a meeting point for ethical and solidarity finance tools linked to the solidarity economy networks.

In this context, REAS launched in 2007 the site economiasolidaria.org. This platform is inspiring a different way of understanding the economy and the relationships based in a collaborative and social paradigm, away from profit. The main objective of this platform is not only focused on "traditional" financial education, understood as the set of skills and knowledge that enable a person or organization to make decisions regarding their finances, but on anything that might lead to a change toward a social and solidarity economy, i.e., fair trade, responsible consumption, ethical finance, social market, or solidarity economy in general. It also reports and denounces the causes that are generating a situation of inequality and injustice. The online platform is a space that provides mutual support and information for all its organizations and society in general, as well as space for exchange of ideas and

---

[1]This case study is part of the ITSSOIN (Impact of the Third Sector as SOcial INnovation) project, funded by the European Commission. The ITSSOIN project (http://itssoin.eu/) investigates the impact of the third sector and civic engagement on society, which goes beyond their economic benefits or the natural virtue of caring for others. To increase its validity, we used the Process-Tracing Methods (Beach and Pedersen 2013). According to this methodology, several types of data sources were used (among them semi-structured interviews). A comparative version of the case study, with other online financial education platforms of several countries (Czech Republic, Denmark, and Spain), can be consulted in Hyánek et al. (2016).

experiences. All networks that are part of REAS are involved in updating the platform with news and content, which has also enabled to extent the network of collaborating people to other parts of the world. In this case, the dynamic of implementation has followed a "bottom-up" logic, inasmuch as it has been boosted by nonprofit organizations highly involved in social problems, with the predisposition and involvement of citizens as well.

Economiasolidaria.org hosts more than 10,000 online contents, with around 300,000 different users and more than 30,000 total subscriptions. During the last years, the site has been the subject of a major renewal with the aim to provide a more personalized service and space for the portal encouraging an optimal connectivity through social networks and the adaptation to mobile devices in terms of responsiveness. Another goal for the renovation of the portal has been to define a specific section for financial education and for particularly advance financial education on responsible consumption activities.

According to this background, the economiasolidaria.org platform can be considered as a SI activity or project, to the extent that this website "(1) is oriented towards a social goal, aiming to satisfy or solve social problems; (2) is a collaborative process, involving different stakeholders; (3) implies an improvement in comparison with the previous situation; and (4) assumes an effective change in certain behaviors/social practices" (Alvarez-González et al. 2017: 27).

The case study of the economiasolidaria.org platform shows, first, how the principles and values that underlie the social marketing strategy of any current organization are very present in the implementation and sustainability of the platform. In addition, the importance of social marketing is also observed in the fact that several operative variables of this strategy had been key elements in the growth and the scope of the platform (visits, users, subscribers, etc.). We refer specifically to the design of the platform itself (product variable) and its implementation and dissemination through online channels (promotion and place variables). We develop further below this evidence in separate subsections.

Strategic Marketing

Strategically, REAS and its platform of financial education stand out for their high degree of market orientation and, consequently, by the adoption of the marketing concept. Specifically, the management of the platform is characterized by several of the key dimensions of the concept of marketing in the private nonprofit sector (Alvarez-González et al. 2002).

Firstly, this site is highly oriented to satisfy social needs of vulnerable groups or those at risk of exclusion, although ultimately the target of their actions is the society as a whole. This approach entails targeting socially vulnerable people, directly or through the organizations (mainly, small nonprofit organizations and, even, social firms) which integrate the network promoting the site. In addition, the site organization is fairly oriented to satisfy urgent or especially important social issues, even if this orientation carries some risks, and it advocates, with high intensity, for different politically neglected social issues and carries out the promotion of social activities (e.g., the organization of awareness campaigns or the promotion of specific policies). There is no doubt that the importance given to pro-social values (solidarity and caring for others and equality) is very high. Relationship with the main beneficiaries and stakeholders is direct; in other words, the site is clearly focused on improving the well-being and living conditions of their beneficiaries.

To achieve this high degree of orientation toward the social needs, the organizational management remains "quite" decentralized, since employees and volunteers can participate in organizational decisions related to (1) the design and development of ideas (to create new services, process, and/or structures) and (2) the implementation of projects and services. Also, the nonmanagerial employees can speak on behalf of the organization and participate in direct contact with external stakeholders, of course with prior authorization of managers.

Secondly, the platform is characterized by its external organizational openness, to the extent that their external stakeholders and beneficiaries are actively involved in many organizational decisions and in the development of projects and services. The external stakeholders actively participate in the following activities: (1) design and development of ideas, (2) implementation of projects and services, and (3) mobilization. The platform is heavily involved in projects in cooperation with other entities; the platform participates with them in formal or informal networks, and the managers are considering the external communication and the social networks (Facebook, Twitter, etc.) as a key concern for the organization. In recent times, the platform is actively engaged in policy dialogue with authorities, in order to participate in the design, monitoring, or evaluation of public policies, and as a result of the changes that are taking place in the regional governments of territories in which REAS has a strong presence (Madrid, Barcelona, Aragon, and some territories of Andalusia).

The site beneficiaries are involved in the same activities mentioned above for stakeholders, and they are also informed about the planned projects/services. In recent years, the exchange of information and knowledge with beneficiaries has increased (the site has a formal feedback channel) with the objective of empowering them. The site tries to enable her beneficiaries to (1) be able to act together toward achieving their objectives, (2) access to valuable resources, (3) control key aspects of their life, (4) participate in the community, and (5) be able to identify their problems, assess possible solutions, and act accordingly.

Thirdly, this site is embedded, directly or indirectly through its partners and/or activities, in their local/regional surrounding community. The site interacts with their key external stakeholders (partners, competitors, public regulators, etc.), being these networks of contacts very wide, heterogeneous, and interconnected. In this particular issue, REAS plays a central and essential role within her global network of contacts, not by her position of power, but by her central ideological position which provides cohesion to the members of the network. As a result, the relationship among REAS and the entities of the network (in terms of conflict resolution, equal sharing of costs and benefits among participants, personal relationships beyond just professional, constant rebalance of relations, etc.) is seen as "very good." They share the same language, objectives, values, and the ways of interpreting the reality.

Fourthly and lastly, the financial resources of the platform had been, mainly and almost exclusively (95%), own. Basically, the resources came from the dues paid by the organization networks that are part of REAS. However, as of 2015 the site financial structure begins to diversify with European public funding for a project (25% of annual income) and even private funding (5% of annual income). If this trend is confirmed, the site financial structure will be similar to the any Spanish nonprofit organizations, in which public funding has always had a significant weight. This same path toward diversification must also be assumed in terms of human resource management. Until now, the human resources of the site have low diversity from the point of view of academic training, professional experience, social characteristics, and contractual relationships, perhaps as a result of the small number of employees managing the site. Only some gender heterogeneity is identified in the organizations that are part of the platform, predominantly female.

"Product" Variable

The analysis of the web economiasolidaria.org from the point of view of marketing reveals how the platform, as a whole, is structured according to the basic benefit it intends to generate in its users: disseminate relevant information not so much about "traditional" financial education but about any informative input that might lead to a change toward a social and solidarity economy in this context. From this social basic benefit, the platform is organized into three main sections (Fig. 1):

1. News. In the first section, the most outstanding news of the Solidarity Economy is collected. approximately, a dozen of news per month, one every 2–3 days. In each case, its content is described and classified according to its source (mainly, some of the networks that are part of REAS) and its tag (banking or ethical finance, responsible consumption, fair trade, etc.).

Fig. 1 Economia Solidaria website. Source: economiasolidaria.org

Fig. 2 Corporate image of economiasolidaria.org. Source: economiasolidaria.org

2. Events. In this section, relevant information is loaded about conferences, workshops, training sessions, presentations, meetings, congress, etc. related to the key topics of the platform. Again, events are classified by organizing entity and type of activity.
3. Library. Finally, the users of the platform can download documents, reports, research, descriptive online videos, etc. on the same topics. The website has in both the main page and each one of its sections specific search engines that favor, as facilitating or convenience services, the search processes of contents and organizations made by the users.

In order to make the platform as valuable as possible for users, it has been equipped with other links that complement the information available in main sections. For example, the platform has specific links that help users understand what the principles that define solidarity-based economy, ethical finance, fair trade, responsible consumption, etc. are. It also has a direct link to the organization that promotes and manages the platform (REAS), and in the latest update, it was adapted to the recent changes in the socioeconomic environment including new contents on the web. For example, as a consequence of the recent period of economic crisis, this platform promotes, together with other representative organizations, new initiatives based on the idea of a new social market. This social market[2] is understood as (1) a network of production, distribution, and consumption of goods and services and (2) the result of a common learning process that works under ethical, participatory, ecological, and solidarity criteria in particular territories. The main objective is to create a network in which citizens can visualize in an integrated manner an endless number of products and services that have not been previously presented as the result of social and solidarity economy. This is intended to (1) enhance the visibility, viability, and sustainability of solidarity economy organizations and, especially, to create alternative circuits to conventional trade from the perspective of responsible consumption and (2) encourage the responsibility of each consumer, producer, or distributor to change the market. Financial market represents an important support for this social market initiative through the financial services of cooperatives, the investment funds of credit sections, or the solidarity bonds to cover financing needs.

Similarly, it is interesting to focus on the recent change in the corporate image of the platform (Fig. 2). On the one hand, strides have been made in trying to provide

---

[2] http://www.economiasolidaria.org/mercado_social

the platform its own personality and independence from the promoter entity (REAS), by eliminating a graphic representation in the form of network that identified this entity. On the other hand, the font of the platform name has been changed, highlighting in capital letters the name (ECONOMÍA SOLIDARIA/SOLIDARITY ECONOMY, in English) and changing its color from green to purple in order to emphasize the gender equality as a key principle of the platform.

"Promotion and Place" Variables

Economiasolidaria.org has been created by REAS with the communication as one of the main purposes upon which this organization provides services relating to:

1. The sharing agenda on network activities
2. Communication tools, such as a database of member entities; networking information; last news and relating events sections; and educational, instructional, and training materials such as reports, specific documents, literature references, and audiovisual tools
3. A specific section focused on responsible consumption with a social market database
4. An intranet including internal documentation and an extranet with public information on the activities performed by territorial networks and the state network
5. A monthly online solidarity economy newsletter

The type of financial education promoted and developed by REAS is different from the "top-down" model promoted by public and corporate institutions through their Financial Education National Plan.[3] In the case of economiasolidaria.org, the dynamic of implementation has been following a "bottom-up" logic. The aim is to encourage a different way of understanding the human relationships based in a collaborative and social economy. Thus, REAS, and consequently the economiasolidaria.org platform, is not focused solely on financial education but on anything that might encourage a change toward a fairer and more social economy, trying to generate a sole message and enhancing public awareness on basic issues (i.e., the use of money, among others) in order to develop a more solidarity society.

All the territorial and sectorial networks adhered are involved in updating the contents of the platform. In particular the financial section includes not only information and instructional materials to be used by citizens to improve their financial education but also makes visible the alternative ethical finances throughout the whole country and is being added to build broader proposals in a collective way. Therefore, financial education is being part of a more global project. Actually, the platform is generally perceived as an online space that provides information and mutual support to all member and nonmember entities and also to society by

---

[3]https://www.cnmv.es/DocPortal/Publicaciones/PlanEducacion/Planeducacion_een2en.pdf

extension. Furthermore, it is a space for exchanging ideas and experiences in the alternative financial services field, serving as both a meeting point for personal encounter and a bridge between business and social movements.

As aforementioned, cooperation among the member entities and territorial/sectorial networks is crucial for the regular development of the online platform. In this sense, economiasolidaria.org has been making possible the creation of alliances with other organizations that would have been otherwise impossible. The regular updating of the contents had also enabled to extend the range of the network to other parts of the world, in particular to Latin American countries.

Furthermore, the platform is being currently updated in terms of responsive design to new technological uses and demands given the virulence with which new technologies become obsolete. One of the objectives of this renewal is to improve the usability of the portal through mobile devices and also the interaction with potential users through the social media and networks. However, an important drawback of the potential usability of the economiasolidaria.org platform is relating to the fact that online contents are not accessible for the entire population (i.e., digital literacy inequality). In addition, another obstacle is related to the possible limits of virtual tools to the extent to which some collective projects still require the face-to-face interaction to generate network collaborations. Although virtual tools are essential in this case in particular, the organization promoter also considers that face-to-face relationships from specific social movements are also indispensable.

Conclusions

There is consensus among the main academic and professional associations of social marketing that this discipline "seeks to develop and integrate marketing concepts with other approaches to influence behaviors that benefit individuals and communities for the greater social good" (Boards of iSMA, ESMA and AASM 2013). In this context, the main conclusion of the case study of REAS, and its online financial education platform economiasolidaria.org, is that the core social marketing principles and concepts are key for developing and implementing socially innovative activities and projects by a CSO.

In particular, it is currently considered that the facilitation of personal and social good is the core necessary principle of all social marketing program (Boards of iSMA, ESMA, AASM and SMANA 2017). The reading of the case shows how the core principle of REAS and economiasolidaria.org is to encourage a different way of understanding the economy and the relationships based in a collaborative and social paradigm. To fulfill this principle, the platform tries to:

1. Influence the citizens' beliefs, attitudes, and opinions about the functioning of the economy and its agents.
2. Adopt a citizen-centered orientation by identifying his problems, developing solutions, and implementing them.

3. Develop value propositions via the social marketing intervention Mix (marketing-mix variables described in the case).
4. Gather relevant understanding about the potential users and beneficiaries of the platform.
5. Have influence on other stakeholders (such as other financial education platforms) that can condition the economic or financial behavior of citizens.
6. And all of this with a critical thinking, reflexivity, and ethical practice.

In short, REAS and economiasolidaria.org adopt in a high degree the six core concepts necessary in any current social marketing campaign or program, according to the latest debates or discussions about the present of the discipline (Boards of iSMA, ESMA, AASM and SMANA 2017). Likewise, REAS use commercial techniques to implement its core social marketing principle and concepts. Specifically, the development of the case study serves to underline how different key aspects in the design, use, and dissemination of the platform through online communication channels are adjusted to the design of any social service according to the current marketing-mix concept. These key aspects are, for example, (1) the platform structure in three main sections according to the basic social problem that justifies its origin and development or (2) the availability of a wide range of facilitating, convenience, or incremental additional sections that complement them. This is why REAS is a good illustrative example of how a CSO can encourage and promote a successful social innovation project by integrating the core principles, concepts, and techniques of the new social marketing.

Discussion Questions

1. Justify why the economiasolidaria.org platform can be considered a social innovation project according to the proposed definition in the case study.
2. Is the economiasolidaria.org platform really market oriented, as stated in the case study? Look for specialized literature and justify your answer.
3. Describe the product "economiasolidaria.org" from the point of view of the current concept of marketing, distinguishing between basic product and the increased service offer.
4. Design a communication strategy through social networks that can help to increase the number of users of economiasolidaria.org
5. Identify a CSO in your surrounding that in recent years has promoted projects or activities that can be considered as social innovations. Then, design an online social marketing campaign targeting potential beneficiaries and other key stakeholders.

References

Alvarez-González, L. I., Santos-Vijande, M. L., & Vázquez-Casielles, R. (2002). The market orientation concept in the private nonprofit organisation domain. *International Journal of Nonprofit and Voluntary Sector Marketing, 7*(1), 55–67.

Alvarez-González, L. I., García-Rodríguez, N., Rey-García, M., & Sanzo-Pérez, M. J. (2017). Análisis multidimensional del concepto de innovación social en las organizaciones no lucrativas españolas. Evidencias prácticas. *Revista Española del Tercer Sector, 36*, 23–48.

AMA. (2013). *Definition of marketing*. Retrieved from https://www.ama.org/AboutAMA/Pages/Definition-of-Marketing.aspx

Anheier, H. K., Krlev, G., Mildenberger, G., & Preuss, S. (2015). *Country selection for the ITSSOIN project*. Deliverable 2.4 of the project: 'Impact of the Third Sector as Social Innovation' (ITSSOIN), European Commission – 7th Framework Programme, Brussels: European Commission, DG Research. Retrieved from http://itssoin.eu/site/wp-content/uploads/2015/09/ITSSOIN_D2_4_Country-selection.pdf

Beach, D., & Pedersen, R. B. (2013). *Process-tracing methods: Foundations and guidelines*. Ann Arbor, MI: University of Michigan.

Boards of iSMA, ESMA and AASM. (2013). *Consensus definition of social marketing*. Retrieved from http://www.i-socialmarketing.org/assets/social_marketing_definition.pdf

Boards of iSMA, ESMA, AASM and SMANA. (2017). *Global consensus on social marketing principles, concepts and techniques*. Retrieved from http://www.europeansocialmarketing.org/wp-content/uploads/2017/08/ESMA-endorsed-Consensus-Principles-and-concepts-paper.pdf

Borzaga, C., & Bodini, R. (2012). *What to make of social innovation? Towards a framework for policy development* (Euricse Working Paper, N.036/12).

Hyánek, V., Navrátil, J., Placier, K., Akinyi, E. A., Figueroa, M., Alvarez Garcia, B., et al. (2016). *Social innovation in consumer protection in alternative financial services*. Deliverable 6.5 of the project: "Impact of the Third Sector as Social Innovation" (ITSSOIN), European Commission – 7th Framework Programme, Brussels: European Commission, DG Research. Retrieved from http://openarchive.cbs.dk/bitstream/handle/10398/9453/ITSSOIN_D6%203_20160901.pdf?sequence=1

Krlev, G., Anheier, H. K., & Mildenberger, G. (2019). Introduction: Social innovation – What is it and who makes it. In H. K. Anheier, G. Krlev, & G. Mildenberger (Eds.), *Social innovation. Comparative perspectives* (pp. 3–35). New York: Routledge.

Phillips, W., Lee, H., James, P., Ghobadian, A., & O'Regan, N. (2015). Social innovation and social entrepreneurship: A systematic review. *Group & Organization Management, 40*(3), 428–461.

Sakarya, S., Bodur, M. B., Yildirim-Öktem, Ö., & Selekler-Göksen, N. (2012). Social alliances: Business and social enterprise collaboration for social transformation. *Journal of Business Research, 65*(12), 1710–1720.

Spear, R. (2012). Innovation and collective entrepreneurship. *Universitas Forum: International Journal on Human Development and International Cooperation, 3*(2).

Van der Have, R. P., & Rubalcaba, L. (2016). Social innovation research: An emerging area of innovation studies? *Research Policy, 45*, 1923–1935.

The Social Role of Awareness Campaigns on Consumer Protection: An Extension of the Social Marketing Area

Ani Matei and Carmen Săvulescu

Abstract

The chapter presents the social marketing campaign "Ask the fiscal receipt!" as a case study for revealing the relevant contribution of consumers as actors of the fiscal policies.

The campaign developed in Romania since 2010 has powerful resonance, being compatible with practices in other European states or countries on other continents, namely, the Tax Lottery, as well as with the regional or continental policies on improving VAT collection, as a source of enhancing development and diminishing fiscal evasion.

The case study represents an example of an analysis on indirect social marketing, designed to highlight the necessity to involve the citizen within adjacent processes with impact on the general and individual welfare.

Learning Objectives
The chapter analyses the social marketing campaign "Ask the fiscal receipt!", developed in Romania in the context of broader international and European initiatives, dedicated to consumer protection through the stimulation of their actions as actors of the fiscal processes, thus triggering better tax collection and increasing individual welfare.

The study has the following objectives:

- Substantiating and formulating a general framework in view to present and evaluate, in general, the role of social campaigns concerning consumer protection and, in particular, their indirect impact on enhancing consumer welfare
- Identifying the types of strategies used in the implementation and delivery of the campaign *Ask the fiscal receipt!* in view to reach its objectives, highlighting the marketing mix and the type of informational approach
- Integrating the social marketing campaign from Romania within a comparative framework of other similar campaigns and emphasising the need for improvement and compatibility
- Presenting the impact of the campaign *Ask the fiscal receipt!* on the change of behaviour and attitude of consumers, as actors/part of the fiscal processes, with consequences on the general and individual welfare

Introduction

Worldwide, the preoccupations concerning consumer protection have been on the agenda of international bodies and organisations, such as the European Union (EU), Organisation for Economic Co-operation and Development (OECD), United Nations (UN), etc.

For the time being, the EU Action Programme for the consumer protection policy is based on two measures: the European Consumer Agenda, representing the new EU strategy for consumer protection according to the EU Strategy, Europe 2020, and the Consumer Programme 2014–2020, the financial framework. The European Consumer Agenda has four main objectives: improving consumer safety, enhancing knowledge, improving implementation, stepping up enforcement and securing redress, and aligning rights and policies to economic and societal change (Valant 2015: 1).

Proposing the development or maintaining of "a strong consumer protection policy" by national governments, as general principle, the UN (2003: 3) reveals at the same time "consumer education, including education on the environmental, social and economic impacts of consumer choice" as an adjacent principle.

In our opinion, this principle incorporates also the necessity of awareness campaigns, designed and operationalized by international or national bodies in the framework of their own social marketing programmes.

Complementary to those principles, OECD conceptualises and publishes complex regulations and directions on financial consumer protection, as a result of broad consultations and debates in the framework of G20. The document (OECD 2011: 6) states that "financial education and awareness" represent an important principle, encouraging "to implement the international principles and guidelines of financial education developed by the OECD International Network of Financial Education (INFE)".

In this context, the preoccupation of the national public authorities in several states is to ensure the adequate legislative framework, initiating normative deeds and actively participating in the update of the national legislation, thus aiming to ensure a high consumer protection degree on a fair competition market, for the consumers' benefit. At the same time, the NGOs are preoccupied to deliver social marketing campaigns, aimed at informing the consumers, taking measures to avoid safety risk, monitoring of product safety and traceability and coordinating campaigns in most cases together with the public institutions.

The current case study fits into those preoccupations on consumer financial education through social marketing campaigns, aimed to determine both the prevention and diminishing of fraud and fiscal evasion, and indirect consumer protection, by ensuring greater resources for social protection, enhancing welfare, etc.

Case Development

General Framework

In the latest two decades, an important initiative/instrument on reducing fiscal evasion and enhancing consumer protection, social security or welfare has been noticed.

We refer to the Tax Lottery, involving consumers in the processes of legal registration of the financial transactions and fair payment of the corresponding taxes and charges to the state.

"The idea of the lottery schemes is to provide consumers with an incentive to ask for a receipt. The incentive is that the receipt is not just a piece of paper documenting the transaction made, but serves as a (potential) lottery ticket, giving consumers eligibility to participate in a tax lottery" (EU 2015: 3).

Analysing and undertaking the experience on the design and operationalisation of the Tax Lottery campaign, the National Association for Consumer Protection and Promotion of Programs and Strategies from Romania (ANPCPPSR) launched in October 2010 the campaign "Ask the fiscal receipt!", with a duration of 1000 days, aimed at better educating the population on fiscal issues.

In April 2015, the National Association for Consumer Protection and Promotion of Programs and Strategies from Romania-InfoCons launched the National Campaign "Ask the fiscal receipt!" section "Pay by card!".

In the same context, in 2015, the Ministry of Public Finance implemented several measures to fight against fiscal evasion. The lottery of fiscal receipts is the most successful one, being organised also nowadays.

We notice that this information and education campaign is supported both by the non-governmental organisations and the public institutions. The lottery of fiscal receipts represents a measure of active population involvement in combating fiscal evasion.

Fiscal evasion constitutes the consequence of illegal facts, based on the following factors: imperfections of the law; non-uniformity in the activity of the financial bodies concerning the establishment and charging of taxes; conduct of several categories of tax payers; and lack of exigency or corruption of civil servants (Amarita 2017: 6).

Taking into consideration its objectives, organisation and finality, the campaign "Ask the fiscal receipt!" is integrated within similar above-mentioned initiatives. Complementarily, the campaign in Romania has involved, to a large extent, non-governmental organisations, media and private financial entities, such as the banks.

The Tax Lottery: An International Perspective

Various initiatives in the practices of states as China, Brazil, Portugal, Malta, Slovakia, Greece and Georgia aim to valorise the potential consumer contribution and involvement in the fiscal processes corresponding to the value added tax (VAT) collection and to the fight against fiscal evasion.

Naritomi (2013) uses a suggestive expression on consumer and government involvement in monitoring the companies and tax collection. This expression refers to "consumers as tax auditors", including also other initiatives for administrative-fiscal databases creation and consumer involvement by the Tax Lottery.

The European Commission (2015) provides a relevant synthesis, aimed at "improving VAT compliance", which comprises information and analyses on initiatives similar to the Tax Lottery (Table 1).

The modalities for Tax Lottery organisation are similar, but there are differences concerning the public or private institutions involved.

Table 1 Use of the Tax Lottery initiative in some European states

State	Year of introducing the Tax Lottery	Open problems
Malta	1997	• The eligibility of foreigners to the lottery • The further use of receipts by the tax authorities • The data that is collected in the process and what it is used for
Slovakia	2013	• Cross check of fiscal receipts • Highlighting the "problematic candidates" for fiscal evasion • The data that is collected and what it is used for
Portugal	2014	• Situation of returned products • Storage of consumer data
Georgia	2012	• The lottery impact was not rigorously evaluated due to simultaneous introduction of several fiscal measures

Source: European Commission (2015: 12–16, 18–21)

Methodology

The empirical and qualitative methodological research has been structured in several parts:

- Describing the way of organisation and delivery of the campaign in Romania and its integration, based on a comparative study, in the general context of similar initiatives from Europe and other continents, delivered under the aegis of Tax Lottery
- Study and analysis of the marketing methods used in implementing the campaign in Romania
- Revealing the consumer perception through a relevant survey, structured on categories of consumers in Romania
- General description of the campaign impact and revealing the contents of the "indirect impact" in the framework of the social marketing campaigns dedicated to consumer protection

Consumer Perception

Research Design In view to reach the research objectives, we have applied a questionnaire concerning the citizens' fiscal behaviour.

Defining the Sample We used the non-probabilistic sampling technique, more specifically, convenience sampling. The questionnaire was applied to the citizens from Bucharest, Romania's capital, 18–80 years of age. The questionnaire results were used to perform a descriptive study.

Data Collection The questionnaire initially identified the respondents' sex and age and also comprised seven questions, designed to determine the respondents' perceptions concerning the importance of releasing the fiscal receipt by traders. Thus, we aimed to identify the citizens' fiscal behaviour, as well as the impact of the campaigns developed by the National Association for Consumer Protection and Promotion of Programs and Strategies from Romania.

Data collection took place in the period 25 January–28 February 2018.

235 online questionnaires were applied and all were validated.

Results 73.8% of the respondents were female, and 26.2% were male. Concerning the age, 59.4% of the respondents are 18–30 years of age, 21.8% are 31–40 years of age, 13.7% are 41–50 years of age and 5.1% are over 51 years old. The study is focused on these variables, given the absence from the previous analyses of other variables, such as income, profession, level of education, etc.

Concerning the question "As a consumer, do you know your rights? Do you consider that the public organisations focused on consumer protection should implement more awareness campaigns?", the responses were as follows: 5.6% of the respondents know their rights and do not feel the need of awareness campaigns on consumer rights; 62.4% know their rights, but the awareness campaigns on consumer rights are welcome; 30.8% do not know their rights, and the awareness campaigns on consumer rights are welcome; while 1.3% do not know well their rights and are not interested in the awareness campaigns on consumer rights.

At the same time, for the question "When you go shopping, do you take the fiscal receipt from the seller?", 54.3% responded yes, always; 43.6% responded yes, sometimes; and 2.1% responded negative.

For the question "If the seller does not give you the fiscal receipt after you pay the products/services, do you ask for it?", the responses were as follows.

Answers	%
Always	27.4
Only for valuable shopping	25.2
Sometimes	38.5
No	9

And for the question concerning the reason for taking/requiring the fiscal receipt, the responses were as follows.

Answers	%
It is normal that everyone pays taxes	26.3
To have evidence of payment	72.8
Lottery of fiscal receipts	0.5
I do not ask it	0.4

Taking into consideration the above responses, we see that over half of the respondents exhibit taxation-centred behaviour.

The Campaign "Ask the Fiscal Receipt!": From Concept to Accomplishment

In 2010, the National Association for Consumer Protection and Promotion of Programs and Strategies (NACPPPS) President explained that the campaign comprised two parts, the first for promoting the things achieved with the money paid by taxes and charges and the second to explain the effects of asking a fiscal receipt, as well as the reversed situation. He stated that the campaign should last 1000 days, aiming especially at the pupils from pre-university education, respectively, the 11th and 12th grade, the elderly and the employees in financial banking institutions.

In 2015, ANPCPPSR launched the National Campaign "Ask the fiscal receipt!" section "Pay by card!". Payment by card means taxation of transactions, especially to reduce the possibility to purchase counterfeit or smuggling products, the citizen's safety when purchasing products/services derived from a chain of traceability, monitored and controlled, as well as the existence of a proof for claiming material or moral losses in case of a complaint.

The objective of the campaign in 2015 was to make aware and to educate the citizens, as European consumers, on purchasing safe products, enhancing their trust in the Romanian market, taking also into consideration that most citizens receive their salary on the card, and they withdraw high amounts of money from ATMs for buying products and services that could be non-taxable, unsafe and untrusted.

In the framework of the campaign "Ask the fiscal receipt!", informational, educational and supportive materials have been made (TV advertisements, posters, flyers) for the citizens. Analysing those materials, we notice that the campaign was based on development of knowledge, information in view to enable the change of behaviour, to develop a new one, to modify and/or to support it in any circumstance. The campaign is focused on pertinent information. At the same time, the campaign has addressed the target group with problematic behaviour that should be changed, as well as the target group with positive behaviour that should be encouraged and supported.

The strategy of the campaign "Ask the fiscal receipt!" was an induction one: the attitudes are positive, but socially desirable behaviour does not carry it out. The objective of the strategy is to try to induce the accomplishment of that behaviour (Santesmases Mestre 1999). Its actions aimed at education and information, in order to encourage the target group to ask the fiscal receipt, if it is not issued, and to encourage the payment by card, in order to avoid such situations.

In order to reduce the number of traders who do not issue fiscal receipts, not as direct outcome of the campaign, the public authorities in Romania are performing controls at their headquarters and "punish" them for not issuing the fiscal receipt.

An Analysis of the Social Marketing Contents

The campaign uses the 4 Ps—product, price, place and promotion (Kotler et al. 2002).

In the framework of the campaign "Ask the fiscal receipt!", information is the product, the cost of informing aimed at the change of consumer's fiscal behaviour is the price. The cost comprises intangible prices, as well as the social cost, i.e. the risk to be perceived as different in the age group.

The place refers to the location of the campaign "Ask the fiscal receipt!", delivered in places of interest for consumers, such as working places of companies or by channels of distribution, such as television, written media and websites of the public institutions.

The promotional activities of the campaign "Ask the fiscal receipt!" include advertisements on television channels, websites, printed materials and events (the lottery of fiscal receipts).

The promotional materials and activities enabling the adoption of the desired behaviour have been as follows:

- Broadcasting advertisements by television, produced with the supervision of the Ministry of Public Finance
- Flyers
- Posters, displayed at the working places of companies
- *TelVerde* service of the Ministry of Public Finance
- Organisation of the lottery of fiscal receipts since July 2015

The lottery of fiscal receipts consists in the random draw of numbers, in order to award prizes in money to resident or non-resident persons in Romania, holders of fiscal receipts, thus certifying the purchase of goods and services on the territory of Romania.[1]

The Impact of the "Ask the Fiscal Receipt!" Campaign

In 2015, the Minister of Public Finance stated that "the organisation of the Lottery of fiscal receipts would determine a positive impact, by enhancing company compliance concerning the enforcement of the legal provisions in the area of cash registers with electronic logbook. The Lottery of fiscal receipts would contribute to combating unfair competition, especially for the companies that do not achieve fair taxation. The Lottery of fiscal receipts is embodied in a broader package together with cash registers with electronic logbook. We hope that since 2015 the evasion would decrease by 5% annually".

Referring to the questionnaire, and especially to the questions aiming the impact of the social marketing campaign "Ask the fiscal receipt!", for the following two questions, the answers were as follows.

Questions	Affirmative answer (%)	Negative answer (%)
"Do you know the campaign, ask the fiscal receipt, delivered by the public institutions/NGOs?"	44	56
"Do you believe that the actual awareness campaigns for asking the fiscal receipt are efficient?"	70.5	29.5

---

[1] Ministry of Public Finance, http://www.mfinante.ro/loteriabonurilor.html?pagina=loteriabonurilor

For the question: "Has the 'Ask the fiscal receipt!' campaign influenced your behaviour?", the responses were as follows.

Answers	%
Yes, now I always ask for the fiscal ticket	13.7
Yes, I often ask the fiscal ticket	28.8
No	57.5

Conclusions

Through the social marketing campaign "Ask the fiscal receipt!", Romania has made its anti-evasion practices and measures compatible with those in other European states and, of course, with the policies developed in this field by the European Union.

As in other areas of social life, the citizen, as consumer, becomes an important actor in sustaining an objective of social and economic development, based on the results of fiscal policies.

Before introducing this initiative, in Romania, the fiscal evasion had reached 16.2% of GDP, of which 12.2% derived just from VAT.

The rigorous evaluation of the impact of the social marketing campaign is hard to be performed, as, simultaneously, other measures aimed at diminishing fiscal evasion were introduced: reorganisation of the National Agency for Fiscal Administration (ANAF), introducing the cash registers with electronic logbook, etc.

However, as noticed by a recent report of the Fiscal Council in Romania, during 2014–2016, the index of efficiency for VAT collection increased from 0.65% to 0.77%, while the revenues from VAT were in the beginning of 2017 smaller by 1.1% than those in 2016 (Fiscal Council 2017: 51).

The campaign "Ask the fiscal receipt!" represents an indirect social marketing campaign, its impact on the citizen being the outcome of the redistribution of additional revenues, often influencing the general social welfare. In fact, this aspect has also led to the difficulty of the rigorous evaluation of its impact.

The possible discussion issues on the conceptualisation, operationalisation and finality of the campaign could be partially found among the open questions revealed by similar campaigns (Table 1).

Referring just to the social marketing campaign "Ask the fiscal receipt!", some issues derive from the empirical research of the current case study; 56% of the respondents did not know the campaign, while 67% did not consider it to be a factor for influencing their behaviour.

In this context, referring to the analysed campaign, as an instrument of financial education, in consensus with the statements of the first part of this chapter, persuasion in its promotion remains a problem without an adequate response.

Comparing the campaign from Romania with campaigns from other European states, we could not find an answer as to how the respondent's personal data is used.

We may also add the difficulty of evaluating the impact, the cost-effectiveness analysis, as well as technical aspects during its development.

Discussion Questions

1. The study presented has finality in the financial and economic education of the citizens. Does this represent a solid argument to consider the campaign as an example of indirect social marketing?
2. Considering that you agree without statements, can you also identify other finalities of the campaign, such as the reduction of corruption or fiscal evasion?
3. What could be the complementary statistical variables meant to lead to a deeper analysis of the impact and manner of organising the campaign?

References

Amarita, A. (2017). Evaziunea fiscala in Romania. *Romanian Statistical Review – Supplement nr. 1*, 3–21.
European Commission. (2015). *Improving VAT compliance – Random awards for tax compliance – Report of DG Taxation and Customs Union (TAXUD) and Joint Research Centre (JRC)*. Office for Official Publications of the European Communities, Luxembourg.
Fiscal Council. (2017). *Annual report*. Retrieved from http://www.consiliulfiscal.ro/RA2016roiunie2017.pdf
Kotler, P., Roberto, N., & Lee, N. (2002). *Social marketing, improving the quality of life* (2nd ed.). London: Sage.
Ministry of Public Finance. Retrieved from http://www.mfinante.ro/loteriabonurilor.html? pagina loteriabonurilor
Naritomi, J. (2013). *Consumers as tax auditors*, Harvard University. Retrieved from https://www.sbs.ox.ac.uk
National Association for Consumer Protection and Promoting the Programs and Strategies from Romania (NACPPPS) – InfoCons. Retrieved from www.protectia-consumatorilor.ro
National Authority for Consumer Protection. Retrieved from http://www.anpc.gov.ro
OECD. (2011). *High-level principles on financial consumer protection*. Retrieved from https://www.oecd.org/g20/topics/financial-sector-reform/48892010.pdf
Santesmases Mestre, M. (1999). *Marketing. Conceptos y Estrategias*. Madrid: Piramide.
United Nations. (2003). Guidelines on Consumer Protection, Department of Economic and Social Affairs, New York. Retrieved from http://www.un.org/esa/sustdev/publications/consumption_en.pdf
Valant, J. (2015). *Consumer protection in the EU, policy overview*, European Parliamentary Research Service – EPRS. Retrieved from http://www.europarl.europa.eu/RegData/etudes/IDAN/2015/565904/EPRS_IDA(2015)565904_EN.pdf

Part IV
Social Marketing Cases: Safety and Security

Preventing Youth Violence in El Salvador: A Relational Social Marketing Model

Reynaldo Rivera

Abstract

In 2015 a partnership of two Italian and three Salvadorian NGOs launched "Niños Protagonistas" Project (NPP, www.ninosprotagonistas.org), ["Protagonist Children", in English], an integrated social marketing programme based on a relational model and financed by the Italian Government. Spanning across five Salvadorian cities, this programme intended to prevent and reduce teenagers' involvement in *maras* (gangs). NPP used segmentation, integrated communications and marketing mix strategies to engage 908 youths and 287 teenagers, the latter throughout this 3-year project. With an ecological strategy including the environmental systems with which children interact, the campaign reached out to hundreds of parents, women and relevant stakeholders in order to promote a culture of inclusion and interpersonal peace, diminishing institutional and intrafamily violence. In addition to its international outlook, the NPP case would help researchers, practitioners and policy-makers to apply social marketing principles and models to promote inclusion and social capital, especially among young people.

R. Rivera (✉)
School of Communication, Austral University, Buenos Aires, Argentina

InterMedia Social Innovation, Rome, Italy

University of Navarra, Pamplona, Spain
e-mail: rrivera@austral.edu.ar

© Springer Nature Switzerland AG 2019
M. M. Galan-Ladero, H. M. Alves (eds.), *Case Studies on Social Marketing*, Management for Professionals, https://doi.org/10.1007/978-3-030-04843-3_17

Learning Objectives
In this case study, learners have an opportunity to:

1. Learn about social marketing strategies to diminish interpersonal violence in urban settings
2. Identify best practices
3. Understand how to design, implement and evaluate an integrated marketing programme for social development
4. Build knowledge on social marketing applied to human rights issues
5. Acquire know-how about the application of marketing mix strategies in Latin America

This chapter starts with a literature review, followed by an explanation of the social marketing model and strategy for youth violence prevention in El Salvador, with a focus on youth engagement and growth.

Introduction

Individuals use violence for different reasons: to influence others, to express discontent about unfair situations and regimes, to compensate the lack of positive social and family support (ERIC 2001), etc. Regardless of individuals' motivations, interpersonal violence is a challenge that requires effective societal interventions intended to prevent it or at least minimize its damages, especially among children and youths.

Different strategies have been pursued to fight and reduce violence, from the use of states' police powers to educational programmes. In this massive and long-term social endeavour, interactive social media and social marketing strategies allow prevention programmes to reach effectively wider audiences. However, a small number of programmes are scientifically designed and evaluated (Jewkes et al. 2015), and only a few focus on reducing domestic violence and violence against women and girls relying on social marketing principles and strategies (Lefebvre 2013). This gap proves serious, as a boomerang effect or backlash in a project of this kind would lead to an increase in homicides or social conflicts. Furthermore, planning, implementation and evaluation teams are often isolated and do not create synergies between each other.

El Salvador has the world's fourth highest murder rates (41.2 per 100,000 inhabitants). *Maras* (gangs) and repressive public security strategies implemented by the government (like the "iron fist" or "*mano dura*" approach) stand out as relevant factors in this setting. Yet, interpersonal and family violence, especially against women and children, in a context characterized by poverty and limited educational and professional opportunities are also higher than in other countries.

After years doing research in El Salvador, an Italian NGO based in Rome and focused on youth positive development and participation, InterMedia, identified two interrelated major challenges for Salvadorian children and young people: an increasing adoption among teenagers of risky lifestyles and early engagement in urban gangs (*maras*).

Based on scientific evidence and models, the project team formulated and deployed a character development programme as its key educational resource. This programme included the creation of two youth-led committees, a scientific support group, training sessions for community leaders and families, and nine experts' meetings. Peer mentoring, social media and impact evaluation methods were used during the whole campaign. NPP also features an online programme for future journalists, another for the police department and professional training and development for young women. These training activities were developed to produce a positive impact at social meso-level and create a child-friendly culture and institutions.

Motivated by its organizational mission and following the intervention mapping model (Bartholomew et al. 1998), InterMedia conducted a literature review to identify evidence and best practices that finally guided the child-centred design of Niños Protagonistas (Protagonist Children) Project.

Niños Protagonistas Project (NPP): Gang Prevention Best Practices and Models

Several studies have pointed out predictor factors for urban gang involvement that span the main social development dimensions: family, peer group, school, individual characteristics and community conditions (Brenneman 2011, 2015; Covey 2010). They have highlighted the multidimensional nature of the phenomena and the influence of experiences like interfamilial violence, rape and forced migrations, poverty and social exclusion, social shame and the need for protective environments to replace the lack of a stable family.

Exploring datasets that analyse US-based projects, InterMedia selected, among those that qualified as effective and promising, three evidence-based and scientifically assessed programmes: the Phoenix Curriculum (TPC), Gang Resistance Education and Training (GREAT) and Big Brothers Big Sisters of America (BBBS).

Although GREAT's evaluations revealed statistically significant positive effects on gang membership and acceptance (Esbensen et al. 2011), only TPC and BBBS have a theoretical model of reference and an evidence-based design: they apply the transtheoretical model of change (Prochaska et al. 1992) and social control theory, respectively (McGill 1997).

In Canada, local governments applied the Ottawa Gang Strategy and the End Gang Life Initiative. Both combined different activities (YouDecide and outreach worker programmes, training events, booklet and poster distribution, radio ads, etc.) and two theoretical perspectives: the former used the life course approach (Moule et al. 2013) and community organization and community building approach, while the latter relied on the Transactional Model of Stress and Coping (Glanz et al. 2008).

Although a few programmes feature evidence-based design and evaluations, the NPP team could not identify any using social and integrated marketing strategies, which would improve their results and impact and facilitate their replication in developing countries, especially among special targets like children and teenagers.

NPP Model of Change

The best practices reviewed as well as those used to reduce violence against women and girls or to work with adolescents who engage in violent behaviours provided InterMedia with relevant insights to start a second stage of social marketing intervention design, choosing its change objective and theoretical model. The next project should approach the reduction of teenagers' engagement in *maras* through an adapted relational version of the transtheoretical model of change, based on the positive youth development 5Cs model (Lerner et al. 2005) and community participation. Lerner's 5Cs model considers that positive development (which focuses on strengths rather than weaknesses) involves interpersonal competence, self-efficacy or confidence, positive relationships, character and compassion or empathy.

The life course approach, adopted by WHO Regional Office for Europe as an essential step towards the goals and targets in the United Nations 2030 Agenda for Sustainable Development, zeroes in on the cumulative effect of experiences and social transitions, as well as the influence of social and cultural contexts. Adverse socioeconomic conditions in childhood and exposure to traumatic events like violence influence personal health and development. Therefore, the new social marketing programme should reach parents and adults that participate in teenagers' socialization process (e.g. teachers and social workers), raise their awareness about the relevance of transition phases into adulthood and increase their knowledge on positive parenting and education.

The life course approach is consistent with COCB: community involvement and participation improve perceived control, empowerment and individual coping capacity. The intervention may increase critical consciousness and capacities to identify and solve problems in beneficiaries' communities of reference. The United Nations Convention on the Rights of the Child (UNCRC) and InterMedia's experience in Eurochild network provided valuable insights on this topic.

UNCRC and documented best practices underscore the relevance of youth participation in behavioural change processes. In fact, BBBS promotes mentoring programmes which are "... based on the premise that a predictable, consistent relationship with a stable, competent adult can help youth to cope with and avoid a high-risk lifestyle" (McGill 1997, p. 55). A stable relationship with a positive, properly screened and trained role model (an adult or older youth) could improve social relationships and socialization outcomes—a notion also supported by the social control theory that stresses the influence of relationships, participation in conforming activities and social values to help people to avoid deviance (Roberts et al. 2011). The assistance of a mentor in the socialization process would contribute to changing misperceptions of social norms, encouraging better and protective behaviours (Fabiano et al. 2003).

Recent studies have revealed both the usefulness (for reducing men's violence against intimate partners) and the limitations (to reduce the use of cannabis among adolescents) of the transtheoretical (TTM) or stages of change (SOC) model. Developed by Prochaska et al. (1992), this model considers change as a process that starts with personal precontemplation and guides the individual through

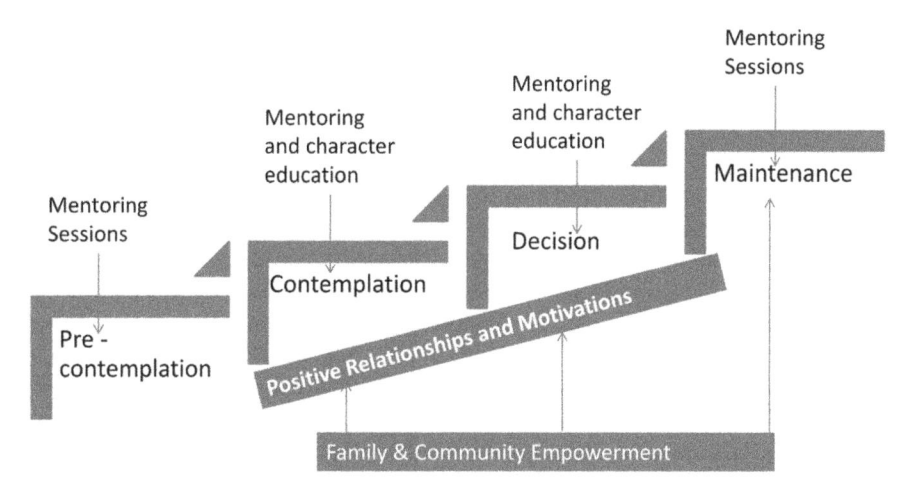

Fig. 1 Revised transtheoretical model of change. Source: Author

contemplation and decision to action and maintenance, with motivation for change as a key success factor throughout this process.

Based on its literature review, InterMedia's team decided to design a revised TTM geared to generating positive experiences and internal motivation via interpersonal relationships (see Fig. 1), including character building in a mentoring programme carried out by older youths, in combination with parents and community participation, as well as empowerment interventions. During mentoring sessions, young peers help teenagers to learn positive habits and skills, to understand the importance of school for personal and future development, to practice positive problem-solving strategies and to change their attitudes towards negative role models in *maras* and other deviant social groups.

The NPP Social Marketing Intervention Design

While InterMedia had experience in behavioural change projects, it needed a partner with a recognized track record on social projects like NPP. In 2014, ELIS NGO joined InterMedia to design an intervention in El Salvador. After identifying reliable partners (Fundación Actúa, Fundación ICEF and Fundación Siramá), InterMedia and ELIS made an initial qualitative assessment of local programmes. Once they confirmed their compatibility with the proposed theoretical model, they started to look for funding. In this project, fundraising was not driven primarily by financial reasons: considering the integrated marketing and communications framework (Kliatchko and Schultz 2014), the partnership decided that the process of securing the necessary resources would play a key role in project design. In fact, it accounted for a learning experience that validated and refined (not only limited) the theoretical model based on public interests, donors' experiences and stakeholders' recommendations, since they provided information on previous interventions and relevant feedback on the future program. As a result, fundraising activities facilitated the co-creation of shared value between the project and its stakeholders throughout its phases.

The NPP partnership submitted two funding requests. Only the second was approved (by the Italian Foreign Office or MAECI). The project started in February 2015 and ended in 2018. After the proposal was approved, InterMedia established the marketing strategy and mix.

This intervention's primary target audiences were (1) schooled adolescents (ages 10 through 16) living in El Salvador's largest cities (San Salvador, La Libertad, San Miguel, Santa Ana, Sonsonate, San Martín and Usulután) and (2) young volunteers (18–29 years old) living in those cities. Secondary audiences included (1) adolescents' parents (especially mothers) and teachers, (2) social workers, (3) journalists and NGO practitioners and (4) law enforcement personnel. Key audience insights informed the development of marketing mix strategies.

The brand, promotional materials and online platforms (webpage, Facebook and YouTube profiles) were designed following IMC principles. All of them focused on the same message: the centrality of primary targets' participation and development as the main path for violence prevention. Accordingly, children and youths, stakeholders and parents participated actively in the design, production and distribution of leaflets, videos, etc. Awareness-raising campaigns using a gaining framework (a shared responsibility for peace building and children's development) were launched in social media and promoted through offline events, like the 2017 Family Run organized by Fundación ICEF, training sessions for policy-makers and practitioners, experts' meetings and an online diploma for young journalists on how to cover and communicate social crises.

The marketing mix strategies to achieve NPP's objectives included partnerships and:

(a) Product: Youth target audiences were encouraged, mainly at universities and other social organizations, to join a 1-year volunteering programme for children's character development, intended to help the latter to improve their social and emotional skills. NPP offered training and personal mentorship for volunteers as well as an accreditation recognized by local universities. Schools were offered 3-year, free-of-charge international training for their students, which complemented their curricula. Teenagers were invited to spend some of their free time at school, attending a programme that may help them, through the assistance of a young mentor, to enhance their academic performance. Programme enrolment was completely free and required parental consent. Mentorship sessions started by building a trust-based atmosphere and talking about school assignments and leisure activities. Depending on the pace of individual relationships, mentors tried to spark some interest (precontemplation) on positive behaviours, like planning, time management, goal setting, etc. After a few weeks, usually there was enough trust between mentor and mentee to deal with issues like interpersonal violence and behavioural change (contemplation). Mentors and students built a personal relationship during an academic year,

which proved very valuable for parents and teachers, as they reported adolescents' progress in academic and social–emotional dimensions. Those products were complemented with training programmes for teachers, social workers, practitioners, single mothers and parents.
(b) Place: Schooling is high among Salvadorian adolescents, at least until they turn 16. Schools provide relatively protected environments, but their neighbourhoods' limits are established arbitrarily by *maras'* leaders. Adults and children cannot ignore them: they cannot move from one "sector" to another without risking their lives. Thus, at urban schools, partners could meet programme's targets, including parents and practitioners, but the limitations imposed by gangs on people's mobility amounted to a serious problem that reduced adult engagement—especially among fathers—in training sessions.
(c) Promotion: NPP could not ignore the fact that gangs might regard its messages as a menace for their recruiting goals and influence. Beneficiaries' and mentors' safety would be at risk if gangs viewed the programme as curtailing their operations. Therefore, partners and mentors did not use keywords like *maras* or *mareros* in public, sticking to terms that expressed a benefit for teenagers' academic performance (which is valuable even for those who lead the *maras*). To identify themselves, mentors used special T-shirts that read, "United for Childhood" and featured the logos of MAECI and partners. Empowerment of women, peace, forgiveness, children's rights, assisted study sessions, virtues, character, positive development and participation were the key concepts used for promotional communications. Unknown parents, youth and children, who did not live in local communities, were portrayed in the campaign. Young volunteers and local NGOs' networks (offline and online) were used as promotional platforms that disseminated information about events and training meetings, using digital leaflets and short videos.
(d) Price: NPP offered free tutoring and sports activities organized by Fundación Actúa as incentives for children to join the programme. Young people were interested on the training and university credits that they would receive for their volunteering service. A few of them were selected as coordinators and enjoyed small financial and nonfinancial benefits.

Parents, women, teachers, social workers, police officers and journalists that participated in the training sessions received materials and a diploma issued by two educational institutions: ICEF and SIRAMA foundations. Women were provided with nonfinancial support to launch their own businesses.

Project Execution, Monitoring and Outcomes

NPP pursued its marketing strategy following an ecological process (see Fig. 2) that reached secondary targets through primary ones: children and youth were key influencers. The campaign used teaching and training materials produced by the

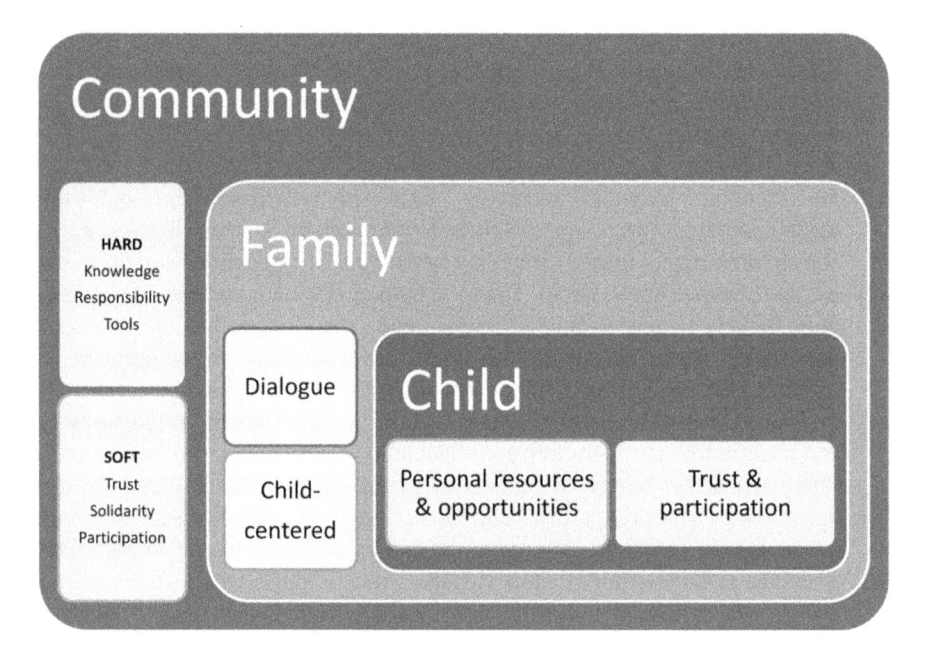

Fig. 2 NPP ecological process. Source: Author

partnership and shared online with trainers and mentors via closed Facebook and WhatsApp groups.

ELIS and InterMedia assisted local partners using online conference services and monitoring trips, which had three main goals: aligning partners' operations with the project's logic framework, conducting capacity-building sessions for management and staff and expanding the program's stakeholder network with experts' meetings, round tables and seminars.

InterMedia crafted several monitoring and research tools that allowed partners to collect data on programme participants as well as to oversee their involvement. The project used QuestionPro's platform, combined with other research software (like NVivo and QDAMiner) to monitor project progress. This evaluation process included surveys for 741 youths and 536 children, as well as a weekly report (7529 records). The baseline information about major targets and the monitoring dashboard provided valuable insights on children's and youths' lifestyles, which were used to adapt the contents to audiences' behaviours. Results were both informative and encouraging: the campaign increased children's self-esteem, conflict management capabilities and positive relationships in peer groups while reducing *maras* engagement by 75%, the number of students carrying knives to school by 13% and violent behaviours by 38%. Based on qualitative data, NPP also improved young mentors' social–emotional and leadership skills.

Conclusions

NPP is a case study that shows the relevance and positive impact of marketing mix and integrated communications strategies to curb interpersonal violence in developing countries. It confirms not only the importance of applying evidence-based theoretical models in social marketing but also their positive impact on communities' capability building. Primary targets' (children and teenagers) active engagement served as a cornerstone strategy for this successful campaign. By design, NPP promoted ongoing interactions among programme staff, mentors and beneficiaries. The flux of data supplied by online dashboards improved monitoring, enhancing the partnership's continuous learning and the project's efficacy.

Discussion Questions

1. Is NPP improving violence prevention policies? Do you think that the applied theoretical model is somehow related with its effectiveness? Why?
2. How were marketing mix strategies applied in the NPP case? Which IMC principles were used in this programme? Which are the commonalities between IMC and the model of change applied in NPP?
3. Does NPP's model seem like a good strategy to reduce crime? Why?
4. How relevant are relationships and participation of young people in NPP's social marketing strategy?

References

Bartholomew, L. K., Parcel, G. S., & Kok, G. (1998). Intervention mapping: A process for developing theory and evidence-based health education programs. *Health Education & Behavior, 25*(5), 545–563. https://doi.org/10.1177/109019819802500502.

Brenneman, R. (2011). *Homies and Hermanos: God and gangs in Central America*. New York: OUP.

Brenneman, R. (2015). Wrestling the devil: Conversion and exit from central American gangs. *Latin American Research Review, 49*, 112–128. https://doi.org/10.1353/lar.2014.0062.

Covey, H. C. (2010). *Street gangs throughout the world* (2nd ed.). Springfield, IL: Charles C Thomas.

ERIC, IDESO, IDIES, IUDOP. (2001). *Maras y pandillas en Centroamérica. Pandillas y capital social* (Vols. 1–5). Managua: UCA Publicaciones.

Esbensen, F.-A., Peterson, D., Taylor, T. J., Freng, A., Osgood, D. W., Carson, D. C., & Matsuda, K. N. (2011). Evaluation and evolution of the gang resistance education and training (G.R.E.A.T.) program. *Journal of School Violence, 10*(1), 53–70. https://doi.org/10.1080/15388220.2010.519374.

Fabiano, P., Perkins, H. W., Berkowitz, A., Linkenbach, J., & Stark, C. (2003). Engaging men as social justice allies in ending violence against women: Evidence for a social norms approach. *Journal of American College Health, 52*(3), 105–112. https://doi.org/10.1080/07448480309595732.

Glanz, K., Rimer, B. K., & Viswanath, K. (2008). *Health behavior and health education: Theory, research, and practice*. San Francisco, CA: Jossey-Bass.

Jewkes, R., Flood, M., & Lang, J. (2015). From work with men and boys to changes of social norms and reduction of inequities in gender relations: A conceptual shift in prevention of violence against women and girls. *The Lancet, 385*(9977), 1580–1589. https://doi.org/10.1016/S0140-6736(14)61683-4.

Kliatchko, J. G., & Schultz, D. E. (2014). Twenty years of IMC. *International Journal of Advertising, 33*(2), 373–390. https://doi.org/10.2501/IJA-33-2-373-390.

Lefebvre, R. C. (2013). *Social marketing and social change: Strategies and tools for improving health, well-being, and the environment*. Hoboken, NJ: Wiley.

Lerner, R. M., Lerner, J. V., Almerigi, J. B., Theokas, C., Phelps, E., Gestsdottir, S., et al. (2005). Positive youth development, participation in community youth development programs, and community contributions of fifth-grade adolescents findings from the first wave of the 4-H study of positive youth development. *The Journal of Early Adolescence, 25*(1), 17–71. https://doi.org/10.1177/0272431604272461.

McGill, D. E. (1997). *Blueprints for violence prevention: Big Brothers Big Sisters of America*. Center for the Study and Prevention of violence, Institute for Behavioral Sciences, University of Colorado, Boulder.

Moule, R. K., Decker, S. H., Pyrooz, D. C., Decker, S. H., & Moule, R. K. (2013). Social capital, the life-course, and gangs. In *Handbook of life-course criminology* (pp. 143–158). New York: Springer. doi:https://doi.org/10.1007/978-1-4614-5113-6_9.

Prochaska, J. O., Diclemente, C. C., & Norcross, J. C. (1992). In search of the structure of change. In Y. Klar, J. D. Fisher, J. M. Chinsky, & A. Nadler (Eds.), *Self change* (pp. 87–114). New York: Springer. Retrieved from http://link.springer.com/chapter/10.1007/978-1-4612-2922-3_5.

Roberts, J., Gunes, I. D., & Seward, R. R. (2011). The impact of self esteem, family rituals, religiosity, and participation in conforming activities upon delinquency: A comparison of young adults in Turkey and the United States. *Journal of Comparative Family Studies, 42*(1), 59–76.

Equality and Gender-Based Violence in the University: A Practical Case of Social Marketing to Implement in the Framework of Non-Profit Marketing Studies

Juan José Mier-Terán Franco and Pedro Pablo Marín-Dueñas

Abstract
This paper proposes a practical case to be incorporated in marketing courses and, more specifically, in courses of non-profit marketing and/or social marketing. From the social marketing model proposed by Mier-Terán (*Igualdad y violencia de género*, https://druidadelmarketing.com/violencia-de-genero/Apuntes-de-clase, 2017a; *Un análisis de los resultados de las estrategias contra la violencia de género en España desde una óptica de marketing social*, 2017b), the main goal is to present to university students with the necessary tools to develop a social marketing campaign: analysis and test of the problem, campaign focus, definition of goals and strategies and, finally, evaluation. The starting point for this is an applied case study, carried out within the University of Cádiz (Spain), which considers the problem of gender-based violence in the university context, with a specific focus on women university students.

Learning Objectives
The case studied that is proposed as a model to sets out and develops the steps for the creation of a support strategy alternative to actions already taken on equality and especially on gender-based violence in the environment of the university; it adopts a focus different from that currently applied and utilizes the principles and techniques of social marketing.

(continued)

J. J. Mier-Terán Franco (✉) · P. P. Marín-Dueñas
University of Cádiz, Cádiz, Spain
e-mail: juanjose.mier-teran@uca.es; pablo.marin@uca.es

The main learning objectives for the students who undertake it can be summarized as follows:

- Know, in the context of social marketing, how to make a diagnosis of the problem under study:
  - Know the context in which the problems of equality and gender violence are encountered.
  - Identify the target public involved in the process and that of most relevance for the strategy.
  - Understand the current behaviours of the segments involved in the process and the associated benefits and barriers.
- Learn to define a proposition and select a campaign focus.
- Learn to set Social Marketing objectives and goals:
  - Define objectives for behaviour, knowledge and belief for the campaign.
- Learn to design social marketing strategies:
  - Product strategy
  - Strategy for costs of adoption (Price strategy)
  - Strategy for facilitation of the proposed behaviour (Placed strategy)
  - Communication strategy (Promotion strategy)
  - Sustainability strategy

Introduction

This project is based on the model of social marketing developed by Mier-Terán (2017a) and is focused on one of the principal problems that affect societies globally: gender inequality and gender-based violence, specifically on the university environment.

Violence inflicted on women is one of the most widespread and habitual forms of violation of human dignity and human rights; it affects a large number of people in the world. In the most conservative estimates, at least 35% of all women have been physically or sexually harmed by their partner or by another man (Nardi 2017). In some countries, especially in Africa and Latin America, this proportion is much higher and can reach extremely high levels. This includes verbal attack, psychological aggression, discrimination and many other sexist practices. In the European Union, this problem is no less serious: in 2014, a study by the *European Agency for Human Rights* found that 25 million women were victims of male violence, 13 million were physically assaulted, 9 million suffered sexual harassment and 3.7 million were subjected to sexual violence. The estimates of mental rather than physical aggression are even higher: 43% of Europeans suffer psychological aggression in one form or another because they are a woman. In Spain, specifically, it is recognized as a state problem; this is reflected in the approval by the Spanish Parliament, in September 2017, of the "State Pact against Gender-based Violence" BOE 2017); the document approved contains more than 200 measures aimed at reducing the incidence of a scourge that has claimed 918 victims since 2003 (the year in which the Government Office for Gender-based Violence established an official register of individuals assassinated). This State Pact is endorsed by the governments of all the autonomous regions and all municipal councils.

The approaches currently adopted to address problems of violence against women in Spain are as follows:

- Political/legal: The State Pact of 2017 and associated document (a study paper for the development of strategies against gender violence, constituted within the Equality Commission); law (legislation at level of state and autonomous regions); ethical codes; special courts to try cases of gender violence (Consejo General del Poder Judicial 2014); and education and training at schools and universities
- Economic measures: Special help under Article 27 of Integral Law LO 1/2004; assistance for victims with change of residence; bonus and replacement contracts; and active insertion income (RAI)
- Technological measures: Dedicated emergency telephone line 016 for victims; ATENPRO (Telephone Service of Attention and Protection to the victims of gender violence); Viogen (System of Integral Monitoring in the cases of Gender Violence); WRAP (Web of Resources for Support and Prevention for cases of gender violence); and electronic bracelets to monitor location of convicted offenders (Consejo General del Poder Judicial 2016)
- Educational/informative measures: Awareness campaigns and educational resources (Ministerio de Sanidad, Servicios Sociales e Igualdad 2015)

Considering in particular the university and as stated in the report "Gender-based violence in the Universities of Spain (2006–2008)", there is hardly any published research on gender-based violence. Therefore there is a clear need to advance in this subject. Various universities around the world are implementing preventive measures and interventions, starting from the assumption that any woman studying or working in the university context is at risk of suffering acts of violence. The working hypotheses considered in national studies on gender-based violence in the university are the following:

- Gender-based violence is a reality that is present in Spanish universities and takes various different forms, as in other social contexts.
- There exist measures that are being implemented in the university context that are intended to contribute to preventing and reducing gender-based violence.

By way of example, in the University of Cádiz (UCA), Spain, a "Protocol for the Attention to Students who are Victims of Gender-based Violence" was approved in June 2016 (Consejo de Gobierno de la Universidad de Cádiz. Bouca n° 210 2016).

The actions carried out in recent years by the university's *Unit for Equality between Women and Men* can be summarized in the following:

- Organization and attendance at congresses
- Meetings
- Working days, seminar and summer courses on the topic
- Making periodic diagnoses of the situation
- Marking International Women's Day with events
- Public manifestos
- Carrying out activities
- Travelling exhibitions
- Projects
- Establishing rules and guidance
- Collaborations with other entities
- Producing reports
- Attention to users
- International collaborations

To date, the UCA has not implemented any big social campaign with the specific objectives of reducing the incidence of this problem.

All the above actions have been carried out with the object of meeting the following goals defined in the equality plan:

- Promoting a commitment to equity and equality between men and women
- Strengthening the inclusion of a gender perspective in teaching and research
- Propitiating the balanced representation of women and men in the university's bodies of representation and governance
- Promoting the conciliation of the personal, family and professional life of all those who work or study in the UCA
- Ensuring the occupational health of all employees, from the perspective of gender; eradicating harassment of a sexual nature or for reasons of gender
- Guaranteeing the normative rights established for the protection of the victims of violence against women

Gender-Based Violence in Social Marketing

Having first contextualized the problem on which the project is centred, the next task is to define the principal steps that will have to be implemented to put the case into practice; as stated before, this is based on the social marketing model defined by Mier-Terán (2017a, b) that is presented as Fig. 1.

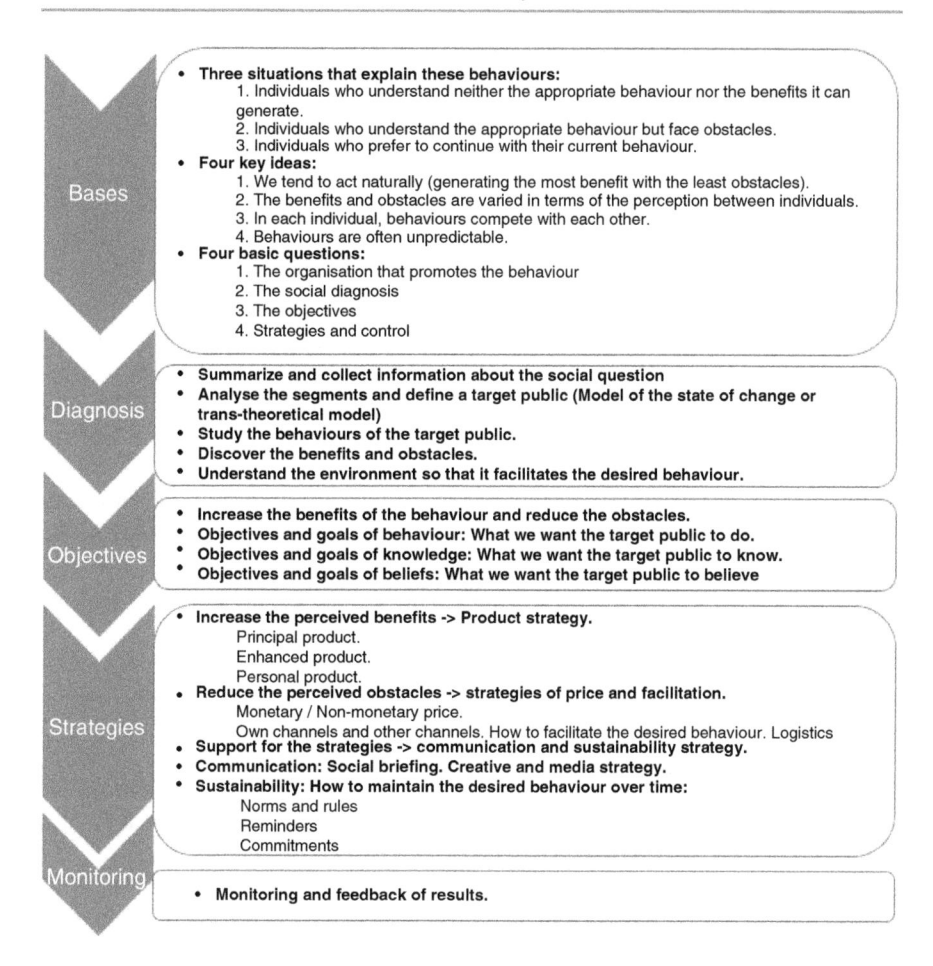

Bases
- **Three situations that explain these behaviours:**
  1. Individuals who understand neither the appropriate behaviour nor the benefits it can generate.
  2. Individuals who understand the appropriate behaviour but face obstacles.
  3. Individuals who prefer to continue with their current behaviour.
- **Four key ideas:**
  1. We tend to act naturally (generating the most benefit with the least obstacles).
  2. The benefits and obstacles are varied in terms of the perception between individuals.
  3. In each individual, behaviours compete with each other.
  4. Behaviours are often unpredictable.
- **Four basic questions:**
  1. The organisation that promotes the behaviour
  2. The social diagnosis
  3. The objectives
  4. Strategies and control

Diagnosis
- Summarize and collect information about the social question
- Analyse the segments and define a target public (Model of the state of change or trans-theoretical model)
- Study the behaviours of the target public.
- Discover the benefits and obstacles.
- Understand the environment so that it facilitates the desired behaviour.

Objectives
- Increase the benefits of the behaviour and reduce the obstacles.
- Objectives and goals of behaviour: What we want the target public to do.
- Objectives and goals of knowledge: What we want the target public to know.
- Objectives and goals of beliefs: What we want the target public to believe

Strategies
- Increase the perceived benefits -> Product strategy.
  - Principal product.
  - Enhanced product.
  - Personal product.
- Reduce the perceived obstacles -> strategies of price and facilitation.
  - Monetary / Non-monetary price.
  - Own channels and other channels. How to facilitate the desired behaviour. Logistics
- Support for the strategies -> communication and sustainability strategy.
- Communication: Social briefing. Creative and media strategy.
- Sustainability: How to maintain the desired behaviour over time:
  - Norms and rules
  - Reminders
  - Commitments

Monitoring
- Monitoring and feedback of results.

Fig. 1 Social marketing model applied. Source: Mier-Terán (2017a, b)

Case Development

Although the project that is presented here is valid for international application, in order to help readers to follow it and to facilitate the learning process, and so that they may get the most benefit from this case study, the development of this project and the data employed are based on an actual process developed in the University of Cádiz (UCA).

Thus, for each learning objective, the basic working tools for the students are shown, and from the example of the project applied and from the research carried out in the context of the UCA, the results obtained in each of the learning objectives are established. This is the reason why this section of the paper is subdivided into four subsections, each of which is identified with one of the learning objectives previously defined.

Objective 1: Know How to Make a Diagnosis of the Problem Studied

General Context of Gender-Based Violence in the University
- Working tools for the student:
  Analyse in greater depth, by means of secondary sources of information, the data on gender-based violence in the university context.

For the first of the objectives, the student will have to undertake a review of the bibliography and an intensive information search in secondary sources that will enable them to place the problem studied into context. This will require the student to employ general sources such as Internet search engines (Google, Bing, etc.), Google Scholar and databases of relevant academic journals—in other words, online resources of all types. At the same time, the student will be expected to access more specific sources, such as:

- Web pages of the organizational units responsible for equality between women and men and similar topics of the particular university in which the study project is being carried out
- Reports issued by the university Equality Unit
- Observatory for gender-based violence
- Research papers on violence against women (VAW)
- Spanish university and VAW reports
- Results obtained for the University of Cádiz

According to the experts, the context in which the problem is framed is the existence of **gender inequality**, discrimination and relationships in which the man holds power over the woman.

According to the data of the "Observatory for Gender-based Violence" of the *Spanish Ministry of Health, Social Services and Equality* (2018), the situation in the province of Cádiz is positive with respect to the overall incidence of gender-based violence in Spain; when a corrective factor for size of population is applied, the incidence is lower than the national average. It is observed that, although in absolute terms the number of telephone calls to the 016 line made in the province place Cádiz in tenth position in the ranking of all Spanish provinces, when the corrective factor for population size is applied, Cádiz falls to the 24th position (out of 52). In the ranking by number of formal complaints/accusations, Cádiz change from the 10th to the 17th position after the correction and, in the ranking by number of deaths attributed to this phenomenon, from the 21st to the 45th position. This indicates that, in relative terms, the province has a lower proportion of cases.

With the object of making an estimate of the degree of incidence in the university and given that there are no specific published data on gender-based violence, we will extrapolate, first, the provincial data to the university population and, second, the data from the national university studies. In particular, we will study the data of official complaints since the orientation of the campaign is aimed in the direction of getting victims to register complaints, and we will consider the population of 18–24 years of age, which is appropriate for the students in the university (Table 1).

Table 1 Extrapolation of the provincial data of complaints/accusations of gender-based violence (GBV) to the women students of the UCA

	Province of Cádiz	Province of Cádiz by women aged between 18 and 24 years (14.5% of all women)	Estimate of complaints that correspond to women students of the UCA (23.35% of all women aged between 18 and 24 years)
Complaints of GBV reported (annual average)	3382	490	115

Source: Authors' own elaboration

Historically, the number of complaints/accusations that are presented annually in the *Unit for Equality* is low—between 2 and 3, on average.

Target Public

- Working tools for the student:
  Analyse the different publics or groups that may be involved in the problem and decide which of those publics the campaign must actively influence.

Once the problem has been put into context and the relevant statistics have been established, the student should be capable of defining the key public affected by the problem of gender-based violence and of describing the principal characteristics of that public. Then the students will need to make the important decision with respect to the public or publics on which the future campaign to be mounted should be centred.

- Results obtained for the University of Cádiz:
  The social phenomenon of gender-based violence involves many different publics or groups, each of which plays a different role in the problem (Potter et al. 2011; Santesmases 1999). The most significant groups identified in the University of Cádiz are the following:
  – Abusers
  – Victims
  – Family members and friends
  – Police and other law enforcement authorities
  – Health system personnel
  – Judicial authorities
  – Associations and organizations

Clearly, in the light of the multiplicity of publics that may be possible targets, any such campaign should follow a clear process of segmentation, with the focus of the campaign aimed at actively influencing each of the selected target publics with differentiated messages. However, for this case we will focus on the possible victims as the target public of highest priority. More specifically, these will be women who are students at the University of Cádiz and who know of cases and/or situations of inequality, physical or psychological abuse, maltreatment or, in general, gender-based violence. In numbers, as can be seen in Table 2, there are 6925 women in this target public.

Table 2 Extrapolation of the national data for universities on gender-based violence to the women students of the UCA

	All Spanish universities (%)	Estimate of cases that correspond to women students of the UCA (10,654 women in total)
Do not know of cases of GBV in the university	35	3729
Have not suffered GBV but do know about GBV	52	5540
Know of cases of GBV in the university	13	1385

Source: Authors' own elaboration

Analysis of Current Behaviours

- Working tools for the student:

    Study the behaviour of the target public that is most important for the campaign and identify the key factors that intervene in that behaviour. Conduct surveys of students of the university and hold personal interviews with the personnel and public who may be involved, in the university in which the project is being undertaken, paying special attention to the priority target public.

In this phase, the students must be capable of identifying and defining the principal behaviours associated with gender-based violence. For this, a key methodology will be to conduct surveys and personal interviews of the principal publics involved, with the objective of identifying the most important factors.

- Comparative results obtained for the University of Cádiz:

    In the case of the University of Cádiz, what has been taken as the reference is the national survey on gender-based violence in Spanish universities (Valls 2008), applying the same questions and scales of measurement for the sample obtained in the UCA. After conducting the surveys (see Annex 1, with the technical data on the survey given in Annex 2) and the interviews held with students of the university, the next step is to identify the following key aspects:

- University students level of recognition of gender-based violence (Table 3)

- Benefits and barriers of current behaviour for the target public identified (results obtained in the personal interviews):
    - Benefits of the behaviour
        Those women victims who have presented a complaint to the Unit of Equality have resolved their problem favourably; the offender has been removed from the classroom, and the victim is now protected.
        The women victims who have not presented a complaint are left with feelings of failure and frustration because of what has happened to them.

Table 3 Recognition of situations that may constitute gender-based violence

	Spain (%)		UCA (%)	
	Yes	No	Yes	No
Making insulting and offensive remarks	86.11	13.89	94.10	5.90
Preventing you from speaking to other persons	77.50	22.50	96.70	3.30
Criticizing and/or denigrating whatever you do	73.06	26.94	90.80	9.20
Making unpleasant observations on your physical appearance	73.89	26.11	91.40	8.60
Stipulating how you should behave in public, what you wear, how you do your hair, etc.	78.61	21.39	98.70	1.30
Demanding to know who you are with and where you are	66.76	33.24	92.10	7.90
Throwing things at you, grabbing you, pushing you violently	95.93	4.07	97.40	2.60
Hitting you or using brutal physical force against you	96.67	3.33	98.00	2.00
Using force to have sexual relations with you	96.57	3.43	99.30	7.70
Systematically scorning you, undervaluing you	85.83	14.17	95.40	4.60
Intimidating and threatening you	95.00	5.00	97.40	2.60
Against your will, touching you, placing hands on any intimate part of your body; trapping you physically in order to kiss you or touch you	93.52	6.48	98.00	2.00
Pursuing you persistently	80.09	19.91	93.40	6.60
Causing you to receive unwanted or malicious calls, electronic mails, letters, messages insisting on maintaining a relationship with you	74.61	25.39	91.40	8.60

Source: Authors' own elaboration and Valls (2008)

- Barriers to the behaviour
  Fear of not being believed or of reprisals by the person accused.
  Shame over what has happened to her.
  Feelings that she is to blame for what happened.
  The victim thinks that she will have difficulty proving her version of what happened due to lack of evidence.
  Lack of support from family and/or friends.

Objective 2: Purpose and Focus of the Campaign

- Working tools for the student:
  In order to define the purpose, it is necessary to establish, in the light of the data obtained from the research, what is the final objective of the campaign in quantitative terms.

In this phase of the project, the students collectively should be capable of interpreting the results of the research carried out in the preceding phase and, from those results, establish the purposes and the key focal point of the social marketing campaign that will finally be put into operation.

- Results obtained for the University of Cádiz

Purpose
To ensure that at least 20% of the total cases of GBV that take place in the UCA are reported by the victim to the Unit of Equality, in a suitable virtual space provided for this

Focal Point
To increase the preliminary complaints/accusations made to the Unit of Equality, in line with the severity of the problem

Objective 3: Objectives and Goals of the Campaign

- Working tools for the student:
    Among other differences, social marketing campaigns are differentiated from generic social campaigns in that three types of objectives are established:
    − Objectives of behaviour: What is it we want our target audience to do?
    − Objectives of knowledge: What is it we want our target audience to know?
    − Objectives of beliefs: What is it we want our target audience to believe?

Once the students have determined the purpose and the principal focus of the proposed campaign, they must then define the specific objectives of the campaign, guided by the social marketing model explained previously.

- Results obtained for the University of Cádiz

Objectives of Behaviour
For any student of the University of Cádiz who considers herself a victim of any kind of gender-based violence perpetrated by any personnel of the University, what we want that student to do is to inform the Unit of Equality so that the student affected can be advised whether or not to present a formal complaint/accusation and, if so, advised to which authority this should be done.

Objectives of Knowledge
We want all students to know that 42% of women university students suffer sexist comments about the intellectual capacity of women or their role in society or comments with sexual connotations that degrade or humiliate women; that 13% state that they know of some situation of gender-based violence in the university context; and that there are 24% of the victims of gender-based violence in the university who do not say anything at all to anyone in respect of a known case. We want them to know that 9.2% of the women students of the UCA do not consider that criticizing or denigrating what they do constitutes gender-based violence (although this is generally recognized as such).

Objectives for Beliefs

We want students to believe that the Unit of Equality has at its disposal mechanisms for the defence of victims already proven on previous occasions and that have resolved problems of this nature. We want them to believe that by reporting behaviours of gender-based violence, it is possible to resolve the specific offence committed against the student and that this is not going to have adverse repercussions on the student's studies or marks awarded.

Objective 4: Proposed Strategies

- Tools for the student:
  The product strategy should facilitate the strengthening of the proposed behaviours. A principal product (the benefits of the behaviour) is defined (Kotler and Roberto 1989), together with an enhanced product (this refers to all those material elements necessary for supporting the principal product) and a personal product (the particular benefit that the person who adopts the behaviour will receive). The price and distribution strategies should facilitate the reduction of the costs incurred in adopting the proposed behaviour. The communication strategy should facilitate the transmission of the information, the persuasion and the proposed behaviour to the target public; it will be implemented in conjunction with the Office of Communication and Marketing of the University. The sustainability strategy should facilitate that the behaviours adopted are maintained over time, after the campaign has ended.

As defined in the social marketing model followed in this research, the last phase to be implemented by the students is the proposal of the main strategies to be followed in order to achieve the objectives. On this point, starting from these objectives, the students should be capable of establishing the five strategies that make up a social marketing plan; these cover product, price, distribution, communication and sustainability. In this phase of the project, a very important role is played by the interpretation that the participants have made of all the information collected and the potential of that information for useful analysis. Equally, a key element in the definition of the strategies should be the creative thinking that the students are capable of doing and putting into effect when formulating the proposals.

- Results obtained for the University of Cádiz

Product Strategy
- Principal product: Registering the complaint/accusation enables information about the problem to be obtained, while at the same time, it activates a protocol that safeguards the victim, protects her rights and freedoms and allows her to describe what happened in her case, freely and anonymously.
- Enhanced product: An anonymous space is provided in the website of the Unit of Equality where the victim can report the offence and request help.
- Personal product: The situation of harassment is eliminated.

Strategy for Costs of Adopting the Behaviour

- The woman student who considers that she is a victim of gender-based violence should report the offender, but that person will sometimes be a friend or a teacher. This will create the fear or worry that her academic performance and her marks may consequently be prejudiced. To reduce this obstacle, it is proposed that the victim's anonymity be guaranteed clearly and evidently when she makes the complaint/accusation. The offender is not accused or made aware of the complaint until the case has been studied, and the Unit for Equality considers that the complaint is viable.

Strategy for Facilitation of the Proposed Behaviour

- To facilitate the desired behaviour, it is proposed that a complaint, message or request for help written by a victim should receive a response in less than 24 h and that a link is included on the principal web page of the Unit of Equality that gives direct access to the complaint/accusation with a closed format and an open space for comments.
- Minimum data to be included: name of the offender, campus school where the offence took place, description of what happened and persons who support the version of the victim.

Communication Strategy

- Media strategy:
    - To circulate the campaign among the students, it is proposed that the main social networks should be used, in particular Facebook and Instagram, both used very frequently by students. Through the *Office of Communication of the UCA*, the campaign is publicized in all the available media. The *Unit of Equality* includes the campaign on its principal web page, and the website of the UCA creates a link from its principal page.
- Creative strategy:
    - What needs to be said? (Core of the message)
        When any instance of this behaviour is suffered, the case must be reported and described on the web page of the UCA's *Unit for Equality between Men and Women*.
        The complaints/accusations are anonymous but are not actively followed up unless the unit considers that it would be effective to do so.
        A protocol that protects the victim is activated.
    - How to say it?
        Language
            Relevant for the victims; bearing witness to the offence
        Images
            Cartoon drawings, illustrative but not amusing

Sustainability Strategy

- Tools for the student:
  The campaigns should continue to be effective over time, since it is a natural tendency for persons to revert back to their habitual forms of behaviour. Therefore, in addition to mounting the campaigns, it is necessary to establish reminders that will be effective over the required period of time.
- Results obtained for the University of Cádiz:
  Reminder 1: Displaying posters in the Campus buildings
  Reminder 2: Maintaining a link on the main web page of the UCA

Conclusions

The university is not insulated from the social phenomena of gender inequality and gender-based violence: these issues are present in the daily life of university students. In this practical case, we have presented a different way of approaching the problem, involving one of the principal publics of the university: its own students. What we have sought with this project is to set up a teaching model derived from work that has been done from the perspective of social marketing and within the framework of subjects related to non-profit-making marketing. This working methodology has proved to be capable of generating a proposed strategy for confronting the problem inside the university itself, from its own initiatives. The project is developed and carried out by the students themselves, utilizing the models that are analysed in the classroom and working in a coordinated way with other units of their university.

Discussion Questions

1. Could it be interesting to do a research study utilizing other quantitative techniques in order to know better the benefits and barriers of current behaviours of men and women? If so, what research techniques would you recommend?
2. What questions should be included to the persons interviewed?
3. What are the differences between social campaigns and those of social marketing?
4. Are there campaigns about gender-based violence in your country? If so, is the object of those campaigns to produce a change of behaviour or are they limited to making people more aware and sensitive?
5. What strategies are employed in your university to reduce the incidence of gender-based violence?
6. Do you think that social marketing campaigns are more effective than generic campaigns? If so, why?

Annex 1 Used Survey

Encuesta Igualdad-Violencia Género

Encuesta sobre VG solo para alumnos/as Uca

Estimado/a alumno/a: Te rogamos contestes esta breve encuesta con total sinceridad, la información será muy importante para mejorar en igualdad. Te garantizamos que los datos facilitados no serán nunca utilizados de forma individual sino agregados.

1. ¿Conoces o has entrado alguna vez en la web de Igualdad de la Uca?
   - No la conozco
   - La conozco pero no he entrado en su web
   - La conozco y he entrado en su web

2. ¿Crees que existe igualdad entre hombres y mujeres en la Uca?
   - Sí
   - No

3. De las situaciones que se pueden dar en una relación (estable o esporádica), marca Sí las que consideres violencia de género y No las que no consideres

	Sí	No
Insultos y ofensas	○	○
Impide que hables con otras personas	○	○
Critica o desvalora lo que haces	○	○
Hace observaciones desagradables sobre tu apariencia física	○	○
Imponerte la manera de vestir, peinar, comportarte en público	○	○
Exige saber con quién y dónde estás	○	○
Lanzarte un objeto, cogerte, empujarte violentamente	○	○

	Sí	No
Pegarte o ejercer otras brutalidades físicas contra ti	○	○
Utilizar la fuerza para mantener relaciones sexuales contigo	○	○
Menospreciarte sistemáticamente	○	○
Intimidarte y amenazarte	○	○
Contra tu voluntad te ha toqueteado o puesto las manos en diferentes partes íntimas del cuerpo o te ha acorralado para besarte o tocarte	○	○
Perseguirte insistentemente	○	○
Recibir llamadas, correos electrónicos, cartas malintencionadas, notas insistiendo en mantener una relación contigo	○	○

4. ¿Conoces alguna situación de violencia de género que haya sucedido en la universidad o entre personas del ámbito universitario (estudiantado, profesorado, Personal de Administración y Servicios, personal de servicios subcontratados –p.e. servicio de limpieza)?

○ Sí
○ No

5. ¿Conoces o has padecido alguna de las siguientes situaciones?

	Conozco algún caso	Lo he padecido	Lo he padecido y conozco otros casos	No conozco ningún caso
Agresiones físicas	○	○	○	○
Violencia psicológica	○	○	○	○
Agresiones sexuales	○	○	○	○
Presiones para mantener relaciones afectivo-sexuales	○	○	○	○
Recibir besos o caricias sin consentimiento	○	○	○	○
Sentir incomodidad o miedos por comentarios, miradas, correos electrónicos, notas, llamadas telefónicas o por haber sido perseguido/a o vigilado/a	○	○	○	○
Rumores sobre vida sexual	○	○	○	○
Comentarios sexistas sobre la capacidad intelectual de las mujeres o su papel en la sociedad o comentarios con connotaciones sexuales que las degradan o las humillan	○	○	○	○

6. En el caso de que hayas sufrido alguna agresión. ¿Consideraste que eras víctima de violencia de género?

○ No es mi caso
○ Sí me consideré víctima de violencia de género
○ No me consideré víctima de violencia de género
○ No lo sé

7. En caso de haber sido víctima... ¿Que hiciste?

○ No es mi caso
○ Denunciarlo en la policía y en la universidad
○ Denunciarlo en la policía
○ Denunciarlo en la universidad
○ No denunciarlo, pero explicarlo a alguien
○ No decir nada a nadie

8. Sexo
- ○ Hombre
- ○ Mujer

9. Edad

Deslice hasta encontrar su edad

0 — 100

10. Título que estudia
- ○ Grado en Marketing e IM
- ○ Grado en Publicidad y RR.PP.
- ○ Grado en Turismo
- ○ Grado en GAP
- ○ Grado en ADE
- ○ Otro (especifique)
- ○ Grado en Derecho
- ○ Grado en Enfermería
- ○ Grado en Criminología
- ○ Grado en Trabajo Social
- ○ Máster

11. Curso que realiza actualmente (aunque le queden asignaturas anteriores)
- ○ Primero
- ○ Segundo
- ○ Tercero
- ○ Cuarto
- ○ Máster

12. Ciudad en la que reside

Annex 2 Data Sheet

Universo	Mujeres estudiantes en la Universidad de Cádiz = 10.564 (female students Uca)
Muestra	154 encuestas válidas (valid surveys)
Nivel de confianza	95.5%
Error de muestreo	8.05% (utilizando el supuesto de máxima indeterminación o varianza para el caso de las proporciones $p = q = 50\%$)
Tipo de muestreo	Por cuotas de titulaciones (By degrees quotes)
Trabajo de campo	Mediante encuestas realizadas en la plataforma de SurveyMonkey. Abril de 2018

References

BOE. (2017). *Ponencia de estudio para la elaboración de estrategias contra la violencia de género*. Constituida en el seno de la Comisión de Igualdad (543/000002). Acuerdo de la Comisión. BOE 134 4 de agosto.

Consejo de Gobierno de la Universidad de Cádiz. Bouca N° 210. (2016). Acuerdo del Consejo de Gobierno de 4 de mayo de 2016, por el que se aprueba el Protocolo de la Universidad de Cádiz sobre atención a estudiantes víctimas de violencia de género.

Consejo General del Poder Judicial. (2014). *Sección del observatorio contra la violencia doméstica y de género*. Informe sobre víctimas mortales de la violencia de género y de la violencia doméstica en el ámbito de la pareja o ex pareja en 2014.

Consejo General del Poder Judicial. (2016). *Informe de violencia de género por provincias*.

Kotler, P. & Roberto, E. (1989). *Social marketing: Strategies for changing public behavior*. New York: Free Press.

Mier-Terán, J. J. (2017a). *Igualdad y violencia de género*. Retrieved from https://druidadelmarketing.com/violencia-de-genero/Apuntes-de-clase

Mier-Terán, J. J. (2017b). *Un análisis de los resultados de las estrategias contra la violencia de género en España desde una óptica de marketing social*. In 16th Congress on Public and Nonprofit Marketing, Badajoz.

Ministerio de Sanidad, Servicios Sociales e Igualdad. (2015). *Macroencuesta la violencia contra la mujer*. Retrieved from http://www.violenciagenero.msssi.gob.es/violenciaEnCifras/estudios/colecciones/pdf/Libro_22_Macroencuesta2015.pdf

Nardi, A. (2017). *Predicción de la ejecución y aceptación de conductas precursoras de violencia de género en población adolescente*. Tesis doctoral. Universidad Miguel Hernández. Retrieved from http://dspace.umh.es/bitstream/11000/4533/1/TD%20Nardi%20Rodr%C3%ADguez%2C%20Ainara.pdf

Potter, S. J., Moynihan, M. M., & Stapleton, J. G. (2011). Using social self-identification in social marketing materials aimed at reducing violence against women on campus. *Journal of Interpersonal Violence, 26*(5), 971–990.

Santesmases, M. (1999). *Marketing. Conceptos y estrategias* (4a Edición). Madrid: Pirámide.

Valls, R. (2008). *Violencia de género en las universidades españolas*. Ministerio de Igualdad, Instituto de la mujer.

Social Marketing and Their Related Challenges for the Limited Access for People Living with a Disability: A Serbian Case Study

Ana Vulevic, Dragan Djordjevic, Rui Alexandre Castanho, and José Cabezas-Fernández

Abstract Accessibility in Serbia is defined through the Strategy for Improving the Position of Persons with Disabilities. Commitment activities started in 2010–2012, through the project "No Obstacles" developed by the Centre for the Development of an Inclusive Society (CRID) and the Accessibility Audit Association in Serbia (AAAS) with the support of the Norwegian Embassy in Belgrade. Contextually, the chapter aims to present a practical case regarding social marketing campaign that was developed by NGOs, through the support of local governments, major local agencies (urban planning, communal and architecture inspection bodies) on a municipality level—a Serbian case study. The implementation of this social marketing project creates the preconditions for increasing accessibility upon the principles of Design for All and building communities where all citizens have

---

A. Vulevic (✉) · D. Djordjevic
Institute of Transportation – CIP, Belgrade, Serbia
e-mail: vulevica@sicip.co.rs; djodjevicd@sicip.co.rs

R. A. Castanho
ICAAM—Institute for Agrarian and Environmental Sciences, Évora, Portugal

Environmental Resources Analysis Research Group (ARAM), University of Extremadura, Badajoz, Spain

VALORIZA – Research Centre for Endogenous Resource Valorization, Portalegre, Portugal

Faculty of Applied Sciences, WSB University, Dąbrowa Górnicza, Poland

Institute of Research on Territorial Governance and Inter-Organizational Cooperation, Dąbrowa Górnicza, Poland
e-mail: racastanho@uevora.pt

J. Cabezas-Fernández
Environmental Resources Analysis Research Group (ARAM), University of Extremadura, Badajoz, Spain

VALORIZA – Research Centre for Endogenous Resource Valorization, Portalegre, Portugal
e-mail: jocafer@unex.es

equal opportunities. The project used all the elements of the marketing mix and/or primary intervention methods.

> **Learning Objectives**
> Ensuring access to the built environment and reducing the isolation of persons with disabilities can be summarized through the learning objectives:
>
> 1. Architectural accessibility provides guidance for improving access to the built environment for persons with disabilities with reducing and overcoming barriers through good practice.
> 2. Architects, planners, policymakers, government officials and NGOs, decision-makers in the construction sector and persons with disabilities should promote and improve architectural accessibility.
> 3. Support better understanding of the core social marketing concepts and principles.
> 4. Assistance in the promotion and the commissioning of social marketing services.

Introduction

The present study aims to promote social marketing-related challenges for limited access to people with reduced mobility's (PwRM) social and community cooperation in relation to their access as well as challenges to improve sustainability by changing the behaviour of people for social well-being. Fully understanding social marketing impact on changing behaviours amongst, and for, PwRM requires a thorough systematic review. Access as the term can refer to many areas such as transport, education, employment, buildings and public spaces, and most of these areas are interdependent (CBM 2008). Low level of access leads to the marginalization of people with reduced mobility (PwRM) in all spheres (the social, economic and political) in an environment of the community (Levinson et al. 2006; Djordjevic et al. 2017). The provision of an accessible building involves the following phases: pre-planning phase, planning and design phase, approval or permission and construction and on-site monitoring and maintenance. These phases involve a multidisciplinary stakeholder—e.g. architects and governmental authorities—fundamental for the successful implementation is the awareness on the need for accessibility is guaranteed throughout the whole process and amongst all stakeholders, a high level of coordination and monitoring for which appropriate mechanisms (CBM 2007, 2008). Social marketing planning approach offers a good social planning framework regardless of whether social goals will be achieved or that the costs will be acceptable

(Kotler and Levy 1969; Kotler and Zaltman 1971; Kotler 2000; Hastings 2003; Kotler and Lee 2008). In this regard, social marketing is seen as an effective approach for people living with a disability—PwD—once it offers a useful framework for effective social planning in a time when social issues become more relevant in Serbia. Kotler and Lee (2008) define social marketing as "process that applies marketing principles and techniques to create, communicate, and deliver value in order to influence target audience behaviour that benefits society (public health, safety, the environment, and communities) as well as the target audience".

Although in the Republic of Serbia (RS) has a good legal basis for accepting basic principles of creating an accessible environment for all citizens, especially for people with disabilities still, several issues remain to be addressed, as precondition for social inclusion.

Throughout the research, successful (practical) examples were identified as well as the role of social marketing, community and structural changes—regarding the RS reality. The exclusion of PwRM from infrastructure, services, social contact and community activities results in limited social, educational and economic opportunities, increasing the vulnerability risk of persons with disabilities to become poor or falling further into poverty.

The struggle to create an accessible environment has begun through the association initiatives (2006–2013), stakeholder engagement, education in 2012, individual civil initiatives in 2013 and support at local level authorities in order to develop local action plans (2014) and to reach them in individual cities of Serbia. These centres also considered successful examples of social marketing in Serbia (Initial Report 2012; Government of the Republic of Serbia 2011). By the same time (2010–2012), the Centre for the Development of an Inclusive Society (CRID), within the project "No Obstacles", carried out the work with local organizations of people with disabilities in the cities as Majdanpek, Uzice, Pirot, Veliko Gradiste and Novi Pazar. This Project was supported by the Embassy of Norway and realized in partnership with the Accessibility Audit Association in Serbia (AAAS). Thus, the main goal of the project is increasing of accessibility upon principles of Design for All[1] in five municipalities in Serbia by education and formation of Councils for accessibility in municipalities and the implementation of concrete solutions to inaccessible objects. In addition, promoting conditions for increasing the mobility of persons with disabilities, the elderly, parents and young children and other people with walking impairments and communication on the territory of the five municipalities, through education and cooperation with municipalities, presents important goals. From education and other activities of the project is expected to increase the visibility of people with disabilities in five municipalities and to ease

---

[1]Design for All is a concept that considers all potential users of a building or environment. According to the Stockholm Declaration 2004, Design for All aims to "enable all people to have equal opportunities to participate in every aspect of society. To achieve this, the built environment, everyday objects, services, culture and information".

living conditions for their independence. Other residents will facilitate movement through the city (CRID and AAAS 2012).

In line with those activities, the campaign establishes links to all NGOs and governmental bodies involved in reconstruction providing technical advice, resources and support on architectural accessibility both in the planning and implementation phases through an Accessibility Map as one of the main marketing tools (CRID and AAAS 2012). The above-mentioned Map is the project of the AAAS—which started in 2011 with constantly updated visually and functionally and with new content—through internal and donor funds. The interactive "Accessibility Map" provides PwRM and other citizens with relevant information on the accessibility of locations in Serbia. Citizens, civil society organizations, local self-government units, state bodies and other public administration bodies collected the data for the Map. In addition to representing a basis for constant monitoring of the situation in this field, the Accessibility Map also promotes good practice examples.

Ensuring access to the built environment and reducing the isolation of persons with disabilities can be summarized through the learning objectives:

1. Architectural accessibility provides guidance for improving access to the built environment for persons with disabilities by reducing and overcoming barriers through good practice.
2. Architects, planners, policymakers, government officials and NGOs, decision-makers in the construction sector and persons with disabilities should promote and improve architectural accessibility.

Used methods and approaches in this campaign are financially and practically sustainable. Throughout the promotion, all the elements of the marketing mix (product, price, place and promotion) and primary intervention methods (inform, educate, support and design) were applied (Cannon 1992; Grier and Bryant 2005; Pilloton 2009).

Case Development

Background to the Project and to the Selected Practice There are no accessibility-specific strategies and action plans in the Republic of Serbia. Accessibility issues are a significant part of the Strategy for Improving the Position of Persons with Disabilities in the RS.[2]

---

[2] The new strategy and action plan for the implementation of the Strategy for Improving the Position of Persons with Disabilities in the Republic of Serbia until 2020 is at the public debate (still not adopted, waiting for the consent of relevant ministries includes time frames and responsible actors' ministries, organizations of persons with disabilities and directorates and departments of relevant ministries and other state institutions) http://www.minrzs.gov.rs/cir/aktuelno/item/6712-javna-rasprava-unapredjenja-polozaja-osoba-sa-invaliditetom (Serbian).

Additionally, there have been several initiatives during 2011 and 2012 for accessibility action plans on a local level. These strategies and action plans provide a framework for the establishment of bodies (teams for accessibility) at a local level for support and monitoring of implementation, which would include representatives of civil society and disabled people's organizations and should report on the results of the implementation to local governments/parliaments on an annual basis. Several nongovernment organizations and organizations of persons with disabilities working in the field of accessibility are members of the European Concept for Accessibility Network. Their activities and efforts are calling for an application of the concept and principles of the Design for All in strategic documents and policies. The state bodies are referring to both Universal Design and Design for All (DfA) in relevant documents, with general reference to accessibility standards on a European or international/world level.

AAAS and CRID in Serbia are advocating for the development and implementation of accessibility standards in order to create an environment that benefits all people. Individuals and organizations that make AAAS and CRID are also active members of the European networks—European Concept for Accessibility Network (EuCAN). AAAS is committed to the implementation of the concept "Universal Design/Design for All". As the project "No Obstacles" was done in partnership with these two organizations, there was a decision-making body regarding the action plans for the implementation, with the members. All the five organizations from the above-mentioned cities that participated in the project had a local coordinator, responsible for his organization activities.

The proposed activities represented a direct support to efforts made by the RS towards the inclusion of persons with disabilities, the elderly and other groups with mobility difficulty (PwRM) through the ratified UN Convention on the Rights of Persons with Disabilities and adopted strategy of the position of persons with disabilities in Serbia (2007–2014). One of the main priorities in every area of Serbian social plans is accessibility, which is a prerequisite for all other social services.

Process/Strategy Used to Implement the Selected Practice Inaccessible environment is not a problem only to a person with a disability but affects up to 40% of the population (according to the research experts EuCAN). The basic idea of this project was to strengthen the organizations of persons with disabilities in the cities over study to identify barriers to mobility in the environment and to map it in detail and to motivate local people.

The main parts of action were the training of PwRM from organizations in these five cities, which are involved in the project, animating the public through various channels of communication, production of coarse picturesque solutions for the perceived barriers and their presentation to the public and authorities. Training was carried out to inform and to bring together activists and organizations of persons with disabilities and also to provide many channels for communication with citizens. Training included accessible chain movement (observation of architectural, communication and sociological barriers to the vulnerable PwRM—the elderly, the disabled, pregnant women, children) for organizations of persons with disabilities. In addition to this central theme, the training had included advocacy skills, communication, representation of interests, the establishment of partnerships at the community level of organization and social action (CRID and AAAS 2012). Between training partner organizations' working team worked to strengthen the participants of education in the direction of forming the Council of accessibility in each of the five municipalities. The formation of the Council of accessibility is one of the most important activities of the project because the Council is a link to the cooperation with local governments and other stakeholders for accessibility within each municipality. The Council operates as an independent body from the local authorities (non-political); it consists of persons with disabilities, who have been trained during the first year of the project. They worked with the local authority on solving the problem of inaccessibility of their city.

Also, seminars on accessibility were held in all five cities. During the seminars, in every city, an overview of the situation was made. The seminar was attended by representatives of the municipality. Same representatives took an active role in the writing and implementation of the action plan. The action team formed and team members signed the declaration of accessibility. The project lasted 12 months and had six main groups of activities (Table 1).

Table 1 The ordering of activities based on approved Action plan

Ordering	Activities
1.	Preparation activities of the project
	First meeting with local partners
	Signing the agreement on cooperation with local partners
2.	First seminar in Veliko Gradiste, Pirot, Uzice, Novi Pazar and Majdanpek
	Meeting of team members for accessibility at the local level
	Media presentation of the project in the Media Center in Belgrade
	Second seminar in Veliko Gradište, Pirot, Uzice, Novi Pazar and Majdanpek
3.	Strengthening of organization capacity of local partners
	Second meeting with local partners from five cities in Serbia—evaluation of previous work and agreements on the next 6 months' plan
4.	Forming of the action team for accessibility, in five municipalities, and meeting of the accessibility team members on the local level
	Work protocol for action team for accessibility was formed
	Tasks for action team for accessibility were formed
	Presentation/promotion of action team for accessibility to interested factors on local level (institutions, organizations of persons with disability, social work centres, business, media)
5.	Cooperation with local municipality authorities
	Dissemination of action team for accessibility to municipal authorities
	Design ideas for removal of architectural and other barriers in some municipalities
6.	Media campaign; media presentation of the project in Belgrade in Media Center
	Media appearances on local radio and TV stations and printed media
	Forming of visual identity of the project (project logo)
	Dissemination of notifications about the project on organization sites
	Preparation and printing of leaflets for media activities of the project

Source: CRID and AAAS (2012)

Changes Achieved In accordance with the main objective (increasing of accessibility upon principles of Design for All/Universal Design in five municipalities in Serbia), improvements in the area of accessibility in four municipalities are gained. Six new ramps were built, in Veliko Gradiste, accessible children's playground was built in Novi Pazar and a new swimming pool in Pirot includes elements of accessibility (after the intervention from the local partner). A summary of the project goals, indicators and interventions is shown in Table 2.

According to McKenzie and Smith (1999), "The goal of social marketing is to influence the societies to change through interventions aimed at individuals. To achieve large-scale behavioral change, social marketing campaigns are tailored to target population that share common characteristics and who are expected to adopt the desired behavior through the use of incentives and removal of barriers". The main idea of this project was to create conditions for increasing the mobility of

Table 2 Social marketing—target behaviour changes and outcome

Project goal, effect on the target group (intended outcome)	Indicators	Interventions
Increasing of accessibility upon principles of Design for All in five municipalities in Serbia by education and formation of councils for accessibility in municipalities and the implementation of concrete solutions to inaccessible objects	Municipalities that comply with accessibility standards in accordance with relevant laws[a]	Local government welcomes forming local action teams in Uzice, Novi Pazar and Pirot, and, in these towns, action plans are made with municipality support as soon as possible for the implementation of accessibility standards and relevant laws
	Trained 100 persons with disability in five municipalities	Total number of trainees was 130. Representatives of the municipality attended the seminar. Each city has been analysed
	Formed at least five solutions for inaccessible objects	Local partners have defined sketches for eight solutions for inaccessible objects in targeted cities
	Accessibility action team in each municipality	Accessibility action teams formed in each municipality. Representatives from municipalities took active role in the writing and implementation of the action plan. The action team formed and team members signed the declaration of accessibility

Source: CRID and AAAS (2012)
[a]This indicator can be measured only for newly created public objects and spaces and/or by analysing local governments' actions over prolonged period of time

persons with disabilities, the elderly, parents and young children and other people with walking impairments and communication on the territory of the five municipalities, through education and cooperation with municipalities. The brief analyses of the social marketing products and interventions is an achievement in Table 3.

The present results can be grouped into different areas of interventions. The practice achieved changes in the following areas (Table 4): urban layout, promotion of accessibility and advocacy and awareness. The summary of application of social

Table 3 Analyses of social marketing products and interventions

Product and services (planned output)	Interventions
From education and other activities of the project was expect to increase the visibility of people with disabilities in five municipalities and to ease living conditions for their independence Other residents will facilitate movement through the city	Resolved architectural and other barriers on the principles of universal design in five municipalities with solutions that not only include access ramps but also communication barriers for people with sensory disabilities
	Increasing visibility of local actors trained to point out problems in inaccessible environment. Activities monitored by regional television stations, Facebook groups have 1265 members and a video from seminars, posted on YouTube have 762 views
	Increased capacity for the project implementation of local partners is gained
	Around 100 people from five municipalities are networked and educated in skills and knowledge necessary for advocating accessibility issues in local communities
	General overview of the situation (concerning accessibility) in each municipality is written
	At least one feasible idea per municipality for improvement of accessibility in local communities is proposed during the period after the first round of training seminars
	Increased capacity of local partners for their everyday work is gained
	Action team/working group for accessibility on the local level is formed in each of five municipalities
	Increased capacity for project advocacy on local level is gained
	Established dialogue with local authorities/institutions
	Increased visibility of project and its goals is gained
	Awareness about accessibility issues on local levels is raised

Source: CRID and AAAS (2012)

Table 4 The application of social marketing—studied component data through the present study

Area of intervention	Urban layout, promotion of accessibility and advocacy and awareness
Target audience	PwRM
Target behaviour	Increasing of accessibility upon principles of Design for All
Behaviour outcomes	Positive change
Use marketing methods	Marketing mix and interventions methods

Source: Authors

marketing, which was carried out in different areas of interventions through the present study, is shown in Table 4.

How Change Was Monitored and Evaluated Monitoring of project activities is one of the key elements for the success of the project implementation and is important for a local organization that encounters problems and also for project partners. The basic goal for all the monitoring activities of this project was to achieve maxim results of the project justifying the investment from the Embassy of the Kingdom of Norway in Belgrade, through achieving the important goals. By monitoring the activities of local partners, through regular reports, certain risks that could occur because of the geographical distance between the organization and the partner have been overcome. By the constructive and positive implementation of monitoring and exchange of information throughout the project implementation, the primary stated project frames are overcome and that the opportunities for dissemination of positive experiences and good praxis examples have been given. Through evaluation of educations, we had an insight into the quality of the programme that has been implemented. Considering work progress the organizations had established a new system of achieving of set goals and noticing of problems and the need for changing the approach, providing quality. With the beginning of implementation for this project, a new approach was introduced, regarding its monitoring, in which the accent is put on strengthening the capacities of organizations—follow-up through work reports and live meetings. Both kinds of monitoring consolidate three functions: (1) preventive, giving the information about procedures and rules; (2) advisory, recommendations about the content and financial aspects; and (3) regulatory, audit and evaluation of the success of the set goals (CRID and AAAS 2012).

Citizen protector organized a public invitation to municipalities and city municipalities in the RS to apply for awards for contribution to the development of all forms of accessibility on their territory in period from 2015 to the end of 2017. The Citizens' Protection Award was awarded to local self-governments that contributed most to the development of all forms of accessibility on their territory, "to draw public attention to the disadvantage of people with disabilities, who account for 8% of the total population".

With initiatives for developing accessibility for 2016, three local communities applied (from the initial five covered by the "No barrier" project). In all three applications (Table 5), it is stated that certain accessibility elements that they applied for the award contribute to better mobility not only of people with disabilities but

Table 5 The main initiatives for improving accessibility in the cities Pirot, Uzice and Novi Pazar

Initiatives	Pirot	Uzice	Novi Pazar
(1)	1. Construction of the building of an inclusive centre for people with disabilities 2. Reconstruction of the sidewalk in the central street "Srpskih vladara" 3. Reconstruction of the sidewalk in the street Danila Kiša and Save Kovačević 4. Construction of a space around the indoor swimming pool and connecting it with the surrounding streets and primarily with the primary and secondary school "Mladost" 5. Local action plan: "Pirot accessible to all 2013–2023"	Adaptation of facilities for public and private purposes in the goal of removing architectural barriers: design and installation of a mobile platform on the promenade along the river Djetinja which is an area of special features	Local action plan for the improvement of the position of persons with disabilities for the period 2017–2021 was adopted The city of Novi Pazar has a significant number of associations dealing with problems and positions of PwD The city administration of the city of Novi Pazar finances the programme activities of all associations that operate in the areas: associations for the mentally underdeveloped people, the Society for Cerebral Palsy, paraplegic associations and interstitial organizations, civil invalids of the war and Association of Psychologists Novi Pazar
(2)	1. From 2015 to the end of 2017 year 2. From March 2016 to June of 2016 3. From July of 2016 to April 2017 4. From December 2016 to September of 2017	2016	2016
(3)	1. "Molijerova street" 2. "Srpskih Vladara" street 3. "Danila Kiša" and "Save Kovačević" streets 4. "Koste Abrasevica" street		
(4)	1. Disability people 2. PwRM 3. All citizens 4. All citizens	PwRM	PwRM

Source: Application form for public invitation to municipalities in the RS to apply for Citizens' Protection Award for contribution to the development of all forms of accessibility on their territory in 2016

(1) Description of the main initiatives for improving accessibility in the city/municipality, (2) the time period in which the initiative was implemented, (3) address at which the initiative was implemented, (4) target group of initiatives

also of other groups of citizens, such as parents with children, elderly people, bikers, etc. In addition, it is noticeable that in the years after the completion of the project "No Obstacles", the said local community (Pirot, Novi Pazar, Uzice) are planning to build an accessible environment, specifically public amenities and spaces.

The city of Pirot was awarded, and the municipalities of Novi Pazar and Uzice received prizes for contributing to the development of all forms of accessibility for persons with disabilities on their territory. Table 5 shows the main initiatives for improving accessibility in the cities Pirot, Uzice and Novi Pazar in an application form for public invitation to municipalities in the RS to apply for awards for contribution to the development of all forms of accessibility on their territory in period from 2015 to the end of 2017 (application form fill-out the responsible individual persons in the municipality—municipal presidents).

Conclusions

This project contributes to improving the environment for civil society, with more effective dialogue between civil society and the government in five less developed areas in Serbia. It results in more active and effective civic participation in policy processes leading to strengthening the rule of law. This can be achieved through strengthening the capacity of local organizations to act in the direction of creating an accessible environment for all citizens, especially for persons with disabilities.

The main strategy is to further help and improvement of social inclusion and accessibility services, evaluation and strengthening liaisons with other civil society organizations' (CSOs) and stakeholders. Promotion action team in the cities of network members as an example of good practice. That lead to fostering other PwDs in their business-oriented motivation and promotion of the concept of social inclusion. Strengthening synergies and cooperation between stakeholders through multimedia platform, web portal and form new initiatives, is basis for future new services. Finally, project activities created foundation and social enterprises as a key sustainability strategy. A strong media campaign is continued in all five cities by the members of the No Barriers network as a sequel to activities that took place in the first year of realization of the project. In the years after the completion of the project "No Obstacles", the mentioned local communities (Pirot, Novi Pazar, Uzice) are planning the construction of an accessible environment, according to principles of DfA, and have been rewarded for contributing to the development of all forms of accessibility for PwRM on their territory in 2016.

Discussion Questions

1. Does the implementation of the project contribute to the improved environment for PwRM with more effective dialogue between civil society and the government in the five analysed cities?

2. Could there be any gaps identified? Does Serbia have adopted standards on accessibility and foreseen satisfactory sanction measures?
3. Can the education interventions change these behaviours?
4. Which strategies and tools existing face the exposed issues? Does the public media should send out positive, yet informative, messages about this issue or about adequate training on accessibility standards for architects and local committees that issue building permits and use permits?
5. Are in fact the interventions responsive to the different needs and aspirations of the various social groups?
6. Is social marketing being used correctly with maximum effectiveness?
7. In which way such good practice examples could have been improved?

The experience through this project shows the usual capacity gaps to monitor indicators of strategic documents regarding the development and infrastructures as well as timely given attention to the omissions. In fact, it should be highlighted the great dependence of the organizations of disabilities persons from the local government funds and absence of constructive dialogue between them. In other words, organizations of persons with disabilities are rarely willing to criticize the work of local institutions as well as to propose structural changes, even in cases of the law violation and subordinate regulations.

Thus, the implementation of the project will contribute to the improvement of the environment for PwRM with more effective dialogue between civil society and the government in five Serbian cities. It also will result in long-time more active and effective public participation in policy processes leading to strengthening the rule of law, through strengthening the capacity of local grassroots organizations to act towards the creation of an accessible environment for all citizens, especially for persons with disabilities.

Acknowledgements We would like to express our sincere gratitude to CRID and URP organizations, which are working for the last few years, alone or in partnership, on the advocacy for accessible environment and for capacity building of various NGOs, institutions and companies to implement Design for All in their environment, for their insightful comments and encouragement but also for the hard question which incanted us to widen our research from various perspectives.

References

Cannon, T. (1992). *Basic marketing: Principles and practice* (3rd ed.). London: Cassell.
CBM. (2007). *Disability and development policy*.
CBM (International Christian development organisation). (2008). *Promoting access to the built environment guidelines*.
CRID & AAAS. (2012). *Final reports for Grants for Norwegian Ministry of foreign Affairs* (MFA).
Djordjevic, D., Stojic, G., & Vulevic, A. (2017). Rail network spatial approach methodologies for achieving better access to people with disabilities: A brief literature review. In *Proceeding book, International Conference Towards a Humane City, Smart Mobility – Synergy between Sustainable Mobility and New Technologies* (pp. 183–190). Novi Sad. ISBN: 978-86-7892-962-5.

Retrieved from http://www.vbs.rs/scripts/cobiss?command=DISPLAY&base=COBIB&RID=31743744

Government of the Republic of Serbia. (2011). *Strategy for improving the position of persons with disabilities in the Republic of Serbia (2011)*. Official Gazette of the Republic of Serbia, No 1/07. World Health Organisation, World Report on Disability.

Grier, S., & Bryant, C. (2005). Social marketing in public health. *Annual Review Public Health, 26*, 319–339.

Hastings, G. (2003). Relational paradigms in social marketing. *Journal of Macro-marketing, 23*(1), 6–15.

Initial report on the implementation of the Convention on the Rights of Persons with Disabilities. (2012). Government of the Republic of Serbia, Belgrade.

Kotler, P. (2000). *Marketing management* (Millennium Edition). Upper Saddle River, NJ: Prentice Hall International (Google Scholar).

Kotler, P., & Lee, N. (2008). *Social marketing: Influencing behaviours for good* (3rd ed.). Thousand Oaks, CA: Sage.

Kotler, P., & Levy, S. J. (1969). Broadening the concept of marketing. *Journal of Marketing, 33*, 10–15 (Google Scholar, Crossref, Medline).

Kotler, P., & Zaltman, G. (1971). Social marketing: An approach to planned social change. *Journal of Marketing, 35*, 3–12.

Levinson, D. M., Wasfi, R., & El-Geneidy, A. M. (2006). *Measuring the transportation needs of people with developmental disabilities*. Paper presented at the 86th Annual Meeting of the Transportation Research Board, Washington, DC. Abstract retrieved from http://papers.ssrn.com/sol3/papers.cfm?abstract_id=1743631

McKenzie, M. D., & Smith, W. (1999). *Fostering sustainable behavior*. Gabriola Island: New Society.

Pilloton, E. (2009). *Design revolution: 100 products that empower people*. New York: Metropolis Books.

Social Marketing in the General Directorate of Traffic's Campaign Called "Caminantedigital"

Estela Núñez-Barriopedro

Abstract

Faced with the problem of a high accident rate in Spain, the campaign called "Caminantedigital" is an important shift in the marketing strategies of the General Directorate of Traffic (Dirección General de Tráfico or DGT in Spanish). For the European Road Safety and the United Nations Global Road Safety Week, the DGT focusses on the target audience. In this case it focuses not only in drivers but also pedestrians, who have not been taken into consideration in past campaigns. The main goal is to raise awareness through a photographic competition of the high accident rate and to encourage walking as opposed to using motorized vehicles, as well as promoting the enjoyment of public spaces. An innovative factor is that this campaign has introduced a marketing strategy based on "Creative Gamification." One of the keys for its success is that the receiver of the information goes from being considered as a mere passive subject to being considered an active participant.

E. Núñez-Barriopedro (✉)
University of Alcalá, Alcalá de Henares, Spain
e-mail: Estela.nunezb@uah.es

Learning Objectives
The current case study tries to achieve the next learning objectives:

- Identify what does the most creative social marketing campaign developed by the General Directorate of Traffic (DGT) consists of.
- Define who the target audience of this campaign is, meaning, to whom the behavioral change is directed.
- Analyze what the social problem is and what behavioral change do we want to achieve in the target audience.
- Study how innovative, creative, and highlight has the marketing mix been developed.
- Discover why and how creativity is especially valued.

Introduction

The General Directorate of Traffic—in Spanish called Dirección General de Tráfico (DGT)—founded in 1959, is an autonomous public organization dependent of the Ministry of Interior of Spain. The DGT is responsible for the execution of the current road safety policies, and among its powers are traffic and road safety enforcement (Núñez et al. 2014).

The target audience is divided into two large groups: on the one hand, the drivers and all items related to the security and awareness in the use of vehicles and, on the other hand, the pedestrian, for whom the DGT has started various specific campaigns.

Therefore, its objectives are multiple and diverse:

- Road safety and reduction of accidents: carrying out awareness actions to both drivers and pedestrians, as well as the improvement of the road infrastructure and the intervention for the improvement of accident blackspots
- Traffic information and management: so that citizens have better accessibility to public roads at all times
- Health: linked to issues that may affect driving, consumption of substances that reduce driving abilities, visual impairments that can substantially influence driving, etc. Undertake and develop specific research and articles and advice about the effects and consequences of these substances and impairments
- Sustainability of the environment: sustainable mobility, encouraging the use of public transportation and commuting by foot or bicycle as one of the measures that reduces the environmental impact that is related to the use of the private vehicle
- Research and development: issues related to the increase of safety in vehicles (researching child safety systems, etc.), on roads, urban areas, etc.

The annual budgets available to the DGT to achieve its objectives are around 840 million euros, of which it assigns 2% to road safety. This percentage is distributed among three causes: education and dissemination, victims of traffic accidents, and research in road safety.

The promotional strategies carried out by the DGT encompass traditional channels and an increasing use of new ones based on information and communication technologies (ICT), such as those used in their latest campaigns highlighting the use of social networks. Among them, we can point out the following:

- A Website, from which the bulk of the information is managed, centralized, and disseminated and strategized
- Monthly digital magazine, digital broadcast channel with interactive content
- Publications and specific research works, related to road safety, to the use and improvement of elements of safety in vehicles, health, etc.
- Advertising campaigns, which not only broadcast and converged in traditional channels, such as television, radio, and press but also via the Internet to convey them in other digital ecosystems (e.g., YouTube)
- Conducting events, with public institutions (town halls, meetings between cities, etc.), and others
- Trainers and talks to raise awareness among the entire population and especially in children. In addition, the work done with victims of traffic accidents that incorporate them into their awareness strategy toward other groups through their collaboration
- Mobile application, launched in 2013 to help and provide the driver with traffic information and about your safety constantly
- Social networks, Facebook, Twitter, Instagram, etc. where it has its own Website

Case Development

#Caminantedigital is a different campaign led by the DGT where citizens' participation and involvement are essential.

The target audience at which the campaign is directed to is primarily the pedestrian, due to the high accident rate in Spain. The global data reaches 89,519 accidents and 1680 annual fatalities (DGT 2018), high figures if we remind ourselves that pedestrians are the most seriously affected by traffic accidents in this environment because they represent half of the victims in urban areas.

The data shows that for each accident, there are at least two people injured and around ten are serious or fatal accidents in urban areas. To try to mitigate this, DGT has undertaken a specific strategy to involve society and local public institutions. In its "Road Safety Strategic Plan 2011–2020," there are two of its strategic priorities listed out, the protection of the most vulnerable users and the promotion of safe mobility in urban areas (Table 1). These are topics that are aimed at the urban space and the groups that coexist in it.

In the current dynamics, using the potential offered by the Internet and the new information and communication technologies (ICT), the DGT launches this

Table 1 Road safety strategic plan 2011–2020

Strategies	Target	Aims
1. Protect most vulnerable users	Children	Provide safe environments and journeys when walking school
	Elderly	Provide safe mobility spaces
	Pedestrians	Promote commuting on foot as a way of economic and healthy mobility Provide safe mobility spaces Improve knowledge about pedestrian accidents and mobility
	Cyclists	Promote the use of bicycles as efficient means of transportation Improve training and attitudes of cyclists and other users Provide safe mobility spaces
2. Enhance mobility safety	Urban zone	Provide an urban public space and safe environments Promote discipline in urban areas

Source: DGT (2018)

campaign as completely new and different from the traditional or classic marketing strategies that they have been doing so far, in search for pedestrian involvement and collaboration, one of its main objectives. The hashtag for this campaign #Caminantedigital was born on May 2013.

This campaign is part of the actions framed within the "World Road Safety Week" of the United Nations and the "European Road Safety Day" of the European Union, held on the 6 May 2013. In the case of Spain, various events and actions carried out the following messages:

- Promote walking
- Provide safe mobility spaces for pedestrians
- Improve knowledge about pedestrian accident and mobility

Its slogan is "Let yourself be contagious and participate!"

#Caminantedigital developed through a photo contest that aims to raise awareness through photography to the pedestrian, and also encourages travelling on foot opposed to using motorized means of transportation, and promotes the enjoyment of urban public spaces.

The organization invited anyone who wanted to express their vision as a pedestrian by taking a picture that could be uploaded to the Instagram platform, the digital tool selected for that purpose, with the hashtag #Caminantedigital.

The campaign was launched on May 6 and it was in effect until the 26th of that month. Immediately, it had a large impact on social media and high participation. Nearly seven million people visited the Website and commented on different blogs, and approximately 15,000 pictures were submitted on Instagram by a multitude of participants.

In addition, PHotoEspaña, one of the main means of dissemination of photography and the visual arts of Spain, collaborated in the campaign by organizing a subsequent exhibition with selected and awarded pictures.

The use of mobile devices is key in the success and in such large amount of participation, because digital marketing is more specific and allows a quicker exchange of information with the user, thus, achieving a most direct communication.

Creativity is especially valued in every field (Núñez-Barriopedro and González del Valle Brena 2016; Núñez and Ravina 2017). Therefore, an interesting and innovative factor of this campaign in contrast to previous ones by the DGT is that it has introduced a marketing strategy based on "Creative Gamification," which encourages the participation of people in the photographic contest, using the game and the subsequent social recognition (publishing all the pictures on the Website and displaying an exhibition of the winning ones) as the main element of "engagement" with the target audience.

The two previous events resulted in a high participation and citizen involvement, even when the duration of this campaign was only of 20 days, which helped make society more aware of these issues.

The judges of the contest were staff from the DGT and PHotoEspaña; they selected the 23 best pictures, which had in common the day-to-day representation of people who walked through the different cities, turning the streets into a space of more conviviality, safety, and kindness.

Furthermore, every picture sent by citizens was published in the specific "microsite" created by the DGT with direct access through its Website. The subsequent photographic exhibition, with the 23 winning photographs, was organized by PHotoEspaña and the private sector collaborated through *Fnac*, which participates in the initiative by lending its facilities located in Avenue Castellana in Madrid to host the exhibition free of charge.

According to the marketing mix used by this campaign, the following could be summarized:

- Given that the main aim of the campaign was to try to make pedestrians aware of the importance of road safety for protection, the product in this case is an intangible idea.
- The use of ICT and social media was the channel chosen by the DGT for its rapid distribution, due to its easy accessibility through mobile devices.
- The promotion of this campaign was initiated by the DGT together with PHotoEspaña, which launched it on social media, blogs, etc. and traditional media, such as the written press, radio, or television. This made references to it multiplying its repercussion.
- The time and effort expended constituted to the price that, in these types of strategies, tends to be very high because it involves many people, both in the design and implementation of the campaign, as in the subsequent participation phase.

Conclusions

The reorientation that the DGT has made of its marketing strategies in the face of a problem that had not been previously addressed with enough attention (high number of accidents and victims in urban areas) has been an advancement, both in the strategy itself and in the target audience. The DGT, with this campaign, adopts a position that moves away from the traditional, with a search for greater involvement and participation of the pedestrian.

This qualitative leap started with these new marketing actions; they have been very positive and have managed to engage pedestrians in the initiative "Caminantedigital," establishing an emotional link with them through which messages are shared, that being the main objective of the campaign. Listening to the target audience is, currently, one of the keys to the new marketing strategies, trying to solve problems or needs that arise using the media technologies available as the main channel of communication.

The use of new technological tools (ICTs) and participation in social media are fundamental in the DGT's new strategy, providing new and more rapid dissemination channels appropriate to marketing actions (Santesmases 2009, 2012). The speed and immediacy of interaction provided by mobile devices to users is today's key tool for receiving and transmitting information, because it is the ideal channel in which they can be heard by companies or entities.

Along with the abovementioned strategy, the use of a "Creative Gamification" marketing approach to the target, the pedestrian, has been very effective and has become a decisive factor in this campaign.

The fact that the receiver of the information goes from being considered as a mere passive subject to being considered an active participant, with the ability to provide information, to feel heard by the institution, etc., is a breakthrough.

The implication of the user is immediate, because of the feeling of being part of a game (since people like to play and compete in these type of contests), being part of something collective (with the publication of the participants' photographs on a webpage accessible to everyone), and receiving recognition or a prize (through selection and participation in a photo exhibition sponsored by PHotoEspaña). These actions foster participation. Alongside, this enables the creators of the campaign to have the perfect vehicle to promote the slogan or message on what they want to raise awareness, which is the main objective sought.

The sum of both has produced a viral spread in the media and in social networks, considerably multiplying the impact of the campaign, both in traditional media (press, radio, television, etc.) and in specialized pages and online media (blogs, Facebook, etc.). It is a good example that with a small investment and an attractive campaign, a powerful message can be achieved (Goel and Goldstein 2014).

This first step or experience has served to verify that these types of strategies can contribute to a public institution like the DGT, and it is a train of thought that would be convenient to continue advancing and innovating with new similar actions. These types of actions allow channeling different messages in a more direct and effective way toward the target audience.

The high participation and repercussion achieved in social media should be taken advantage of by gathering more information, problems, etc. provided by the pedestrian, in order for it to be used as support to the DGT. Other objectives and actions should be considered when dealing with problems, like looking for solutions or improvements on the urban road network or pedestrian public spaces or even raising awareness focusing on the driver and the pedestrian, leading to a decrease in the accident rate in these areas.

Discussion Questions

1. Considering the repercussion of the campaign, have the objectives been achieved?
2. Until now, the DGT has led to a shift in the marketing strategy used with the target audience, that is, from a consumer receiving information to a consumer that can be heard. What changes have this marketing strategy introduced with respect to those that have been made previously?
3. May have the use of new technological resources available to everyone been the key to success?
4. Has the full potential of this type of strategies and tools been exploited?
5. What could be the future line of action and the new marketing strategies from the DGT?

References

DGT. (2018). *Dirección General de Tráfico*. Retrieved March 9, 2018, from http://www.dgt.es/
Goel, S., & Goldstein, D. (2014). Predicting individual behavior with social networks. *Marketing Science, 33*(1), 82–93.
Núñez, E., & Ravina, R. (2017). Análisis del nivel de competitividad empresarial en el panorama publicitario colombiano fundamentada en el éxito creativo y la responsabilidad ética y jurídica. *JURÍDICAS CUC, 13*(1), 9–28. https://doi.org/10.17981/juridcuc.13.1.2017.1
Núñez, E., Carrillo, F. J., Rojas, P., Uceta, A. T., & Vadillo, V. (2014). Caminante digital como caso de aplicación del marketing digital en una entidad pública. En *VI Congreso internacional de casos docentes en marketing público y no lucrativo "Marketing for people: Let's go digital"* (Vol. 6, p. 22). Coimbra: Asociación Internacional de Marketing Público y No Lucrativo.
Núñez-Barriopedro, E., & González del Valle Brena, A. (2016). Ranking de publicidad en Iberoamérica ¿cuáles son las principales agencias? *Opción, 32*(8), 360–372.
Santesmases, M. (2009). *Fundamentos de Marketing*. Madrid: Pirámide.
Santesmases, M. (2012). *Marketing: Conceptos y Estrategias* (6a ed.). Madrid: Pirámide.

Combat to Abandonment and Mistreatment of Animals: A Case Study Applied to the Public Security Police (Portugal)

Bruno Sousa and Daniela Soares

Abstract
Social marketing is based on the adaptation of the contemporary commercial marketing theory and practice as a means of guiding and aiding social change campaigns. In this context, animals are abandoned and mistreated every day. Rescue organizations and public institutions spend countless hours working to save these animals. Because animal cruelty has traditionally been seen as a minor crime, basic quantitative information as to the nature and extent of animal cruelty has been limited. Therefore, the main objective of this study is to systematize the main determinant aspects of a campaign for the abandonment and mistreatment of animals as a social marketing case study (i.e., "animal mistreatment is a crime"— promotion). The case study is applied to the Public Security Police (in Portuguese contexts), but the problematic evidence in this manuscript is common to several countries in the world.

B. Sousa (✉)
IPCA – Polytechnic Institute of Cávado and Ave, Barcelos, Portugal
e-mail: bsousa@ipca.pt

D. Soares
School of Economics and Management, University of Minho, Braga, Portugal

> **Learning Objectives**
> 1. The present case study aims at gaining a deeper understanding of social marketing campaigns in specific contexts (i.e., combat to abandonment and mistreatment of animals).
> 2. This study intends to present and discuss a social marketing campaign that has been developed by case study Public Security Police in Portugal in 2015.
> 3. This manuscript is explored from the scoping and research stage to evaluation, providing the reader with an overview of the social marketing theory and how these can be applied to the real context of combat to abandonment and mistreatment of animals.
> 4. Under an interdisciplinary perspective, this case study brings together inputs from social marketing and local development.

Introduction

Since the 1970s, social marketing has been highlighted by its impact on social issues in the areas of public health, safety, and protection of the environment and communities (Andreasen 1994; Kotler and Lee 2011). Social marketing is not a theory in itself, since it is a system that brings together several areas of knowledge from psychology, sociology, anthropology, and communication theory, in order to understand the mechanism of influence of human behavior (Kotler and Zaltman 1971; Peattie and Peattie 2009). Social marketing involves "influencing behaviors through a systematic planning process that applies marketing principles and techniques, focusing on priority audience segments, providing a positive benefit to society." The principles and techniques employed aim to "create, communicate, and deliver value" to the consumer (Kotler and Lee 2011). Human behaviors are at the root of many social and health problems, including the spread of the HIV virus, dangerous driving, death from tobacco use, or abandonment and maltreatment of animals (MacFadyen et al. 2003). Thus, "social marketing provides a mechanism to address these problems by encouraging people to adopt healthy lifestyles" (Hastings et al. 2003: 694).

The phenomenon of maltreatment of animals and their abandonment is a problem of a social nature that has gained importance every year. There are many reasons that someone might abandon a family pet. Sometimes people receive pets as Christmas or birthday presents, and by the summertime, the novelty has worn off, and the real responsibility of having a pet has set in. The institutions speculate that longer daylight hours and struggling to find someone to pet sit while families go on vacation could be big contributing factors as well. Pets will never be able to understand why they have been abandoned by the ones they love. Social marketing success relates to the success of the influence of desired behavior (Kotler and Lee 2011). In this way, the chosen target public is free to accept, reject, modify, or abandon behavior in favor of society and individual good (Kotler et al. 2002). According to Kotler and Lee (2011), the most challenging aspect of social marketing (and also the greatest contribution) lies in the "reward of good behavior" rather than the punishment (legal, economic, or coercive) of wrongdoing. The present case study addresses the "animal mistreatment is a crime" (Portuguese campaign)—combating abandonment and mistreatment of animals (by PSP—Portugal).

Public Security Police in Portugal

The Public Security Police (PSP) is the oldest police in Portugal. At the age of 150, this government organization was created in 1867 by King D. Luís. The law published in that year created the Civil Police Corps in Portugal and with it lays the foundations for the creation of the current Public Security Police, designated since 1927. According to PSP (2018), today, it is defined as "a security force, uniformed and armed, with a public service nature and endowed with administrative autonomy." Also designated by PSP Portugal, this security force, enshrined in the Constitution, has the task of ensuring democratic legality and guaranteeing internal security and citizens' rights. PSP Portugal works for the protection of the community (public service). "Providing citizens with a sense of security" is a priority and a fundamental one, as well as establishing a close relationship between police and citizens with the aim of preventing crime (e.g., mistreatment and abandonment of animals).

The main functions of the Public Security Police (PSP 2018) are as follows:

- Guarantee security conditions that allow the exercise of rights and freedoms and respect for the guarantees of citizens, as well as the full functioning of democratic institutions, while respecting the legality and the principles of the rule of law.
- Ensure public order and tranquility and the security and protection of people and property.
- Prevent crime in general.
- Ensure compliance with laws and regulations relating to road transport and promote and guarantee road safety, in particular through roadworthiness, traffic management, and discipline.
- Protect, assist citizens, and defend and preserve assets that are in dangerous situations, due to human or natural causes.
- Prevent and detect situations of trafficking and consumption of narcotic drugs or other prohibited substances by monitoring and patrolling the zones referred to as places of trafficking or consumption.
- Ensure compliance with legal and regulatory provisions related to the protection of the environment, as well as prevent and investigate their illegal activities.
- Contribute to training and information on the security of citizens.

Communication: PSP Portugal

At the end of 2015 and beginning of 2016, the Public Security Police (PSP—Portugal) adopted a disruptive, relaxed, and creative communication posture characterized by the relevance and timeliness of the messages transmitted. Currently, the communication made by PSP is focused on social networks, although communication on the ground takes place in various ways and takes on some dimensions. The actions of raising awareness among the schools about the themes of "Safer Internet," "Bullying," "Psychoactive Substances," and "Preventing Dating Violence" among the young are examples of interpersonal communication established with the population and materialized along with social networking policing. However, one of the major concerns of PSP Portugal in the last 2 years is the combat to abandonment and mistreatment of animals.

With more than 600,000 followers, PSP is the institutional page of Facebook with more followers in Portugal (i.e., represents a lot of interaction between the citizen and the police force). With such a wide target, ranging from the smallest to the oldest, it is necessary to adopt different languages and approaches, and therefore it is difficult to be consistent and always have the same style in the publications. If the communication is aimed at a younger audience, they use the logic of the *trending topic*; on the contrary, if it is intended for an older age group, they resort to more emotional and formal messages. The presence of PSP online, specifically through social networks, arose from the need to pass messages without a filter and to establish a more direct communication with the public, without being dependent on traditional media. Through a smoother message, an informal tone, and the use of intelligent humor, the PSP was able to establish a greater relationship of closeness and affectivity with the consumer that, until then, had not reached.

The combat to abandonment and mistreatment of animals is a very sensitive subject, which requires closeness. Proximity and trust established between citizens and agents of the PSP are essential to create "bonds" that allow the exchange and sharing of information, with the aim of preventing crime and changing wrong behaviors toward animals. The publication of Internet posts, sometimes irreverent but emotional and informative, has strengthened the relationship between citizens and the PSP Portugal, leaving this institution to be seen as a distant and austere element. Proximity policing came to humanize the figure of the police agents. PSP marketing strategy reinforced the affective side, deconstructing the image of the serious police. The publication of photographs, and even self-images, of smiling agents on Facebook, alone or interacting with people of all ages or even caressing and assisting the animals, makes the Public Security Police "cool" and transmits the image of a safe Portugal, without prejudice to the authority, seriousness, impartiality, and respect that characterizes this police institution. Facebook has not only had an impact on the external communication of the PSP Portugal. It proved to be important in the internal communication of the organization, since it came to feed the sense of belonging of the agents and of the police, occupying the role of internal aggregator of motivation. In addition, it served as a vehicle to break with misinformation and speculation, taking over an official source of real and authentic information. It is concluded that, in addition to the information component, it has become necessary for the PSP brand to create value in order to increase proximity, involvement, and commitment of the police to the consumer. Currently, PSP is the top of mind of Portuguese police brand.

PSP Portugal Campaign: Combat to Abandonment and Mistreatment of Animals

In Portugal, the law that criminalizes mistreatment and abandonment of animals entered into force on October 1, 2014. Approved for more than 3 years, Law 69/2014 provides that "who, without legitimate cause, inflict pain, suffering or any other physical ill-treatment of a companion animal is punished" (Art. 387 of the Penal Code) and also protects pets by stating that "who, having a duty to guard, watch or watch pet society, abandoning it, thereby endangering their food and the care they are owed, is punished" (Art. 388 of the Penal Code). In this context, the Metropolitan Command of Lisbon of the Public Security Police launched in July 2015 a campaign entitled "Animal misconduct is crime" (animal abuse is a crime) with the aim of alerting society to this awareness.

Thus, to facilitate complaints of these situations, PSP created a direct contact line with the address defensaanimal@psp.pt and the telephone contact 21POLICIA. This awareness campaign also went through the placement of posters in schools, parish councils, and municipal councils with images of dogs, in which one could read: "Abandonment of Animals is Crime" (Table 1).

The Animal Defense Project eventually became permanent and spread throughout the country. PSP publications on this subject continue to alert the population to denounce these cases, reminding that the law criminalizes with imprisonment and fines the abandonment and mistreatment of animals. Recently, the Statute of Animals (Law no. 8/2017) recognized animals "their nature as living beings with sensibility and object of legal protection," leaving them to be considered as "things."

Table 1 Campaign summary table

Campaign	"Animal mistreatment is a crime"—combating abandonment and mistreatment of animals
When? Who?	Started on July 22, 2015, by the Metropolitan Command of Lisbon (Portugal) of the Public Security Police
Where?	The initiative is currently implemented throughout the police system: 2 regional commands (Azores and Madeira); 2 metropolitan commands (Lisbon and Porto); 16 district commands (remaining district capitals)
Duration	Permanent
Actions	Creation of the email and phone contact 21POLICIA to report cases of mistreatment and abandonment of animals; disclosure of posters with the message "Abandonment of Animals is Crime" in schools and municipal services; awareness-raising and enlightenment of actions through proximity policing; protocols with animal associations; participation of public figures as "padrinhos" (godfathers) and "madrinhas" (godmother) of the initiative
Promotion	Social networks and media
Target	Portugal residents and visitors
Results	Recording an average of 1600 complaints per year since 2015. In 2016, PSP treated 3098 crimes related to ill-treatment, neglect, and other animal-related irregularities (903 were ill-treatment crimes)

Source: Authors (based on PSP Subcommittee interview)

The marketing promoted by the PSP in Portugal is strongly based on the idea of affectivity and with appeal to the emotions. The following images (Fig. 1) show the sense of greater proximity between the police forces and the local community, and the abandonment of animals is a very sensitive issue for society. The figures illustrate the feeling of belonging and the affective bonds with animals, and sometimes humor

Fig. 1 "Animal mistreatment is a crime"—Promotion. Source: PSP (2018)

is used to capture the public's attention and make the message clearer and more efficient. In one of the images, you can read "Report, they cannot" or "Hi, I have a complaint. My owner abandoned me."

Conclusions

The use of social marketing to design and implement programs that promote socially beneficial behavioral changes has grown in popularity and use in the public health and wellness community in general (Grier and Bryant 2005). Generally, in social marketing, products are actually complex behaviors and intangible elements (Andreasen et al. 2008), which makes it difficult to create a simple and meaningful product concept (Hastings 2007). For instance, cause-related marketing (CRM) has proliferated as a marketing strategy and is being employed by numerous brands across product categories (Galan-Ladero et al. 2015). Social marketing has experienced substantial growth over the last decades, and its utilization has spread into various areas of social and public life (Alves 2010). In this context, the present case study showed the problem of maltreatment and abandonment of animals as a way to reinforce the importance of social marketing in changing people's behavior.

The phenomenon of animal disrespect is of great importance to the general population and to future generations. Abandoned pets are companion animals that are either inadvertently or deliberately cast off by their owners. This commonly occurs when an owner dies, when a pet becomes disruptive or grows too large, or if the pet was acquired impulsively. Typical of this group are pets left behind when the owner's home is foreclosed. These animals can be left alone on the property or dropped off at an animal shelter. They are often discovered after the foreclosure process, when the realtor or bank enters the home. Animal abandonment is a serious (social marketing) problem. Some pets find homes and, sadly, some do not.

The PSP Portugal case study reinforces the role of communication in social marketing as a successful strategy for behavior change. Social marketing can mimic the success of commercial marketing and mitigate the damage it sometimes causes. Social marketing recognizes the value of new research techniques to help build robust evidence to guide its regulation and helps avoid the less desirable effects of conventional marketing. In this sense, the PSP Portugal is a successful case in the fight against abandonment and mistreatment of animals as a phenomena transversal to many world populations.

Discussion Questions

1. How can abandonment and mistreatment of animals affect the quality of life of society in general?
2. How can social marketing combat this phenomenon (i.e., combat to abandonment and mistreatment of animals)?

3. Do you consider the communication elements of the Public Security Police (Portugal) adequate for the proposed objectives?
4. What recommendations would you give to PSP Portugal to minimize the effects of abandonment and maltreatment of animals and improve this social marketing campaign?

References

Alves, H. (2010). The who, where, and when of social marketing. *Journal of Nonprofit & Public Sector Marketing, 22*(4), 288–311.
Andreasen, A. R. (1994). Social marketing: Its definition and domain. *Journal of Public Policy & Marketing, 13*(1), 108–114.
Andreasen, A. R., Kotler, P., & Parker, D. (2008). *Strategic marketing for nonprofit organizations* (pp. 44–53). Upper Saddle River, NJ: Pearson/Prentice Hall.
Galan-Ladero, M. M., Galera Casquet, C., & Singh, J. (2015). Understanding factors influencing consumer attitudes toward cause-related marketing. *International Journal of Nonprofit and Voluntary Sector Marketing, 20*(1), 52–70.
Grier, S., & Bryant, C. A. (2005). Social marketing in public health. *Annual Review of Public Health, 26*, 319–339.
Hastings, G. (2007). *Social marketing: Why should the devil get all the best tunes?* Amsterdam: Butterworth-Heinemann.
Hastings, G., MacFadyen, L., & Stead, M. (2003). Social marketing. In M. J. Baker (Ed.), *The marketing book* (5th ed., pp. 694–725). Amsterdam: Butterworth-Heinemann.
Kotler, P., & Lee, N. R. (2011). *Social marketing: Influencing behaviors for good* (4th ed.). Thousand Oaks, CA: Sage.
Kotler, P., & Zaltman, G. (1971). Social marketing: An approach to planned social change. *Journal of Marketing, 35*, 3–12.
Kotler, P., Roberto, N., & Lee, N. (2002). *Social marketing: Improving the quality of life*. Sage Publications.
MacFadyen, L., Amos, A., Hastings, G., & Parkes, E. (2003). 'They look like my kind of people'—Perceptions of smoking images in youth magazines. *Social Science & Medicine, 56*(3), 491–499.
Peattie, K., & Peattie, S. (2009). Social marketing: A pathway to consumption reduction? *Journal of Business Research, 62*, 260–268.
PSP. (2018). *Polícia de Segurança Pública*. Retrieved from www.psp.pt